Temples IN THE TOPS OF THE MOUNTAINS

Temples
IN THE TOPS OF THE MOUNTAINS

Sacred Houses of the Lord in Utah

Richard O. Cowan

Clinton D. Christensen

RSC BYU

DESERET BOOK

On the cover: *Payson Princess Timpanogos*. On the title page: *From on High: Draper Utah Temple*. Both by Alan Fullmer, temples.alanfullmer.com. Used with permission.

Published by the Religious Studies Center, Brigham Young University, Provo, Utah, in cooperation with Deseret Book Company, Salt Lake City. Visit us at rsc.byu.edu.

Printed in China by Book Printers of Utah.

DESERET BOOK is a registered trademark of Deseret Book Company. Visit us at DeseretBook.com.

Cover and interior design by Carmen Durland Cole.

ISBN: 978-1-9503-0439-4

Library of Congress Cataloging-in-Publication Data
Names: Cowan, Richard O., 1934– author. | Christensen, Clinton D., author.
Title: Temples in the tops of the mountains : sacred houses of the Lord in Utah / Richard O. Cowan and Clinton D. Christensen.
Description: Provo, Utah : Religious Studies Center, Brigham Young University : Salt Lake City, Utah : Deseret Book, [2023] | Includes index. | Summary: "This book shares the story of Utah's temples, now numbering more than twenty-five. Early chapters treat the iconic pioneer-era temples. Later chapters consider temples built during the twentieth and early twenty-first centuries and pioneer-era temples renovated during the 2020s"—Provided by publisher.
Identifiers: LCCN 2022056170 | ISBN 9781950304394 (hardcover)
Subjects: LCSH: Church of Jesus Christ of Latter-day Saints—Utah—History. | Mormon temples—Utah—History.
Classification: LCC BX8643.T4 C689 2023 | DDC 246/.958933209792--dc23/eng/20230208
LC record available at https://lccn.loc.gov/2022056170

Contents

Foreword

Mountains in Zion National Park, Utah, by Daniel Olah/Unsplash.

Let us go up to the mountain of the Lord, to the house of the God of Jacob; and he will teach us of his ways, and we will walk in his paths: for out of Zion shall go forth the law, and the word of the Lord from Jerusalem

—Isaiah 2:2–3

Even from ancient times, prophets of God looked forward to the building of temples in the latter days. In the eighth century BC, Isaiah wrote, "And it shall come to pass in the last days, that the mountain of the Lord's house shall be established in the top of the mountains, and shall be exalted above the hills; and all nations shall flow unto it. And many people shall go and say, Come ye, and let us go up to the mountain of the Lord, to the house of the God of Jacob; and he will teach us of his ways, and we will walk in his paths: for out of Zion shall go forth the law, and the word of the Lord from Jerusalem" (Isaiah 2:2–3). Micah, Isaiah's contemporary, echoed this prophecy in almost identical language (see Micah 4:1–2). In this book, we see the fulfillment of these prophecies, with the construction of not just one but two dozen houses of the Lord in the mountainous state of Utah. Truly all nations have flowed here, and from this place the law of God has gone forth.

The two authors bring significant but different backgrounds to this project. After earning his doctorate in history at Stanford University in 1961, Richard O. Cowan was a member of the Religious Education faculty at Brigham Young University for over fifty years, retiring in 2014. His research has focused on the Doctrine and Covenants and Latter-day Saint history during the twentieth century. He has authored or coauthored more than a dozen books related to these topics, including five about Latter-day Saint temples. Clinton D. Christensen earned his master's degree in English at BYU in 1998. While at BYU, Clint was a student in one of Dr. Cowan's graduate Church history classes. Following graduation with a master's degree in library and information science at Wayne State University in Michigan, he joined the staff at the Church History Library in 2001. Among other things, he has been assigned by the Temple Department to oversee local committees writing temple histories throughout the world at the time of dedications or rededications. One of these committees he guided and assisted was writing the history of the Provo City Center Temple in 2016; it was chaired by Brother Cowan. Hence, these two authors have experience in working together.

Temples in the Tops of the Mountains shares the story of Utah's temples, now numbering twenty-eight. The book is organized chronologically. Early chapters treat the iconic pioneer-era temples. Later chapters consider temples built during the twentieth and early twenty-first centuries. These include the unique Provo and Ogden Temples, the first of President Gordon B. Hinckley's "small temples" at Monticello, older tabernacles that were transformed into temples in Vernal and Provo, the completely reconstructed temple in Ogden, pioneer-style temples built in Brigham City and Cedar City, and several others. Another chapter returns to the pioneer-era temples to describe how they were thoroughly renovated during the 2020s. The final chapter reviews temples that had been announced or were under construction but not yet dedicated at the time of publication.

An important feature of this book is the large number of insightful photographs. The authors are grateful to those that have assisted in the Church History Library, including Ben Whisenant, Jeff Thompson, Jay Burrup, Gary V. Davis, Debra Dixon, and Steven and Alene Dinger. Lee R. Cowan drafted maps and diagrams, contributed a number of original photographs, and provided helpful advice concerning illustrations in this volume. The authors are grateful for a publication grant from the Church History Department that paid for the graphic illustrations.

We also acknowledge Alan Fullmer for the use of his beautiful photographs of Utah's temples on the covers, at the beginning of the chapters, and throughout the book. His talented eye for creating amazing photographs of temples in their mountainous environments has greatly enriched this project. We thank Carmen Cole for identifying Alan's work and providing exceptional photographs to create the final touches to the book as she created a masterful graphic design. Further, we acknowledge the additional donors that helped offset the printing costs so that this book could be printed in color, so that the reader's experience would be visually enhanced.

Several individuals have provided vital information needed for this work. These include Andy Kirby, director of historic temple renovation, and his public relations specialist Georges Bonnet.

Others have made important contributions as well. Scott Esplin was publications director at Brigham Young University's Religious Studies Center when this manuscript was submitted. He was succeeded in 2021 by Jared Ludlow, who has provided counsel and encouragement as he shepherded this project through the publication process. Devan Jensen, executive editor at the RSC, kindly answered repeated questions regarding style and form as well as many other substantial matters. Brent Nordgren, production supervisor, generously provided technical assistance with illustrations. Carmen Cole is the capable graphic designer of this book. We express thanks to RSC editing interns Erica Smith, Adi Marshall, and Emma Taylor. Richard and Clint are especially grateful for the encouraging and helpful support they have received from their wives, Dawn and Angie, respectively.

We, the authors, hope that you will find this book to be interesting and inspiring. In addition to information about the history of Utah's temples, we hope you will gain insights that will enrich your service in these or any other Latter-day Saint temples.

We see the fulfillment of these prophecies with the construction of two dozen houses of the Lord in the mountainous state of Utah.

Utah mountains with the Logan Temple in the foreground, by Nathan Blaylock/Unsplash.

1853
1893
HOLINESS TO THE LORD

1 Beginnings

Detail, Salt Lake Temple exterior doors. *Eternal Doors*, by Alan Fullmer.

Almost from the beginning, Latter-day Saints have been a temple-building and temple-attending people.[1] For them, temples are more than ordinary meetinghouses; they truly are the "house of the Lord." Since Old Testament times, temples have served two major functions: first, they have been places where heaven and earth meet—a place of revelation between God and man—and second, places where sacred ceremonies or "ordinances" have been performed by which the faithful enter covenants with God. Holy instructions and promises connected with these ordinances testify of humankind's ultimate eternal destiny and set forth how it can be attained.

ROB MARTIN/UNSPLASH

Two temples had been built by the Latter-day Saints before the Saints entered the valley of the Great Salt Lake in 1847. Church leaders like Brigham Young and Wilford Woodruff brought in their hearts and minds the ordinances of the temple as instructed by the Prophet Joseph Smith. They planned to build more temples as the Restoration continued. The Kirtland and Nauvoo Temples were preparatory temples to what Latter-day Saints would later associate with the fullness of temple ordinances we see today. The Lord was laying the foundation for the work to redeem the dead with these temples.

In Kirtland, Ohio, the Latter-day Saints overcame poverty and persecution to build their first temple in the mid-1830s. Their sacrifice surely did bring forth the blessings of heaven. As the temple neared completion, the Saints enjoyed a rich outpouring of spiritual gifts, including prophecy, speaking in tongues, and visions of angels. Joseph Smith declared that "this was a time of rejoicing long to be remembered."[2] These events climaxed with glorious experiences during the day-long dedication of the temple on Sunday, March 27, 1836. One week later, on April 3, the Prophet recorded that Jesus Christ appeared in glory to accept the temple and that Elijah the prophet, in fulfillment of Malachi's prophecy, restored the sealing keys that were "to turn the hearts of the fathers to the children, and the children to the fathers" (Doctrine and Covenants 110:15; see Malachi 4:6). Within a few years, the first genealogical societies were organized in both Europe and North America. Latter-day Saints often refer to this interest in ancestors as "the spirit of Elijah."

Temples are more than ordinary meetinghouses; they truly are the "house of the Lord."

Clearly the first function of temples—a place of revelation—had been restored. The Kirtland Temple, however, had no facilities for ordinances—the second function of temples. Instead, it was designed more for general meetings, consisting mostly of two large halls, one above the other. Being the Church's only building, it needed to be a multipurpose structure accommodating various activities. However, Joseph Smith did make the first step toward future temple ordinances within the Kirtland Temple. On January 21, 1836, Joseph Smith "administered" and other elders performed the ordinances of washing and anointing, which at the time were performed in preparation for the elders to

take the gospel to the nations.[3] Also on the same day that washing and anointing were performed in the Kirtland Temple, Joseph received the revelation known as Doctrine and Covenants 137. In this vision, Joseph saw his unbaptized brother Alvin Smith in the celestial kingdom, learning that he too would be an "heir to salvation."[4] God taught Joseph that there was a plan for the dead to receive exaltation. It is fitting that this revelation occurred in the first temple of the restored Church, as temples would be an essential place for ordinances to be carried forward for the living and the dead.

Above: Kirtland Temple. Courtesy of Church History Library, Salt Lake City. Below: Joseph Smith. Courtesy of Intellectual Reserve, Inc.

Temple Ordinances Restored

A greater fullness of sacred ordinances unfolded while the second temple was being built at Nauvoo, Illinois. In 1840, Joseph Smith taught the Saints that they could be baptized on behalf of the dead (compare 1 Corinthians 15:29). They eagerly went into the Mississippi River to perform this ordinance, thus making gospel blessings available to their loved ones who had died without this opportunity. In 1842 the Prophet presented the endowment, which was a "course of instructions" describing the path which leads back into the

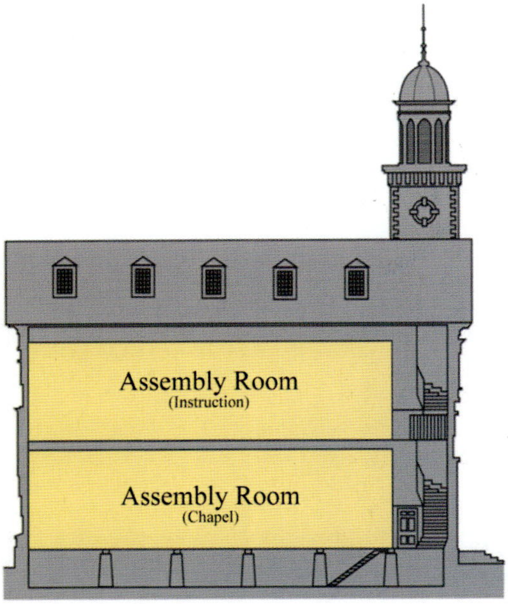

Kirtland Temple (1836)

Diagram of Kirtland Temple. Courtesy of Lee R. Cowan.

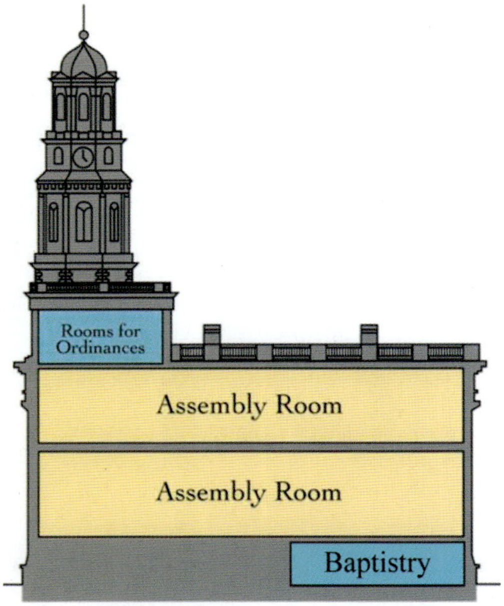

Nauvoo Temple (1845)

Diagram of Nauvoo Temple. Courtesy of Lee R. Cowan.

presence of God.[5] Joseph recorded that on May 4 he had "spent the day" with a select group "instructing them in the principles and order of the Priesthood, attending to washings, anointing, endowments, and the communication of keys pertaining to the Aaronic Priesthood, and so on to the highest order of the Melchizedek Priesthood" and teaching all the "principles by which any one is enabled to secure the fullness of those blessings" and be prepared to dwell in the presence of God "in the eternal worlds."[6] Soon couples were also being "sealed," or married, making solemn covenants "for time and for all eternity" (see Doctrine and Covenants 132:7–20). Children could also be linked to their parents through sacred ceremonies performed by priesthood authority.[7]

Thus, the second function of temples—sacred ordinances—had been restored. When completed, the Nauvoo Temple repeated the pattern of two large meeting rooms but added a font in the basement and facilities for other ordinances on its uppermost floor.

Temples in Utah

Unfortunately, the forces of religious bigotry climaxed with the murders of Joseph Smith and his brother Hyrum in 1844. As anti-Mormon persecution continued, the Saints in Nauvoo—under the leadership of Joseph's successor, Brigham Young—made their well-known trek across the plains to new homes in the Rocky Mountains. The endowment they had received in the Nauvoo Temple fortified them for this ordeal. "What was it that gave those early Church members such strength?" asked Elder David A. Bednar. "What fueled their devotion and enabled them to press forward in overwhelmingly adverse conditions? It was the fire of the temple covenants and ordinances that burned in their hearts."[8] For example, of the trek across muddy Iowa, Sarah Rich wrote, "If it had not been for the faith and knowledge that was bestowed upon us in that temple . . . , our journey would have been like . . . taking a leap in the dark."[9]

Soon after the first pioneers entered the Salt Lake Valley in 1847, Brigham Young sent scouts north and south to locate possible sites for additional settlements. During his lifetime, some 350 communities would be established in "the top of the mountains" (Isaiah 2:2). Utah became a territory of the United States in 1850 and was admitted to the Union as a state in 1896. Four temples were dedicated here during the last quarter of the nineteenth century. With the dedication of these temples, additional knowledge would be received by Church leaders for the work of redeeming the dead, which will be shown in the following chapters.

During the twentieth century, the number of Latter-day Saints continued to grow in Utah and in other areas, particularly in the western United States. Rapid international growth came during the second half of the century. In all these areas, the Church built holy temples.

As the twentieth century drew to a close and a new millennium dawned, the population and number of Latter-day Saints in Utah mushroomed. People were drawn by expanding economic opportunities and by the area's wholesome lifestyle. Over the years, twenty-eight temples would grace the landscape, enhancing the spiritual lives of the Saints in the Beehive State.

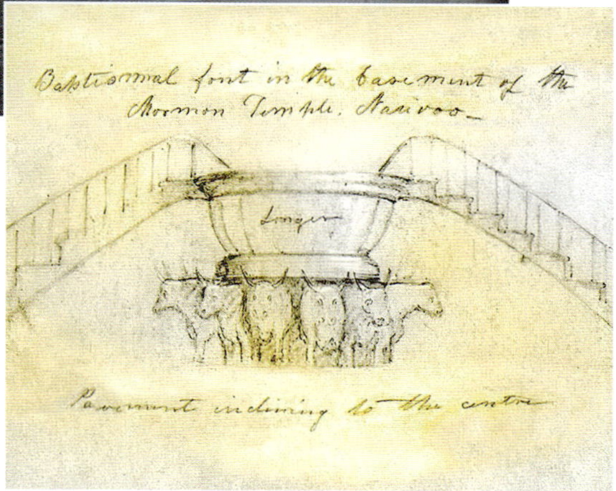

Top: Nauvoo Temple. Courtesy of Church History Library. Above: Drawing of Nauvoo Temple baptistry. Courtesy of Intellectual Reserve, Inc.

Notes

1. For a discussion of Latter-day Saint temples, see James E. Talmage, *The House of the Lord* (Salt Lake City: Bookcraft, 1962); Boyd K. Packer, *The Holy Temple* (Salt Lake City: Bookcraft, 1980); and Richard O. Cowan, *Temples to Dot the Earth* (Springville, UT: Cedar Fort, 1997).
2. History, 1838–1856, volume B-1 [1 September 1834–2 November 1838], http://josephsmithpapers.org/paperSummary/history-1838-1856-volume-b-1-1-september-1834-2-november-1838?p=156.
3. https://www.josephsmithpapers.org/event/washings-and-anointings.
4. https://www.churchofjesuschrist.org/study/scriptures/dc-testament/dc/137?lang=eng.
5. Talmage, *House of the Lord*, 99–100.
6. *Teachings of Presidents of the Church: Joseph Smith* (Salt Lake City: The Church of Jesus Christ of Latter-day Saints, 2007), 414; *Saints: The History of the Church of Jesus Christ in the Latter Days* (Salt Lake City: The Church of Jesus Christ of Latter-day Saints, 2018), 1:453–55.
7. *Saints*, 1:578–80.
8. Jason Swensen, "Elder Bednar Declares Miracles Have Not Ceased," *Church News*, January 23, 2021, 6.
9. Quoted by Ronald A. Rasband, "Recommended to the Lord," *Ensign*, November 2020, 24.

2 Temples in the Tops of the Mountains

Salt Lake Temple. *Ramparts*, by Alan Fullmer.

Endowment House and announced Utah temples of the nineteenth century. Courtesy of Lee R. Cowan.

When the Latter-day Saints left Nauvoo and headed toward the Rockies, they were forced to leave their nearly completed temple behind. Their interest in temple service did not diminish, however. If anything, it became stronger as they were deprived of the opportunity to receive these blessings. At Winter Quarters, for example, President Brigham Young said that when the Saints should reach their resting place in the mountains, his intention was to labor hard to build another temple. This matter was constantly on the pioneers' minds during their trek across the plains.[1]

Preparations for Building a Temple in the Salt Lake Valley

Within two days of President Young's arrival in the Salt Lake Valley, he designated the site for the future temple. On July 26, 1847, he and a few others were walking across the area that one day would be Temple Square. He stopped between the two forks of City Creek as he saw the future Salt Lake Temple in vision, struck the ground with his cane, and declared, "Here will be the Temple of our God." Wilford Woodruff placed a stake in the ground to mark the spot that would become the center of the future building. Many years later President Woodruff would call the construction of the temple on the designated site "a monument to President Young's foresight and prophetic accuracy."[2]

Marshalling Resources

As early as December 23, 1847, an official circular letter from the Twelve invited the Saints to gather and bring precious metals and other materials "for the exaltation . . . of the living and the dead," for the time had come to build the Lord's house "upon the tops of the mountains."[3] Soon afterward, Brigham Young named Truman O. Angell as temple architect, a post he would hold until his death in 1887. His previous work as a wood joiner on both the Kirtland and Nauvoo Temples provided useful background for his new assignment. He would have an able assistant, William Ward, who received his architectural training in England and was skilled in stone construction (Angell's experience was primarily with wooden structures). A skilled draftsman, Ward prepared the drawings for the Salt Lake Temple under Angell's direction.[4]

To aid with this and other building projects in the valley, Church authorities established the Department of Public Works in January 1851, with Daniel H. Wells

Brigham Young. Courtesy of Church History Library.

Truman O. Angell. Courtesy of Church History Library.

(a military and civic leader and future member of the First Presidency) as superintendent. Soon carpentry, paint, stonecutting, and blacksmith shops were set up in the northeast corner of the temple block where they could get power by means of a waterwheel in City Creek. Public Works provided an immediate job for newly arrived immigrants and channeled their skills into building the community. During the 1850s, as many as five hundred workers were employed on various projects.[5]

Meeting in the Bowery on Temple Square in April 1851, the general conference accepted by acclamation the resolution "to build a Temple to the name of the Lord our God" and appointed Daniel H. Wells as building superintendent specifically for the temple.[6] Because of a lack of materials and manpower—fewer than five thousand Saints lived in the immediate area of the projected temple—construction could not commence immediately. In 1852 Public Works put men to work building a fourteen-foot wall of sandstone and adobe around the temple block. This project not only provided security for the construction site but also created worthwhile employment for men who otherwise would have been idle.

The general conference of October 1852 considered which material would be best for building the temple. Some favored sandstone from nearby Red Butte Canyon. Brother Brigham suggested adobe, because brickmaking materials were readily available; he observed, perhaps tongue in cheek, that harder rock had already reached

Salt Lake Temple cornerstone ceremony. Courtesy of Church History Library.

its zenith of perfection and so was now subject to the processes of decay.[7] Heber C. Kimball, Brigham Young's first counselor, asked the conference whether they should build the temple of sandstone, of adobe, or of "the best stone we can find in these mountains." The congregation unanimously voted that "we build a temple of the best materials that can be furnished in the mountains of North America, and that the Presidency dictate where the stone and other materials shall be obtained."[8]

Elder James E. Talmage later concluded that this significant decision reflected the faith and determination of the Saints: "The Temple they were about to rear should be in every particular the best the people could produce. This modern House of the Lord was to be no temporary structure, nor of small proportions, nor of poor material, nor of mean or inadequate design." The Saints knew that the temple would not be finished for many years. By that time "the few would have grown to a multitude of souls. The Temple was to be worthy of the great future."[9]

Site Dedicated and Cornerstones Laid

The temple site was dedicated on a chilly Monday, February 14, 1853. Standing in a small buggy, President Brigham Young addressed the crowd of several thousand who had gathered for the occasion. The band played "Auld Lang Syne," and then Heber C. Kimball offered the dedicatory prayer. Because the ground was frozen, it had to be broken with a pick. President Young then declared the ground officially broken for the temple.[10]

During the next several weeks, trenches twenty feet wide and up to sixteen feet deep were excavated for the temple's foundation. Cornerstones were laid on April 6, 1853, the twenty-third anniversary of the Church's organization. Large stones, measuring approximately two by three by six feet, had been placed in convenient positions ahead of time. They were of "firestone," quarried in nearby Red Butte Canyon. On this beautiful spring day in the valley, general conference convened in the old adobe tabernacle on the southwest corner of the temple block.

Accompanied by military honor guards and the music of three bands, a procession headed by Church leaders marched to the spot where the First Presidency and patriarch laid the southeast cornerstone. President Brigham Young then spoke, explaining that the temple had to be built in order that the Lord "may have a place where he can lay his head, and not only spend a night or a day, but find a place of peace."[11] The southwest cornerstone was next laid by the Presiding Bishopric, representing the Lesser Priesthood. The presidency of the high priests, the stake presidency, and the high council then placed the northwest cornerstone. Finally, the northeast cornerstone was laid by the Twelve and representatives of the seventies and the elders. The laying of each stone was accompanied by special music, speeches, and a prayer. On this occasion, Elder Parley P. Pratt perceived "by the power of the Spirit" that Joseph Smith and others "hovered about us."[12] These proceedings lasted from 10:00 A.M. through 2:00 P.M., at which time President Brigham Young blessed the assembled congregation "in the name of Jesus Christ of Nazareth," and prayed that God would "encircle you in the arms of His love and mercy, and protect us until we have finished this Temple, received the fullness of our endowments therein, and built many more."[13]

President Brigham Young then spoke, explaining that the temple had to be built in order that the Lord "may have a place where he can lay his head, and not only spend a night or a day, but find a place of peace."

How the Temple Was Designed

After a one-hour break, the April 6 conference resumed in the Old Tabernacle. Concerning the future temple, President Young declared,

> I scarcely ever say much about revelations, or visions, but suffice it to say, five years ago last July [1847] I was here, and saw in the Spirit the Temple not ten feet from where we have laid the Chief Corner Stone. I have not inquired what kind of a Temple we should build. Why? Because it was represented before me. I have never looked upon that ground, but the vision of it was there. I see it as plainly as if it was in reality before me. Wait until it is done. I will say, however, that it will have six towers, to begin with, instead of one. Now do not any of you apostatize because

Tower sections, Salt Lake Temple architectural drawings by Truman O. Angell. Courtesy of Church History Library.

Old and New Tabernacles, Salt Lake City. Courtesy of Church History Library.

> it will have six towers, and Joseph only built one. It is easier for us to build sixteen, than it was for him to build one. The time will come when there will be one in the centre of Temples we shall build, and on the top, groves and fish ponds. But we shall not see them here, at present.[14]

Some temples built in the twentieth century, including Hawaii, Los Angeles, and Oakland, would represent a fulfillment of President Young's prophecy, as would the Conference Center across the street from Temple Square.

William Ward, Angell's assistant, later recalled how the prophet shared his vision: "Brigham Young drew upon a slate in the architect's office a sketch, and said to Truman O. Angell: 'There will be three towers on the east, representing the President and his two counselors; also three similar towers on the west representing the Presiding Bishop and his two counselors; the towers on the east the Melchisedek priesthood, those on the west the Aaronic priesthood. The centre towers will be higher than those on the sides, and the west towers a little lower than those on the east end'."[15] Then Angell sketched "a rough vertical section" as President Young described his concept of the temple's interior.[16]

In 1854 architect Truman O. Angell published a detailed description of the future temple. Measurements of the towers match the building as it ultimately was completed.

In 1854 Angell published a detailed description of the future temple. Measurements of the towers match the building as it ultimately was completed. Brigham Young's original plan for the interior, however, was different. It followed the Kirtland and Nauvoo pattern, having two large halls for general meetings. A font and rooms for other ordinances all would be confined to the basement.[17] Three decades later, this concept would be modified (see chapter 5).

The great temple would not be completed for forty years. In the meantime, the Saints would need to have access to temple blessings, so temporary facilities needed to be provided.

Ensign Peak. Courtesy of Church History Library.

Temporary Accommodations for Sacred Blessings

At Various Locations

During the pioneers' early years in the Salt Lake Valley, the endowment was given in a variety of places. In the fall of 1849, Elder Addison Pratt, who had served as a missionary for several years in the South Pacific, was appointed to a second mission in that same area. Before his departure he received his endowment on Ensign Peak, just north of the center of Salt Lake City.[18] This action was consistent with the Prophet Joseph Smith's earlier instructions that under certain circumstances these sacred blessings could be received on mountain tops, as had been the case with Moses.[19]

Beginning in February 1851, the endowment was again given to living members on a regular basis, but these blessings continued to be received at various locations. Some temple ordinances during this time were administered in Brigham Young's office, for example. By 1852 endowments were being given in the Council House, located on the southwest corner of what are now South Temple and Main Streets. This two-story structure measured forty-five feet square. The outer walls of the first story were of red sandstone, while those above were adobe. The building was surmounted by a square tower. There was a large hall and two offices on each floor. The large room on the second floor was divided by white canvas screens into sections representing the various stages of humankind's eternal progression, much as had been done in the upper room of the Nauvoo Temple. During the years 1851, 1852, and 1854, more than two thousand received their endowment here. (None were recorded in 1853.) Because the Council House also was the site for a variety of

Council House. Courtesy of Church History Library.

ecclesiastical and governmental gatherings and the *Deseret News* was even printed there, there was a need for a separate building where endowment blessings could be given in seclusion without interruption.[20]

The Endowment House, a Temporary Temple

Construction on the "new endowment rooms" or "Endowment House," as the structure soon came to be called, commenced during the summer of 1854. The building's architect, Truman O. Angell, referred to it as a "temple pro tem," reflecting how the Saints regarded this new structure. Located in the northwest corner of the temple block, the Endowment House was a two-story adobe structure that measured forty-four by thirty-four feet and had a twenty-by-twenty-foot one-story annex on its north side. Construction was relatively simple and thus progressed rapidly. The building was completed by the spring of the following year.

The Endowment House was dedicated May 5, 1855. President Brigham Young declared that "the house was clean and named it 'The House of the Lord'" and explained that "the spirit of the Lord would be in it, for no one would be permitted to go into it to pollute it." Over the years this prophetic statement would be confirmed by repeated spiritual experiences in the Endowment House. The dedicatory prayer was offered by Heber C. Kimball, who would preside over the work in this holy house. The first endowments and sealings were performed that same day.[21]

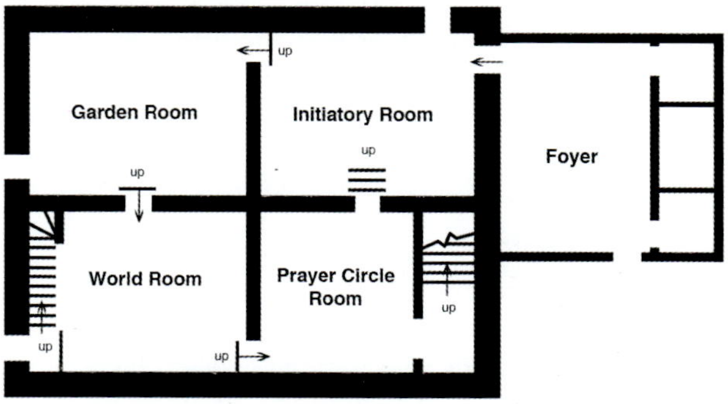

Endowment House floor plans. Courtesy of Lee R. Cowan.

The ground floor had an area for initiatory ordinances, rooms representing the Garden of Eden and the "lone and dreary world," and a room with an altar for special prayers—each room one step higher than the preceding one. Those receiving the endowment would then proceed up a wide staircase to an instruction room and then through the veil into the celestial room. There was also a sealing room on this upper floor. A few months after the building's dedication, William Ward painted a beautiful mural depicting animals, birds, trees, and flowers on the north wall in the garden room. Thus, the Endowment House had several "firsts" that anticipated features that would be familiar in many temples—separate rooms, some with murals, in an ascending series suggesting upward progress. In 1856, the year after the building opened, a large addition on the west provided a baptismal font, which was dedicated on October 2.[22]

For the next three decades, the Endowment House would be an influence for good in the lives of thousands of Latter-day Saints. Here the Saints renewed their covenants through rebaptism as they prepared to enter important new phases of their lives; baptisms for the dead would also be performed here. From six hundred to over three thousand received the endowment each year, between twenty-five and thirty people receiving these blessings on a typical day.[23] Outgoing missionaries received instructions from Church leaders and were set apart here. The Endowment House also provided the setting for as many as 2,500 eternal marriages annually. President Heber C. Kimball continued to have general supervision of this work until his death

Endowment House. Courtesy of Church History Library.

Early stonework on basement level of the Salt Lake Temple. Courtesy of Church History Library.

in 1868. Elder Wilford Woodruff was also heavily involved, spending from thirty to sixty days each year helping to administer the sacred ordinances in the Endowment House.

Work Continues on the Salt Lake Temple

Meanwhile, the Saints maintained their interest in constructing the temple. The temple's footings, composed of large rough-hewn red sandstone blocks called "ashlars," were completed in July 1855. This particular sandstone was very dense and therefore strong. The footings diminished in width from sixteen feet at the base to ten feet at the top and were seven and one-half feet high. The next step was to build the eight-foot-thick basement walls, which would be composed mostly of carefully cut and fitted granite blocks. Sources of this stone had just been discovered in the canyons twenty-three miles southeast of the temple site, and President Young directed that the temple be built of this material. A unique feature of these walls was inverted arches that distributed the temple's massive weight more evenly.[24]

In the spring of 1856, President Young sent architect Truman O. Angell on a special mission to Europe. "You shall have power and means to go from place to place, from country to country, and view the various specimens of architecture," President

Young blessed him. "You will be quick to comprehend the architectural designs of men in various ages. . . . You will increase in knowledge upon the Temple and other buildings, and many will wonder at the knowledge you possess." Specifically, President Young instructed him to make sketches of important architectural works in order to become better qualified to continue his work on the temple and other buildings.[25] It is possible, for example, that Angell refined his idea for the four corner stairways with their supporting central columns after he had seen the Nelson Monument at Trafalgar Square in London.

The Coming of the Utah Expedition

Not knowing the army's intentions, the Saints were concerned that the temple foundation might be in danger.

On July 23, 1857, as the Latter-day Saints were preparing to celebrate the tenth anniversary of their entrance into the Salt Lake Valley, they received the disturbing word that a potentially hostile United States Army force was heading toward Utah. Not knowing the army's intentions, the Saints were concerned that the temple foundation, which by this time included the beginnings of the granite basement walls, might be in danger. On August 13 President Young placed some important records in a stone box in the temple foundation.[26] The following spring, President Young directed that dirt be hauled in to fill the excavation and cover the foundation walls. When the army arrived in June 1858, the entire temple block looked like a freshly plowed field, and there was no visible evidence of the temple's construction. As it turned out, the army marched through the city without harming any property and set up its camp some thirty miles to the southwest near Utah Lake. With the outbreak of the American Civil War in 1861, the army was needed elsewhere, and it departed from Utah in December of that year.

The Saints had been eager to resume work on the temple. By late 1859, while the army was still in Utah, enough of the foundation was uncovered to reveal that its upper surface was not as level as it needed to be. Then during the spring of 1862, after the army had left, the site was fully reexcavated and the temple footings uncovered, allowing them to be inspected more thoroughly. There were cracks in some of the large sandstone ashlars, and some were not adequately set in mortar. There were gaps between some of the more roughly shaped blocks, filled with rubble or even wooden rollers to lift the stones up. Brigham Young was alarmed by this condition. While today, many believe that the sandstone foundation was ripped out and replaced, the Salt Lake Temple renovation project in 2020 uncovered existing sandstone as part of the foundation. After the pioneer workmen found the cracked stones, they replaced the defective stones in the footings, made the top of the footings perfectly level, and then recommenced laying the blocks for the granite walls. "I want to see the Temple built in a manner that it will endure through the Millennium," President Young declared.[27] The work of rebuilding moved more carefully, and the walls did not reach ground level until the end of the construction season in 1867, fourteen years after the cornerstones had been laid.[28]

The Salt Lake Tabernacle

As mentioned in chapter 1, the Kirtland Temple's main use was as a meeting hall. In many of the communities founded in Utah, a large meetinghouse, called a "tabernacle," was built in the center of town. The term was borrowed and adapted from the language of the Old Testament, where the tabernacle was a movable temple at the center of the camp of Israel and the twelve tribes wandered for forty years in the desert. Centuries after settling in the promised land, the Israelites sought for a more permanent structure than the tabernacle. King Solomon directed the construction of a temple in Jerusalem that would become the focal point for worship in Israel (1 Kings 5–8).

For modern Israel, the Latter-day Saints focused on construction of a temple in the center of Salt Lake City, but in this case a tabernacle would also become a fixture of Temple Square. There was a need for a meeting hall and, in particular, a place to hold general conference. However, the first structures erected to provide for meetings of the Saints were outdoor boweries with open sides and a network of leafy branches overhead to provide shade. They were replaced in 1852 by an adobe "tabernacle." Though it was enclosed, its capacity was limited and the numerous support columns blocked a clear view of the stand. Eventually, a permanent tabernacle was erected just west of the temple site and would become a permanent fixture of Temple Square.

Eager to have a more adequate meeting place for the Saints, Brigham Young in 1863 directed William Folsom to draw up preliminary plans for a new tabernacle, 250 feet long by 150 feet wide, that would seat up to ten thousand persons. Henry Grow, an experienced bridge builder, designed and supervised the construction of

Trusses during the Tabernacle construction. In the foreground are granite blocks for building the Salt Lake Temple. Courtesy of Church History Library.

Completed Tabernacle with men standing on Salt Lake Temple construction site. Courtesy of Church History Library.

huge elliptical wooden trusses that would span the full width of the structure without any center supports, "an innovation without parallel for a building of these dimensions."[29] The domed building was completed and entered service in 1867. When the 3,000-seat balcony was added during 1869–70, the auditorium's acoustics were improved to their widely admired quality. The Salt Lake Tabernacle truly was "one of the most impressive achievements of Latter-day Saint architectural design and engineering skill."[30] The building was officially dedicated in 1875 and would be the home for general conference until the twenty-first century. From the Tabernacle's pulpit, Church leaders gave encouragement and direction to the Saints' temple activity.

Renewed Emphasis on Vicarious Service

While the Saints were struggling to get established in the Rocky Mountains, Church-sponsored activities were limited. Emphasis in temple work was on providing needed ordinances for the living, and work for the dead virtually ceased following the exodus from Nauvoo. Even with the opening of the Endowment House in 1855, this pattern did not change. Official records indicate that only thirty-three deceased couples were sealed vicariously during the pre–Endowment House period, and no such ordinances at all were performed during the following decade. Similarly, there is a record of only one baptism for the dead in 1855, of only two in 1857, and of no others during the Saints' first two decades in Utah.

In the mid-1860s, however, ordinance work for the dead resumed. Sealings of six deceased couples were recorded in 1865 and two baptisms for the dead the following year. In 1869 more than four hundred deceased couples were sealed, and more than five thousand vicarious baptisms were recorded. Available records do not state why these ordinances resumed at this time, but several factors may have been involved. The Saints understood that endowments for the dead could be performed only in a temple and may have supposed that this restriction applied to other vicarious ordinances as well. Nevertheless, the Saints who had participated in baptisms for the dead at Nauvoo were growing older. They, together with more recent immigrants, undoubtedly voiced their anxiety to have further opportunity vicariously to provide the saving ordinances for their departed loved ones.

Where would the Saints perform such ordinances? Most looked forward to returning to Jackson County, Missouri, and anticipated that they would have the privilege of building the great temple there in the not-too-distant future. In 1862, for example, Brigham Young felt the Saints would be going back within a few years and wanted to largely complete the Salt Lake Temple before that time. Nevertheless, he believed that no other temple would be completed before the one in Jackson County.[31] Some may have thought that the American Civil War would open the way for the Saints' return. When the war ended in 1865 without having wrought the expected changes in Missouri, however, attention shifted to the possibility of performing vicarious ordinances in Utah.

By this time the pioneers were sufficiently well established to take on additional religious activities. In 1867, for instance, President Brigham Young directed that steps be taken to establish Relief Societies and Sunday Schools in all branches of the Church for the first time. It was at this same time that vicarious ordinances were being performed in increasing numbers under the direction of inspired leaders. Elder Wilford Woodruff recorded in his journal that during 1870 he had personally witnessed 4,400 baptisms for the dead performed by Elders Joseph F. Smith and Samuel H. B. Smith.[32]

The Need for a Temple

The lack of a temple limited the ordinances that could be performed. For example, Brigham Young specified "no one can receive endowments for another, until a Temple is prepared in which to administer them."[33] In 1872 he pointed out, "We are now baptizing for the dead, and we are sealing [couples] for the dead, and if we had a temple prepared, we should be giving endowments for the dead—for our fathers, mothers, grandfathers, grandmothers, uncles, aunts, relatives, friends and old

Unidentified pioneer family, ca. 1860s. Was this family sealed? Couples that were not sealed when first married often had children who were not sealed to them during their lifetime. The sealing of children to parents would not begin until dedication of the St. George Temple in 1877 and the Logan Temple in 1884. Courtesy of Church History Library.

associates." President Young testified that the Lord was "stirring up the hearts" of many people to search out their pedigrees and that "it will continue and run on from father to father, father to father, until they get the genealogy of their forefathers as far as they possibly can."[34]

President Brigham Young had explained that "there are some of the sealing ordinances that cannot be administered in the [Endowment House] that we are now using; We can only administer in it some of the first ordinances of the Priesthood pertaining to the endowment. There are more advanced ordinances that cannot be administered there."[35] He later explained that ordinances designed "to connect the chain of the Holy Priesthood from Father Adam until now, by sealing children to their parents, being sealed for our forefathers, etc., they cannot be done without a Temple. . . . Neither will children be sealed to their living parents in any other place than a Temple."[36] In 1865 he therefore urged couples to be endowed before their marriage and to be sealed by proper authority so that their children would be "born in the covenant." Otherwise the children could not be theirs as "heirs to the priesthood."[37]

An 1876 circular letter from the First Presidency and the Twelve acknowledged these restrictions but challenged the Saints to overcome them: "We feel led to say to the Latter-day Saints throughout these mountains: Let us arise and build Temples unto our God at such places as He shall designate, into which we and our children can enter and receive those blessings that He has in store for us." The Presidency now called for the construction of two temples in addition to those already under way in Salt Lake City and St. George and called on ward bishops to provide donated labor for this task.[38] While ground would be broken for the Logan and Manti Temples the following year, construction on the temple in St. George had begun five years earlier.

Salt Lake Temple at Christmastime, by Michael Hart/Unsplash.

"Let us arise and build Temples unto our God at such places as He shall designate, into which we and our children can enter and receive those blessings that He has in store for us."

Notes

1. Matthias F. Cowley, *Wilford Woodruff: History of His Life and Labors* (Salt Lake City: Bookcraft, 1964), 255.
2. Cowley, *Wilford Woodruff*, 619–20; early published accounts of this event place it on July 28, but a study of diaries suggests that it happened two days earlier.
3. James R. Clark, comp., *Messages of the First Presidency* (Salt Lake City: Bookcraft, 1965), 1:333.
4. C. Mark Hamilton, *The Salt Lake Temple: A Monument to a People* (Salt Lake City: University Services, 1983), 51–53.
5. Leonard J. Arrington, *Great Basin Kingdom* (Cambridge, MA: Harvard University Press, 1958), 109–12.
6. *Deseret News Weekly*, April 19, 1851, 1.
7. Brigham Young, in *Journal of Discourses* (London: Latter-day Saints' Book Depot, 1854), 1:218–20.
8. Heber C. Kimball, in *Journal of Discourses*, 1:160, 162.
9. James E. Talmage, *The House of the Lord* (Salt Lake City: Bookcraft, 1962), 142.
10. James H. Anderson, "The Salt Lake Temple," *Contributor*, April 1893, 250–58; Scott G. Kenney, ed., *Wilford Woodruff's Journal*, February 14, 1853 (Midvale, UT: Signature Book, 1984), 4:195–199.
11. Brigham Young, in *Journal of Discourses* (London: Latter-day Saints' Book Depot, 1854), 2:33, April 6, 1853; James H. Anderson, "The Salt Lake Temple," *Contributor*. April 1893, 252–59.
12. Parley P. Pratt, in *Journal of Discourses*, 1:14, April 7, 1853.
13. Anderson, "Salt Lake Temple," 257.
14. Brigham Young, in *Journal of Discourses*, 1:133.
15. William Ward, "Who Designed the Temple?," *Deseret News Weekly*, April 23, 1892, 8.
16. Ward, "Who Designed the Temple?," 8.
17. Truman O. Angell, "The Temple," *Deseret News*, August 17, 1854.
18. Brigham H. Roberts, *A Comprehensive History of The Church of Jesus Christ of Latter-day Saints* (Provo, UT: BYU Press, 1965), 3:386.
19. "Discourse, 1 May 1842, as Reported by Willard Richards," p. 94, The Joseph Smith Papers, https://www.josephsmithpapers.org/paper-summary/discourse-1-may-1842-as-reported-by-willard-richards/1.
20. Andrew Jenson, *Encyclopedic History of the Church* (Salt Lake City: Deseret News, 1941), 161; Roberts, *Comprehensive History of the Church*, 4:12–14; Journal History July 7, 1852, 1, MS, Church History Library. Elder Roberts's statement that the endowment was given in 1852 for the first time since the expulsion from Nauvoo is in error.
21. Journal History, May 5, 1855, 1–2.
22. Lisle G. Brown, "'Temple Pro Tempore': The Salt Lake City Endowment House," *Journal of Mormon History*, 34, no. 4 (Fall 2008): 1–68.
23. James Dwight Tingen, *The Endowment House, 1855–1889,* (Provo, UT: BYU, 1974), 13–15.
24. Paul C. Richards, "The Salt Lake Temple Infrastructure: Studying It Out in Their Own Minds," *Brigham Young University Studies*, 36, no. 2 (1996–97): 207–9.
25. Richard Neitzel Holzapfel, *Every Stone a Sermon* (Salt Lake City: Bookcraft, 1992), 17; see also Marvin E. Smith, "The Builder," *Improvement Era*, October 1942, 630.
26. Mark Henshaw, *Forty Years: The Saga of Building the Salt Lake Temple* (Salt Lake City: Deseret Book, 2020), 142–43; Richards, "Salt Lake Temple Infrastructure," 208.
27. Brigham Young, in *Journal of Discourses*, 10:254; see also Kenney, *Wilford Woodruff's Journal*, 6:71, August 23, 1862.
28. Henshaw, *Forty Years*, 172–74, 190–97, 234–35.
29. Paul L. Anderson, "Tabernacle, Salt Lake City," in *Encyclopedia of Mormonism*, ed. Daniel H. Ludlow (New York: Macmillan, 1992), 4:1433.

30. Anderson, "Tabernacle, Salt Lake City," 4:1433.
31. Kenney, *Wilford Woodruff's Journal*, 6:71, August 23, 1862.
32. Kenney, *Wilford Woodruff's Journal*, 6:586.
33. Brigham Young, in *Journal of Discourses*, 16:186–87, September 4, 1873; Kenney, *Wilford Woodruff's Journal*, 6:232, July 13, 1865.
34. Kenney, Brigham Young, in *Journal of Discourses*, 15:138, August 24, 1872.
35. Brigham Young, in *Journal of Discourses*, 10:254, October 6, 1863.
36. Brigham Young, in *Journal of Discourses*, 16:186–87, September 4, 1873.
37. Kenney, *Wilford Woodruff's Journal*, 6:232, July 13, 1865.
38. James R. Clark, comp., *Messages of the First Presidency*, 2:278–80.

3 The First Temple Completed in Utah

The St. George Temple

St. George Utah Aerial, by Alan Fullmer.

While the Salt Lake Temple was under construction, three other temples were completed. The first of these would be in St. George in southern Utah.

Anticipation of a Temple in St. George

Cutaway view of the St. George Temple. Courtesy of Lee R. Cowan.

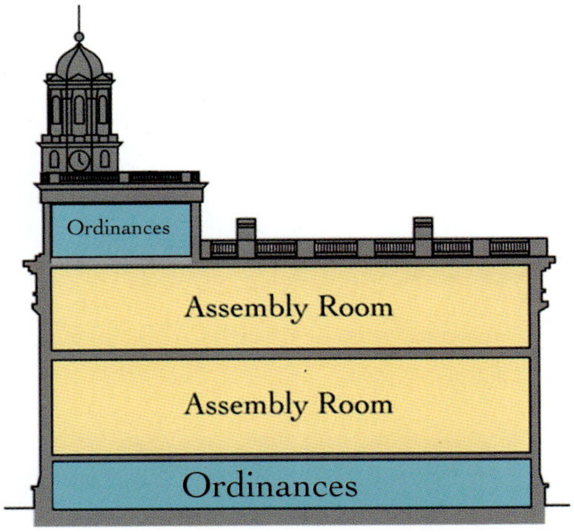

St. George Temple

The first Latter-day Saint colonists were sent to southern Utah in 1861 to raise needed cotton and also to provide a stopping place along the trail connecting southern California and the central areas of colonization surrounding Salt Lake City. After ten years of struggle to gain a foothold in the desert, St. George's population had reached only twelve hundred. At a council meeting with local leaders on January 31, 1871, President Brigham Young proposed that a temple be built in the city. This announcement was received with "Glory! Hallelujah!" from Elder Erastus Snow of the Twelve, who had presided in the St. George area. These feelings were shared by all present.[1]

The construction of this temple had been prophesied as early as 1855, six years before the town of St. George was even founded. While he was in the community of Harmony, about forty miles northeast of the future temple site, President Heber C. Kimball declared that "a wagon road would be made from Harmony over the Black Ridge; and a temple would be built in the vicinity of the Rio Virgin."[2] At that time the construction of such a road and temple seemed highly unlikely.

With such a small population in the area during the early 1870s, many wondered why a temple was to be built in St. George. President John Taylor later pointed out that because "it was found that our Temple in Salt Lake City would take such a long time to build, it was thought best" to erect another one in southern Utah. In the warmer climate, construction could proceed year-round. Furthermore, John Taylor would later say, "There was a people living here who were more worthy than any others. . . . God inspired President Young to build a Temple here because of the fidelity and self-abnegation of the people."[3]

"Brother Young," protested the men, "this land is boggy. There is no place to build a foundation." President Young countered, "We will make a foundation."

Locating the Site

Brigham Young directed local Church leaders to consider possible sites where the temple might be built. Two hilltop locations were proposed. Nevertheless, the group could not agree on which to recommend. A young man who was present later described what happened. When President Young arrived, he "somewhat impatiently chided them, and at the same time asked them to get into their wagons, or whatever else they had, and with him find a location." He had them drive to the lowest part of the valley, a swamp infested with marsh grass and cattails.

"But, Brother Young," protested the men, "this land is boggy. After a storm, and for several months of the year, no one can drive across the land without horses and wagons sinking way down. There is no place to build a foundation." President Young countered, "We will make a foundation."

Heber C. Kimball. Courtesy of Church History Library.

Later, while the brethren were plowing and scraping where the foundation was to be, a horse's leg broke through the ground into a spring of water. The brethren then wanted to move the foundation line twelve feet to the south so that the spring of water would be on the outside of the temple. David H. Cannon Jr., who was there as an eleven-year-old child, recalled many decades later what he could of the prophet's remarks. "Not so," he recalled Brigham Young insisting. "We will wall it up and leave it here for some future use. But we cannot move the foundation. This spot was dedicated by the Nephites. They could not build [the temple], but we can and will build it for them."[4]

Because of the sparseness of the population and the lack of funds, many wondered how the temple could be built. "We do not need capital," President Young responded. "We have raw material; we have labor: we have skill. We are better able to build a temple than the Saints were in Nauvoo." All tithing collected south of Beaver was to be used for the St. George Temple.[5]

Creating the Design

The architect for the temple was Truman O. Angell. Even though he had designed the Endowment House with separate rooms for giving ordinances, he and President Young were reluctant to depart from the pattern established by Joseph Smith for the Nauvoo Temple. Hence his plan for the St. George Temple's interior was like the concept for the Salt Lake Temple described in 1854. There would be two large assembly halls, one above the other, with half stories consisting of a row of small rooms on each side of the large halls' arched ceilings. The basement would include a font and other rooms for ordinances; there would be four entrances directly from the outside at this level, two on the south and two on the north, just as Angell had planned for Salt Lake. Therefore, most of the temple's space was designed for general meetings rather than for ordinances.

Like the Nauvoo Temple, the St. George Temple would have a single front center tower. Its two large halls would be illuminated by tall windows, while each of the small side rooms would have a small round window. Hence, the pattern of exterior windows would be like those of the Nauvoo and Salt Lake Temples. The main difference from the Nauvoo Temple was the St. George Temple's flatter roof with no attic story. Otherwise, the temple in St. George was very similar to the temple in Nauvoo in size, general form of the building, and arrangement of its interior spaces.

Interior rendering of St. George Temple. Courtesy of Church History Library.

Difficulties during Construction

Ground was broken November 9, 1871. Music was provided by a Swiss brass band from nearby Santa Clara. President George A. Smith offered the prayer dedicating the site. "If the brethren undertake to do this work with one heart and mind," President Brigham Young promised, "we shall be blessed exceedingly, and prospered of the Lord in our earthly substance."

Placing his spade in the ground, President Young declared, "I now commence by moving this dirt in the name of Israel's God." All present responded with "Amen." Erastus Snow earnestly prayed "that our beloved President, Brigham, might live to officiate at [the temple's] dedication." The people "gave a hearty Amen." After the congregation sang "The Spirit of God," President Young stood on a chair and led them in the Hosanna Shout. That very afternoon, plows and scrapers began excavating for the foundation.[6]

As the excavation progressed, workmen discovered that the site was filled with water and mud. To provide a firm foundation for the temple, "hundreds of tons" of rock had to be pounded into the ground. Not any rock would do. Black volcanic rock which would not decay in the moisture had to be brought by wagon from a ridge west of the settlement. To pound this rock into place, a primitive pile driver

Right: Exterior rendering of St. George Temple. Courtesy of Church History Library.

THE
TEMPLE
GOD
JESUS CHRIST
LATTER DAY SAINTS
1874
FRONT ELEVATION OF THE TEMPLE
St GEORGE

was improvised. A small brass cannon, which the Mormon Battalion had acquired at Sutter's Mill in California, was filled with lead. A heavy framework about thirty feet high was constructed, and the thousand-pound weight was hoisted by horses and then allowed to fall. "So great was the momentum that the hammer would bounce three times before coming to rest."[7]

During the six years of construction, the whole community demonstrated a spirit of cooperation and dedication. Men took wagons some eighty miles to Mount Trumbull in Arizona to obtain timber of sufficient size. Often eight days of travel across the hot desert were required to bring as few as two huge logs back to St. George.

Local able-bodied men were expected to donate one day in ten as tithing labor, following the pattern which had been established in Nauvoo. Eighteen-year-old John Stucki walked five miles from the nearby Swiss colony in order to work in the stone quarry; he then gave half of his pay back to the temple fund. Also, men from the northern settlements were called on forty-day missions to help with the construction.[8]

On Wednesday, April 1, 1874, President Brigham Young and other general and local Church leaders gathered to place a metal box in the temple's southeast cornerstone. The box contained copies of the standard works, other books, and newspapers of the time. Also placed in the box was a silver plaque listing key events in Church and St. George history and the names of the General Authorities then serving. President Young explained that these items were selected "in token of our faith, to be here preserved until the Savior comes; and then to be subject to His will and pleasure, together with the Temple, for the use of the living and the dead."[9]

The baptismal font and oxen, constructed in Salt Lake City, were a personal gift of President Brigham Young. The font was shipped in sections and assembled in the partially completed St. George Temple. It was dedicated August 11, 1875, and beginning that same day was used for baptisms initiating people into the United Order. When Elder Orson Hyde visited the temple and saw the font in place, he "came out weeping with joy. He thanked God that he had lived to see another font in place in a temple of the Lord."[10]

Men working with stone for the St. George Temple. Courtesy of Church History Library.

The main walls of the temple were of red sandstone, quarried just north of town. These were covered with plaster to give the temple its familiar gleaming white appearance. Visiting the temple just before its dedication, Wilford Woodruff was impressed with the structure that was "as white as snow both inside

Teams prepared to haul the baptismal font to St. George in 1874. Courtesy of Church History Library.

and out and is a beautiful contrast with the red appearance of the surrounding country."[11] The temple's whiteness distinguished it from other buildings in the area and symbolized its holy purposes.

The southern Utah Saints were eager to see the temple completed and to have the opportunity of performing sacred ordinances therein. On Christmas Day of 1876, for example, "forty women were sewing carpets and all the men were at work" to get the temple ready for dedication.[12]

A Piecemeal Dedication

Baptistry and Lower Assembly Hall Dedicated

The Saints gathered at the temple on New Year's Day in 1877 to dedicate the portions of the building sufficiently completed at that time. In the baptistry, Elder Wilford Woodruff, who was to become the temple's first president, reminded the congregation what a privilege it was once again to be able to enter a temple built by the Lord's command and especially dedicated to him. After prayer was offered there, the group moved to the main assembly room on the ground floor where Erastus Snow, also of the Twelve, offered a dedicatory prayer.

St. George Temple before plastering and during the process of making the temple white. Courtesy of Church History Library.

President Young was determined to attend the services even though he was so ill that he had to be carried about in a large chair by four men. He had not expected to speak, but during the service he received enough strength that he was able to walk to the pulpit and address the congregation with great power:

> Now we have a Temple which will all be finished within a few days. . . . We enjoy privileges that are enjoyed by no one else on the face of the earth. Suppose we were awake to this thing, namely, the salvation of the human family, this house would be crowded, as we hope it will be, from Monday morning until Saturday night. . . . What do you suppose the fathers would say if they could speak from the dead? Would they not say, "We have lain here thousands of years, here in this prison house, waiting for this dispensation to come?" . . . When I think upon this subject, I want the tongues of seven thunders to wake up the people. Can the fathers be saved without us? No. Can we be saved without them? No.

One who was present recalled that as President Young spoke, he "brought his cane down very hard on the pulpit. He said, 'If I mar the pulpit some of these good workmen can fix it up again.' He did mar the pulpit, but the people did not fix it up again. They left it for a mark to be carried through the years."[13] The marking can be seen in the St. George Temple pulpit to this day.

Temple Dedicated by Daniel H. Wells

Finally, weeks after ordinance work had begun, the Church's annual general conference was held in the now completed St. George Temple. In connection with this conference the temple was officially dedicated on April 6, 1877, the dedicatory prayer being offered by Daniel H. Wells, second counselor to Brigham Young in the First Presidency. Elements of the prayer acknowledged that the Lord had led the Saints "to this distant land" and that through His "continued blessings they have been enabled to gather together the materials of which this building is composed; to put together and erect the same, even a Temple." In view of the temple's swampy site, the prayer continued: "We dedicate and consecrate the foundation of this building upon which it stands. Cause, O Lord, that it may not give way nor yield in consequence of any

St. George Temple with a new tower. Courtesy of Church History Library.

destructive elements which may be in the soil, but the nature of those elements be changed so as to become strengthening instead of weakening, that the same may always remain firm and sound." The prayer minutely referred to each part of the building. It suggested possible uses of the small "side rooms" above the arched ceilings of the two main halls. "They may be used, by the Priesthood, for prayer, for worship, for councils or meetings, for administering the Holy Ordinances of Thy house that they may be holy unto Thee, the Lord our God." The prayer concluded by petitioning, "Let Thy peace and blessing dwell and abide here in this Holy Temple" and may the St. George Temple "stand as a monument of purity and holiness as long as the earth shall remain."[14]

Many traveled long distances to be present at this special general conference and temple dedication. They had to bring their own provisions because there were only limited accommodations along the way and in St. George. Most camped near the temple or in the yards of St. George friends.

Three temples were needed for the full restoration of temple ordinances: (1) priesthood keys were bestowed at Kirtland, (2) baptisms for the dead and endowments and sealings for the living were inaugurated at Nauvoo, and (3) endowments and sealings for the dead commenced at St. George.

Struck by Lightning

The people of St. George passed down a tradition that Brigham Young was pleased with the temple which the Saints had sacrificed to build, except for in one area. He did not like the short-domed tower, preferring a taller tower that would give the temple a more magnificent appearance. Contemporary accounts do not contain references to Brigham's thoughts about the shorter tower. Yet, a year after his death, during a severe thunderstorm on October 16, 1878, a bolt of lightning struck and destroyed the dome, which was later replaced by the taller tower that President Young had initially wanted. "Brother Brigham finally got his way," the St. George Saints concluded.[15] Whether it really was Brigham or the likelihood that the temple's tower, which was the highest point in the area, would be struck by lightning eventually, there is a more important issue.

Those that were present to assess the damage after the lightning, including John D. McCallister and James G. Bleak, realized that the lightning and subsequent fire could have destroyed the entire temple structure, not just the dome. In a letter to Wilford Woodruff, Bleak stated, "We find in repairing the roof, that the hand of the Lord, and nothing else, must have saved the building from being burned at the time the tower was struck by lightning." He continued, describing how the fire did not go below the tower even though, "the fire must have smoldered for some time, and that too, right in contact with the tar-covered canvas which covers the roof. We acknowledge the preserving hand of the Almighty."[16]

The First Endowments for the Dead

Baptisms for the dead had commenced in the St. George Temple on January 9, 1877, with Elder Woodruff, who was serving as the newly called temple president, personally baptizing and confirming the first 141. President Young also assisted in the laying on of hands.[17] Two days later, for the first time in this dispensation, the endowment was also given in behalf of the dead. Just the month before his martyrdom, Joseph Smith had taught the necessity of these ordinances: "It is not only necessary that you should be baptized for your dead, but you will have to go through all the ordinances for them, the same as you have gone through to save yourselves."[18] Unfortunately, intensifying persecution and the Prophet's death prevented the Saints from inaugurating endowments for the dead at Nauvoo. With the completion of the first temple in the west, this service could be commenced. Heretofore, the Saints could experience the teachings of the endowment only once—for themselves. Now they could return time after time, serving in behalf of their deceased loved ones and gaining a deeper understanding of the endowment's teachings.

Elder Bruce C. Hafen has shared that three temples were needed for the full restoration of temple ordinances: (1) priesthood keys were bestowed at Kirtland, (2) baptisms for the dead and endowments and sealings for the living were inaugurated at Nauvoo, and (3) endowments and sealings for the dead commenced at St. George.[19]

The introduction of endowments for the dead focused greater attention on these sacred instructions. Up to this time, these teachings had been communicated from one person to another only in oral form. As the lone survivor of the original group receiving the endowment from Joseph Smith in 1842, President Young was concerned that this ordinance be preserved. He therefore spent much time during the early months of 1877 giving instructions on this important subject. On January 14, he specifically assigned Elders Wilford Woodruff and Brigham Young Jr. to write these ceremonies "from beginning to end." During the next several weeks, these two Apostles met with President Young, who reviewed what they had written and made corrections as necessary. By March 21, 1877, the project was completed, and a standardized endowment ceremony was taught to the temple workers at St. George.[20]

The original plan was to present the endowment in basement rooms, some areas being divided by white canvas partitions or temporary screens. Baptisms would take place on other days of the week, so the same dressing areas could be used both for baptisms and for the endowment. When the numbers of faithful Saints flocking to

Those that were present to assess the damage realized that the lightning and subsequent fire could have destroyed the entire temple structure, not just the dome.

Ordinance workers ride a wagon to come to the temple. Courtesy of Church History Library.

The temple and the growing St. George community during the nineteenth century. Courtesy of Church History Library.

the temple quickly overwhelmed these facilities, Wilford Woodruff consulted with Brigham Young and others.

By the beginning of March 1877, after just seven weeks, they decided to use the lower of the two large assembly halls, immediately above the basement, to relieve the pressure. Henceforth, the areas representing the Creation and Garden of Eden were in the two basement rooms east of the font, and the larger world room was to the west. Patrons then climbed a flight of stairs into the spacious assembly room above; the western portion, representing the terrestrial kingdom, was separated from the celestial room at the eastern end by one of the white screens. The room in the tower behind the Melchizedek Priesthood pulpits was then used for sealings. This basic arrangement would continue in the St. George Temple until it was remodeled sixty years later.

Permission to Officiate for People Other Than Relatives

Wilford Woodruff, 1877. Courtesy of Church History Library.

While directing the unfolding of vicarious service at St. George, Wilford Woodruff became increasingly concerned about the redemption of his own deceased relatives. Not having any family members with him in St. George, he worried about how this could be accomplished. On February 23 he made this a special matter of prayer: "The Lord told me to call upon the Saints in St. George and let them officiate for me in that temple and it should be acceptable unto him."[21] "I saw an [effectual] door open to me for the redemption of my dead. And . . . I felt like shouting Glory Halleluiah [*sic*] to God and the Lamb."

Up until 1877, temple ordinances were generally not performed for nonfamily members. On March 1, Elder Woodruff's seventieth birthday, some 154 sisters came to the temple to act as proxies for his female relatives. "I feel thankful to you my sisters for this manifestation of kindness," he told them as they gathered at the beginning of the endowment session, "for you might have searched the world over and you could not have found a present as dear to me as this. What is gold or silver in comparison to the redemption of our dead? Nothing."[22] One sister later recalled that when she heard Elder Woodruff needed help, "we prayed that we might be chosen, and our joy was great when we received our notice that we were to be numbered with the proxies of this first company." She and others returned to the temple again and again to officiate for those on the Woodruff list.[23] Thus, the Saints not only had the responsibility to perform vicarious ordinances in behalf of deceased loved ones but also had

Glen Hopkinson, *Redeemed*. Used with permission.

the permission to help others with this sacred work. This precedent laid the foundation for the massive effort that became such an important component of the Saints' temple service in later years.

Wilford Woodruff Visited by Spirits of the Dead

Performing ordinances beyond one's own ancestors was underscored in an unusual way, as one fulfillment to President Brigham Young's question at the temple dedication: "What do you suppose the fathers would say if they could speak from the dead? . . . What would they whisper in our ears?"[24] For two consecutive nights in August 1877, Wilford Woodruff learned the answer to that question. He felt the presence of an esteemed group of men, the signers of the Declaration of Independence, urging him with a desperate request to receive the ordinances of salvation. In his own words, Elder Woodruff described the experience:

St. George Utah Temple. Courtesy of Intellectual Reserve, Inc.

The prophet felt the presence of an esteemed group of men, the signers of the Declaration of Independence, urging him with a desperate request to receive the ordinances. of salvation.

> The spirits of the dead gathered around me, wanting to know why we did not redeem them. Said they, "You have had the use of the Endowment House for a number of years, and yet nothing has ever been done for us. We laid the foundation of the government you now enjoy . . . and were faithful to God.
>
> The men were the signers of the Declaration of Independence, and they waited on me for two days and two nights. I thought it very singular, that notwithstanding so much work had been done . . . nothing had been done for them. . . . Heretofore our minds were reaching after our more immediate friends and relatives.[25]

Following this experience, on Sunday, August 19, 1877, Elder Woodruff studied a work written by Evert A. Duyckinck, entitled *Eminent Men and Women of Europe and America*, identifying those individuals he felt should be the first group of nonrelatives to receive vicarious ordinances. Two days later, on August 21, 1877, Elder Woodruff stepped into the temple baptismal font and was baptized by John D. T. McAllister for one hundred prominent men of the seventeenth and eighteenth centuries, including the signers of the Declaration of Independence and other noted individuals such as Christopher Columbus, Daniel Webster, Henry Clay, John Wesley, and Benito Juárez. Elder Woodruff then baptized Brother McAllister for all the deceased presidents of the United States except three (whose ordinances have been performed by relatives in the Church more recently). Sister Lucy Bigelow Young was then baptized for seventy prominent women, including Martha Washington and Elizabeth Barrett Browning.

Contemporary historians may judge favorably or unfavorably some of these eminent men and women whom Wilford Woodruff decided to put on the list to be baptized and confirmed in the temple. However, it should be remembered that notwithstanding the weaknesses demonstrated in a person's life, all people have the opportunity to continue to grow and change in the spirit world and to accept or reject the ordinances offered to them through the temple. Ultimately, Christ alone will balance justice and mercy and make a final judgment of the lives of God's children.

Historian Jennifer Ann Mackley noted how for Wilford Woodruff this experience "changed not only his view of temple work but has become an important symbol of the universal nature of temple work. His experience underscored the role of the living in providing the opportunity to accept Christ's salvation to all who have ever lived. It also reminded the Saints that those in the spirit world expected them to fulfill their responsibility."[26]

Historian Richard E. Bennett, who has studied how temple work unfolded, concluded, "It is hard to overemphasize the importance of what happened for the first time in the St. George Temple beginning in January 1877. With the introduction of endowments for the dead for both deceased friends and family ancestors, members began returning to the temple on a much more regular basis than before. Such increased temple attendance forged a renewal of their own temple covenants and instilled a heightened sense of family history, temple consciousness, and personal worthiness upon the many who frequented the temple, both men and women."[27]

At about this same time, the publication of a new edition of the Doctrine and Covenants also heightened "temple consciousness." The 1876 edition, prepared under the direction of Elder Orson Pratt, added twenty-three sections for the first time, some directly related to temple service: Section 2 was Moroni's 1823 paraphrase of Malachi's prophecy about Elijah restoring priesthood keys. Section 109 was the dedicatory prayer for the Kirtland Temple. Section 110 included the account of Elijah's coming in 1836 (see verses 13–16). Section 132 explained eternal or celestial marriage (see especially verses 7 and 15–24).

While the far-reaching events were taking place in St. George, steps were being taken which would lead to the construction of yet two other temples in Utah. Of these new temples, Elder Woodruff spoke in general conference and said the Saints would "begin to see the necessity of building others, for in proportion to the diligence of our labors in this direction, will we comprehend the extent of the work to be done, and the present is only a beginning."[28]

Notes

1. Daniel Tyler, "Temples," *Juvenile Instructor*, August 15, 1880, 182.
2. Stanley B. Kimball, *Heber C. Kimball: Mormon Patriarch and Pioneer* (Urbana: University of Illinois Press, 1981), 201.
3. John Taylor, in *Journal of Discourses* (London: Latter-day Saints' Book Depot, 1854–86), 23:14, November 9, 1881.
4. David H. Cannon, Jr., October 14, 1942, quoted in Janice F. DeMille, *The St. George Temple: The First 100 Years* (Hurricane, UT: Homestead Publishers, 1977), 20–21.
5. Juanita Brooks, "The St. George Temple" (MS, Juanita Brooks papers, Utah State Historical Society), 3.
6. Tyler, "Temples," 182; DeMille, *St. George Temple*, 21–23.
7. N. B. Lundwall, *Temples of the Most High* (Salt Lake City: Bookcraft, 1947), 86; DeMille, *St. George Temple*, 26–29.
8. Brooks, "St. George Temple," 3.
9. Southern Utah Mission Historical Record, 1873–1877, MS, Church History Library, 78.
10. DeMille, *St. George Temple*, 39–41.
11. Scott G. Kenney, ed., *Wilford Woodruff's Journal* (Midvale, UT: Signature Books, 1985) 7:291, November 10, 1876.
12. Kenney, *Wilford Woodruff's Journal*, 7:297, December 25, 1876.
13. Brigham Young, in *Journal of Discourses*, 18:304, January 1, 1877. Maggie Cragun interview, "The Dedication of the St. George Temple" (Juanita Brooks papers, Utah State Historical Society);
14. Quoted in N. B. Lundwall, *Temples of the Most High* (Salt Lake City: Bookcraft, 1947), 79–83.
15. DeMille, *St. George Temple*, 88.
16. St. George Utah Stake manuscript history and historical reports, Church History Library, July 30, 1883.
17. Kenney, *Wilford Woodruff's Journal*, 7:321, January 9, 1877.
18. Joseph Smith, *History of the Church of Jesus Christ of Latter-day Saints*, ed. B. H. Roberts, 2nd ed., rev. (Salt Lake City: Deseret Book, 1962), 6:365.
19. Bruce C. Hafen, Evening at the Museum presentation, Church History Museum, May 2014, https://www.churchofjesuschrist.org/media/video/2014-01-0105-may-2014-evening-at-the-museum-bruce-c-hafen.
20. Kenney, *Wilford Woodruff's Journal*, 7:322, 327, and 340, January 14, February 12, and March 21, 1877; see also "St. George Temple: One Hundred Years of Service," *Ensign*, March 1977, 94.
21. G. Homer Durham, ed., *Discourses of Wilford Woodruff* (Salt Lake City: Bookcraft, 1969), 159; Kenney, *Wilford Woodruff's Journal*, 7:329, February 23, 1877.
22. Kenney, *Wilford Woodruff's Journal*, 7:330–32, March 1, 1877.
23. Martha Cragun Cox, "Autobiography," holograph, Church History Library, 150.
24. Brigham Young, in *Journal of Discourses*, 18:304.
25. Wilford Woodruff, in *Journal of Discourses*, 19:229, September 16, 1877.
26. Jennifer Ann Mackley, *Wilford Woodruff's Witness of the Development of Temple Doctrine* (Seattle, WA: High Desert Publishing, 2014), 184.
27. Richard E. Bennett, *Temples Rising* (Salt Lake City: Deseret Book, 2019), 229–30.
28. Wilford Woodruff, in *Journal of Discourses*, 19:229–30, as quoted in Mackley, *Wilford Woodruff's Witness*, 194.

4 A Design More Suited for "Sacred and Holy Purposes"

The Logan and Manti Temples

Manti Sunset Panorama by Alan Fullmer.

The St. George Temple had followed the basic pattern of the earlier Kirtland and Nauvoo Temples—essentially comprising only two large assembly rooms, one above the other, which were well-suited for large meetings. The inauguration of endowments for the dead, however, created a greater need for temple facilities specifically adapted to the presentation of this sacred ordinance. The next decade and a half witnessed a dramatic acceleration in temple construction. Not just one, but three of these sacred edifices—the Logan, Manti, and Salt Lake Temples—were under construction at the same time. They would embody changes made with the guidance of inspired Church leaders.

Inspired Variations in Temple Design

Speaking at the time that the St. George Temple was being completed, several Church leaders had indicated that the design of future temples would meet new needs. In 1879 Elder Orson Pratt pointed out that the Church by then had tabernacles and other buildings for the Saints' regular meetings. Therefore, temples could be designed specifically for more "sacred and holy purposes"—for ordinances associated with "the Priesthood of the Most High God." Elder Pratt insisted that the Lord is "not confined" to a single pattern in temple building any more than he is in the creation of worlds, "but He will construct His Temples in a great variety of ways."[1] Two years previously Elder Pratt explained, "The Lord begins little by little; he does not reveal everything all at once." There were no rooms for ordinances in the Kirtland Temple. When baptisms for the dead were restored at Nauvoo, a font was provided in the temple there. Endowments for the dead, not known in the first two temples, were now being performed at St. George. Therefore, "by and by," Elder Pratt concluded, "we will have Temples, with a great many things contained in them which we now have not."[2]

That there would be variations in temple design had specifically been made known to President Brigham Young in St. George. "Oh Lord," he had prayed, "show unto thy servants if we shall build all temples after the same pattern." People do not build their homes the same when their families are large as when they are small, came the inspired response. "So shall the growth of the knowledge of the principles of the gospel among my people cause diversity in the pattern of temples."[3] Years earlier, at the time ground was broken for the Salt Lake Temple, President Young had taught that the order of priesthood ordinances is made known by revelation, and therefore we should know what facilities must be included in our temples.[4]

Nineteenth-century temples in Utah. Courtesy of Lee R. Cowan.

Exterior plan of the Logan Temple. Courtesy of Church History Library.

In his landmark work *The House of the Lord*, Elder James E. Talmage pointed out that "there is a definite sequence of development in the dealings of God with man." He explained, "While the general purpose of temples is the same in all times, the special suitability of these edifices is determined by the needs of the dispensation to which they severally belong." Therefore, "we may affirm that divine revelation of temple plans is required for each distinctive period of the Priesthood's administration." Consequently, Elder Talmage concluded, the temple buildings themselves are a tangible record of God's unfolding revelations to his people concerning temple work.[5]

A Design for the Two New Temples

During the 1850s, two rather different concepts were advanced for temples and related buildings. First, Church architect Truman O. Angell presented the traditional concept of two large meeting halls that Brigham Young envisioned for the Salt Lake Temple. Then, at the same time, Angell designed the Endowment House, the first building composed of separate permanent ordinance rooms—a plan obviously more suited for performing priesthood ordinances. When he planned the St. George Temple two decades later, he returned to the earlier pattern, providing facilities for giving the endowment only in the basement. As the Logan and Manti Temples were contemplated, Church leaders gave inspired direction on which concept in temple design to follow and how extensive facilities for the endowment would be. Speaking at the October 1876 general conference, President Brigham Young encouraged the Saints to get to work building temples in the Cache and Sanpete Valleys, promising that he would "provide the plan." Just two weeks later, in a circular letter, the First Presidency indicated that these new temples would not be costly, could be built quickly, and would be designed specifically "for Endowment purposes."[6] By the mid-1870s, Angell was tied up with other projects and in poor health, so the task of completing the design for the new temples was turned over to his two capable assistants. William H. Folsom, who had served during the early 1860s as Church architect and helped to design the Salt Lake Tabernacle, became architect for the Manti Temple, while Truman O. Angell Jr. received the assignment to complete the plans for the temple in Logan.

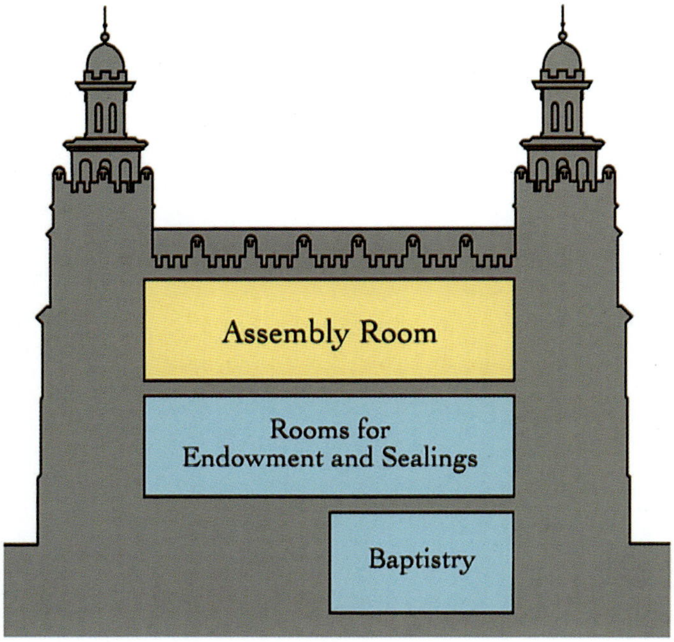

Logan (1884) and Manti (1888) Temples

Manti and Logan Temple layout. Courtesy of Lee R. Cowan.

Though the Logan and Manti Temples were finished under the direction of Young's successor, President John Taylor acknowledged at the Logan Temple dedication that Brigham Young "contemplated and designed" that structure.[7] Both Folsom and Angell Jr. affirmed in 1878 that President Young had instructed that "it was not required that temples should [always] be alike, neither in their interior or exterior design and construction," but they should be arranged for the "convenience of performing the labors therein."[8] This was a departure from the Kirtland, Nauvoo, and St. George Temples.

Both the Manti and Logan Temples would have similar dimensions, be built of local stone in the "castellated" (or castle-like) style. They would each have two towers, the eastern one representing the higher priesthood being slightly taller. They would also have corner turrets enclosing spiral staircases. Hence, these were the first temples to have permanent creation, garden, world, terrestrial, and celestial rooms. In both temples, these rooms would be situated at various levels in a similar ascending clockwise progression. These temples would also be the first to be built with an "annex," which would include space for waiting rooms, administrative offices, record storage, dressing rooms, and other related functions and therefore provide a more suitable entrance to the temple itself. The construction of these two temples was a major focus of the Church during the later 1870s and the 1880s.

A Temple in Cache Valley

Speaking at Wellsville on July 4, 1857, John Thirkell, a convert from England, prophesied that a temple would be built on Cache Valley's east bench.[9] The settlement of Logan at that location would not begin until two years later. Then, in 1863, President Young and other General Authorities visited the valley. Preaching at the bowery in Logan on August 22, Elder Wilford Woodruff was impressed to direct his remarks particularly to the youth: "You will have the privilege of going into the tower of a glorious temple built unto the name of the most high God, east of us upon the Logan Bench." President Young then testified that what Elder Woodruff had said was revelation.[10]

Groundbreaking in Logan

President Young and a large group of general and local Church leaders broke ground on May 18, 1877. Four inches of snow had fallen during the previous night, and the day was brisk yet sunny. Someone in the congregation placed his coat on the ground so that Elder Orson Pratt would not have to kneel in the mud and snow as he offered the prayer dedicating the site.[11] Following the prayer, President Young reminded the Saints that the temple would be constructed by volunteer labor and that "wages are entirely out of the question." Nevertheless, the temple could be built "without any burden to ourselves if our hearts are in the work," he insisted, "and we will be blessed abundantly in doing so. We will be better off in our temporal affairs when it is completed than when we commenced." Speaking on this same occasion, Elder John Taylor quoted the biblical prophet Jacob's affirmation that "this is none other but the house of God, and this is the gate of heaven" (Genesis 28:17). "That is not simply a metaphorical expression, but a reality," Elder Taylor affirmed, "for it is in [temples] that the most sacred ordinances of God are to be performed, which are associated with the interest and happiness of the human family, living and dead."[12]

Construction began immediately. Only two feet of dirt had to be excavated in order to reach bedrock, and by September, the seven-foot-wide foundations were in place. The temple's cornerstones were laid on the nineteenth of that month, just over three weeks following President Young's death. The southeast or chief cornerstone was laid by the Twelve, who were then the presiding quorum in the Church. The

Logan Temple under construction. Courtesy of Church History Library.

other cornerstones were laid at the southwest by Presiding Bishop Edward Hunter, who represented the lesser priesthood; at the northwest by the high priests; and at the northeast by the seventies and elders. Elder Wilford Woodruff testified that a host of departed spirits were "witnessing these proceedings [even] more intently and anxiously" than the ten thousand Saints who were physically present, "for they well know in their prison homes that their salvation depends upon these things."[13]

Charles O. Card was named superintendent of construction. During the next several years, more than two hundred men, including Shoshone converts, were almost constantly engaged in building the temple.[14] Many were volunteers from the various towns in the area, each coming when assigned to donate his skill as a mason, carpenter, plasterer, or in some other way to help build the house of the Lord. For example, each Monday morning Julius Smith left his large family at their small farm near Brigham City and hiked over the mountain about twenty miles to Logan. Although he was a slender man just over five feet tall, he worked all week carrying heavy loads of mortar or plaster up ladders to the workmen. After finishing his work on Saturdays, he walked back home in order to spend Sundays with his family.[15]

Fundraising

More than $600,000 (equivalent to nearly twelve million dollars in the early twenty-first century) was contributed to the Logan Temple, over 60 percent coming from the Saints within the Logan Temple district itself. Only a relatively small amount ($93,000) was donated in cash. The remainder came in a variety of forms: $30,000 in merchandise, $30,000 in livestock, $71,000 in produce, and $3,000 in wagons and teams. The equivalent of $380,000 was donated in the form of labor (using the prevailing wage rate of $1.50 per man per day).[16] Those who worked on the temple received food, clothing, livestock, or other items donated by the wards and stakes in the area. In Bear Lake Valley, for example, all the eggs laid on Sundays were donated for the temple. Some Saints even donated some of their hair to strengthen the plaster in at least two of the sacred rooms. Children of the Cache Stake contributed $2,300 toward the temple by means of a Sunday School "nickel fund." One day a young boy attempted to climb the scaffolding to have a close look at the temple but was stopped by a guard. Permission was granted when he explained that he "had paid his nickel to the temple" and therefore felt he had a right to see it.[17]

One day a young boy attempted to climb the scaffolding to have a close look at the temple but was stopped by a guard. Permission was granted when he explained that he "had paid his nickel to the temple" and therefore felt he had a right to see it.

The Saints established their own quarries, sawmills, mechanical shops, and other facilities in order to supply as many materials as they could for the temple without having to use their scarce finances to purchase goods elsewhere. The temple's construction had a far-reaching impact on the development of the whole area. "One can hardly distinguish the building of the . . . temple from the general building of the community," historians concluded. "The network of temple industries not only supplied the temple itself but provided materials for the construction of homes, barns, and shops." Skills learned by those working on the temple subsequently aided the construction of other important buildings in the area.[18]

A challenge facing the temple builders was to construct a roof to span the large upper assembly room. Mechanical superintendent James Quayle reported that after fasting and praying for guidance, he was pondering and saw how "the roof seemed to fit perfectly on the Temple" and knew "how it was [to be] supported and built."[19] After the roof was completed in 1881, work on the temple's interior could move forward throughout the year.

In about 1882 the temple's dark gray limestone exterior was painted white. This outside paint scheme was maintained until about the turn of the century, after which the temple's stone was allowed to weather back to its original color. The supply of commercially produced carpeting in Utah Territory was not adequate to meet the temple's needs. Just two months before the dedication, the sisters in the temple

Logan Temple. Courtesy of Church History Library.

district received the overwhelming assignment to produce the needed floor coverings. They worked energetically collecting rags, tearing them into strips, matching colors, and then stitching together the carpets. Eventually, the women produced over two thousand square yards of finely woven rag carpeting.[20]

The Logan Temple Dedicated

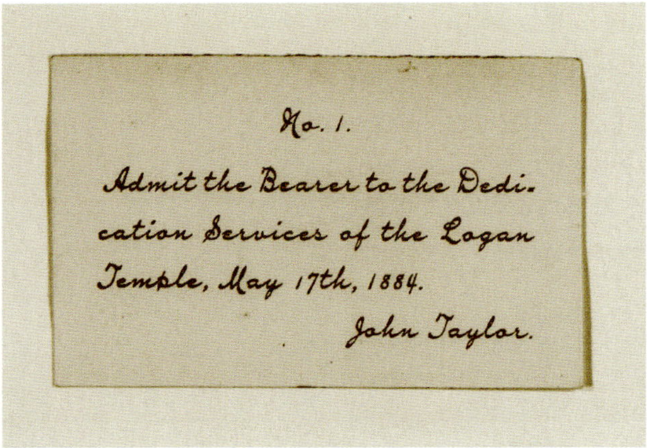

Logan Temple dedication ticket. Courtesy of Church History Library.

Dedication was set for Saturday, May 17, 1884, and the conference of the Cache Stake was scheduled to coincide with this event. This date would mark the seventh anniversary of the groundbreaking for the temple. The railroad offered special excursion rates, so large crowds were anticipated for the events in Logan. The Saints opened their homes, and local Church leaders arranged to feed the crowds; thus, none of the visitors had to pay anything for meals or lodging. Because not all could be accommodated inside the temple during the dedicatory services, bishops were instructed to issue tickets only to those who were worthy to be admitted into the Lord's house.[21] These tickets were personally countersigned by President John Taylor. This was the first time invitations of this kind were used at a temple dedication. The temple's large east doors were opened promptly at ten o'clock Saturday morning. The approximately fifteen hundred Saints bearing tickets to this first dedicatory session climbed the winding corner stairways to the large upper assembly room. The first speaker was President George Q. Cannon of the First Presidency. "Heaven itself and our co-workers of the past are delighted with the accomplishment of this temple," he declared. "We are the representatives of the ages. . . . How boundless should be our gratitude that we are permitted to officiate in the ordinances that will save those who have gone before us." Elder Woodruff testified that "the spirits of Elias, Elijah and other holy men of old are hovering over us and are ready to aid us in any way that is possible." He declared that Joseph Smith, Brigham Young, and the Savior were especially interested in the dedication of this temple, and that "if the veil were taken from our eyes we would behold their faces. . . . God and the heavens are with us today and the Lord is pleased with our labors."[22]

At the conclusion of this dedicatory service, those in attendance were permitted to see other parts of the temple. Led in a procession by Presidents Taylor and Cannon and other Church officials, they walked quietly two by two through the various rooms in the building. As they exited the building, they were greeted by the music of brass bands from Logan and Tooele (the latter having traveled about one hundred miles to be present for this occasion).

Logan Temple ordinance workers, 1880s. Temple president Marriner W. Merrill is in the center left. Courtesy of Church History Library.

President John Taylor dedicated the Logan Temple. Courtesy of Church History Library.

A session of stake conference convened Saturday afternoon in the Logan Tabernacle, about two blocks from the temple. Speaking in this service, Elder Franklin D. Richards of the Quorum of the Twelve referred to the importance of the occasion: "The dedication of the Temple this morning awakens anew in our souls a heavenly, family feeling." Our interest extends beyond this earth to those who are in the spirit world, he explained, and "inspires a feeling that we are part of them and that they are part of us." On such occasions, by the power of faith we view "that portion of the family of God with whom we have before associated, and with whom we expect hereafter to be associated."[23]

To accommodate others who wished to attend, additional dedicatory sessions were scheduled for Sunday and Monday, and about 3,500 more tickets were issued. At one of the three dedicatory sessions, President John Taylor and Charles O. Card stood at the top of the stairs as the throngs were surging into the temple's upper assembly room. President Taylor noticed a woman whom he did not know but instructed Brother Card, "Don't let that woman come into the assembly, she is not worthy." When asked for an explanation, President Taylor replied: "I know not but the Spirit of God said, 'She is not worthy.'" Brother Card therefore told the woman she would have to leave. She offered no resistance. When questioned about the matter, she admitted that she had not been able to get a recommend from her bishop but had purchased one for a dollar from a man on the street.[24]

President John Taylor had also been guided by inspiration in the selection of the first president for the Logan Temple. Several prominent men were under consideration, but because of some prejudiced reports about Marriner W. Merrill, he was not included among the candidates. However, as President Taylor earnestly prayed for guidance, "a voice seemed to say that the man for the post was Bishop Merrill of Richmond." Because of the reports he had received, the president questioned this impression, so he prayed on. "Then there came the distinct and unmistakable impression of a voice, 'Bishop Merrill of Richmond.'" That settled the matter, and Merrill was chosen as temple president. Just five years later, he also was called as a member of the Quorum of the Twelve, and he continued to serve in both positions until his death in 1906.[25]

At the time of the dedication, President Taylor gave instructions concerning the selection of workers for the temple. Except about six who would need to be employed on a permanent basis, men and women should be chosen "who can leave their farms for a season and supply their own necessities for living and doing their work without being dependent on the Temple for their sustenance." These workers should be prepared to stay "as long as shall be needed," from six months to three years. They were to serve much on the same basis as missionaries to the living. President Taylor instructed that this pattern was also to be implemented at St. George and in all other future temples.[26] Two years earlier, a group of nine individuals had been asked to spend several months in St. George working in the temple in order to learn essential procedures. While on this assignment, these individuals were supported by their home wards.

The first ordinances in the Logan Temple were performed two days after the dedication under the personal supervision of the General Authorities still present. Before leaving Logan, President Taylor instructed that the following be placed in the official temple records: "The Lord is well pleased and has accepted this House, and our labors in its Dedication, also the labors of the people in its building and beautifying. . . . I state this as the Word of the Lord. And the Lord will continue to reveal unto us every principle that shall be necessary for our guidance in the future in all matters pertaining to our labors both spiritually and temporally."[27]

The first ordinances in the Logan Temple were performed two days after the dedication under the personal supervision of the General Authorities still present.

A Temple in Sanpete Valley

Although construction on the Manti Temple did not commence until the later 1870s, the idea of a temple in the Sanpete Valley began much earlier. Manti, founded in 1849, was the fourth settlement established by the pioneers in the Rocky Mountains. Only Salt Lake City, Ogden, and Provo preceded it. When the residents of Manti laid out a fifty-nine-acre fort in 1854, they identified a central block as the site for a future temple. At about this same time President Heber C. Kimball prophesied that the temple would be built on the hill above Manti rather than down in the town. "And more than that," he continued, "the rock will be quarried from that hill to build it with, and some of the stone from that quarry will be taken to help complete the Salt Lake Temple."

The rock at Manti, known as oolite, is a warm cream color. President Kimball's prophecy would be fulfilled completely, as stone from Manti was used for decorative work at the east and west ends of the Salt Lake Temple.[28]

Site Selected and Dedicated

As early as December 4, 1873, at a conference in Ephraim, seven miles north of Manti, President Young announced that the temple in Sanpete Valley would be built soon. While in the area, he made some preliminary investigations of possible sites and available materials. By this time, Ephraim had become the principal settlement in the valley. Hence, a controversy arose over where the temple should be built. People in Manti advocated a site in or just above town, while the residents of Ephraim believed the temple should be in their community. This matter was decided at another conference in Ephraim on June 25, 1875, when President Young declared that the temple would be built at the "Manti stone quarry."[29]

The stone quarry was where the first settlers of Manti had lived in dugouts on the side of the rattlesnake-infested hill during the winter of 1849–50. A large stone from this same quarry had been Utah Territory's contribution to the Washington Monument at the nation's capital. Carved by William Ward, the slab bore a beehive, the "all-seeing eye," and the name "Deseret." William H. Folsom had received the assignment as temple architect and superintendent of construction.[30] His work was to be supervised by a committee composed of three members of the Twelve: Elders Wilford Woodruff, Orson Hyde, and Erastus Snow.

On his way back to Salt Lake City from the St. George Temple dedication, President Brigham Young stopped in Manti to dedicate the temple site there. He arrived April 24, 1877, and on that same afternoon he supervised the work of William Folsom and Truman O. Angell Jr. as they surveyed the site and set stakes. Several hundred were present the following day at noon when President Young dedicated the site in connection with stake conference.

A common story dating to this visit is that Brigham Young took Warren S. Snow to the temple site and told him that during the prophet Moroni's wandering years he visited the area and dedicated this piece of land for a temple. Yet Warren Snow's memory of the conversation is the only source for this account. Diligent research by the Church History Department has not turned up any contemporary references to Moroni by any Church leaders who spoke at the groundbreaking, cornerstone ceremony, or dedication. On the contrary, their remarks point to President Young as the one who chose the site. Historian Ardis Parshall notes that John Taylor said in 1879, "Brigham Young . . . selected this ground as a suitable site whereon to build a temple," and at the temple dedication in 1888, Wilford Woodruff said Brigham was "moved to build and to appoint Temples . . . and to designate that one should occupy this delightful spot."[31] While the Moroni story has been very popular and sensational over the years, it distracts from the prophetic role and mantle exercised by the living prophet at the time, who was Brigham Young.

Construction Begins

When President Young dedicated the site for the Manti Temple, he exhorted the people to labor on the temple with "clean hands and pure hearts" so that they might be worthy to receive blessings in the temple and to officiate in behalf of their dead. He explained that the women could assist by giving encouragement to their husbands and sons and by making clothing for those working on the temple. He instructed bishops in the area to have men and their teams come and prepare the site for construction. He hoped that from fifty to one hundred would respond, and explained that they could be rotated as often as necessary. "Now, Bishops," President Young

George Edward Anderson, *Construction of the Manti Temple*. Courtesy of Church History Library.

instructed, "if any person should inquire what wages is to be paid for work done on the temple, let the answer be, 'Not one dime.' And when the temple is completed, we will work in God's holy house without inquiring what we are going to get, or who is going to pay us, but we will trust in the Lord for our reward, and he will not forget us."[32]

Only five days later, some one hundred men with their teams from Manti and surrounding communities reported to the temple site at 8:00 a.m. After kneeling in prayer, they commenced the work of excavation. Work on the hillside was discouragingly slow. Explosions shattered the stillness of the rural valley as men worked to provide a level building site for the temple. In the last blast on June 27, 1878, for example, 875 pounds of powder threw out over 4,600 cubic yards of rock and debris. By the end of the year, rough retaining walls were completed, and material removed from the hill had been graded to form four terraces nearly a quarter mile long. A level plot, about sixty feet above the road at the base of the hill, was now ready for temple construction to begin in the spring. Honoring Brigham Young's vision to turn the spur of the mountain into a temple site, Wilford Woodruff later stated, "The Prophet of God also laid out the Manti Temple, and he did a thing that perhaps no other man on the earth would have done—he removed a mountain at the cost of a hundred thousand dollars to get a place that would suite [*sic*] him for a Temple to stand on."[33]

Manti Temple. Courtesy of Church History Library.

Cornerstones were laid on April 14, 1879. Master mason Edward Parry had prepared the cornerstones and made a treasure box that would include historical memorabilia. Previously, Parry had constructed similar cornerstone boxes for both the Salt Lake and St. George Temples.[34] A steady rain fell most of the morning on the appointed day, but the sun broke through as about four thousand Saints gathered for the 11:30 service. As the Stars and Stripes fluttered overhead, the southeast cornerstone with its zinc box containing historical memorabilia was laid by William Folsom under the supervision of President John Taylor of the Quorum of the Twelve—then the presiding officer of the Church—who also spoke. The Presiding Bishop, representing the Aaronic Priesthood, laid the southwest cornerstone. The presidencies of the high priests and seventies laid the northwest and northeast cornerstones respectively. The two-hour service featured other talks by General Authorities as well as music provided by the Manti choir and by a band from Nephi. As the last Saints left the hill, the rain began to fall again.[35]

Many people became involved in raising funds for the temple. A dramatic company put on two performances, donating half their proceeds. Two brethren were appointed to travel from settlement to settlement soliciting funds. Beaver, over a hundred miles from Manti, contributed $1,500. Less than 4 percent of the donations came in the form of cash. Most contributions were commodities, including beef, chickens, wheat, flour, quilts, shoes, socks, overalls, and other items of clothing. Children gleaned wheat from the fields so that their mothers could make bread for the workmen. A young father gave his only cow even though his small children needed the milk; soon afterward, however, a bachelor neighbor offered to provide from his own cow all the milk the little family needed. The Greenwood United Order provided a wagonload of butter. Such supplies were distributed to the workmen through the local bishop's "tithing office."[36]

The estimated cost to construct the Manti Temple was about $1,000,000 (equivalent to over $20,000,000 in the twenty-first century). Almost all the materials needed for the temple were donated or produced locally. A few items, however, had to be shipped in from the East. Nails were particularly scarce; twenty pounds of nails cost sixty dollars (at this time one hundred pounds of flour sold for only two dollars). Glass was sent from New York to California by ship and then had to be carried carefully by wagon across the desert.[37]

The estimated cost to construct the Manti Temple was about $1,000,000 (equivalent to over $20,000,000 in the twenty-first century). Almost all the materials needed for the temple were donated or produced locally.

Stake president Canute Peterson became the assistant superintendent of construction with the specific assignment to promote and coordinate the donation of materials and labor. Under the direction of his wife Sarah, women of the Relief Society made cheese and donated "temple eggs"; many were convinced that their hens laid twice as many eggs on Sunday for the temple than on any other day of the week. As had been done for the Logan Temple, these women wove hundreds of yards of carpet.[38]

Construction on the temple progressed slowly. Lumber from the surrounding mountains was delivered to the site during the winter when the men were free from farm work and the normally muddy roads were frozen (and hence in the best condition). Furthermore, most of the work had to be done by hand. Craftsmen shaping stones for the walls used hammers and chisels and took pride in their work. By April 1882 the walls reached the height of fifty feet.

A concern for excellence also motivated those who accomplished the intricate wood carving in the temple. "When I see the terrestrial room," a woodworker later remarked, "a feeling of deep reverence comes over me as I imagine myself attempting the pieces of wood work there. These men were inspired with a higher cause."[39]

The spiral stairways in the two west corners are a unique feature of the Manti Temple. They are an outstanding example of pioneer craftsmanship. Unlike most spiral staircases, which wind around and are supported by a central column, those in Manti are open in the center. Even though the temple's floors are not all the same distance apart, each story is reached by one complete revolution of the stairway. The curved panels and perfectly executed curved banisters of imported black walnut are a marvel of woodworking.[40] Large wooden stairways of this design are extremely rare, and two of those in existence are in this temple.[41] In addition to these celebrated staircases, there actually are two others in the temple; they too are open in the center, but they are not as noted because they ascend only one story.

In 1886–87 murals were painted on the plaster walls of the first three endowment rooms. C. C. A. Christensen, a Danish convert who had studied art in Denmark, painted the creation room; he was noted for his large "panorama" painting of Church history scenes featured in his traveling lectures. Dan Weggeland, a Norwegian immigrant who had studied art in Europe, painted the murals in the garden room and probably the world room.

The temple was nearing completion when President Taylor died in the summer of 1887. That fall President Woodruff, his successor, advised Church members that the Manti Temple was ready for its interior furnishings and invited the Saints to make their last donations toward the completion of this temple. Contributions poured in from many locations in Utah and Idaho and from such far-flung places as England, Germany, Switzerland, and Hawaii. Hundreds of Saints responded, most donations ranging from twenty-five cents to five dollars.

Private and Public Dedications

The public dedication of the Manti Temple was scheduled to begin on Monday, May 21, 1888. However, because of the bitter anti-Mormon persecution raging primarily over the issue of plural marriage, most General Authorities were forced to remain in seclusion in the "underground." Hence, a private dedicatory service was scheduled for a few days earlier. President Woodruff, the senior apostle who then presided over the Church, left Salt Lake City on a Sunday night and traveled by private railroad car to Nephi. There he remained in seclusion until the following night when he journeyed by carriage across the mountain to Manti, arriving at 1:00 a.m. on Tuesday. He remained in the temple the next few days conferring with local officials and naming Daniel H. Wells, formerly a counselor to Brigham Young, to be the temple's first president. In the presence of only a few General Authorities and other invited guests, President Woodruff offered the dedicatory prayer at noon on Thursday, May 17. Before leaving the temple on Friday, President Woodruff "consecrated upon the Altar the [white] seer stone that Joseph Smith found by revelation [and which was] carried by him through life."[42]

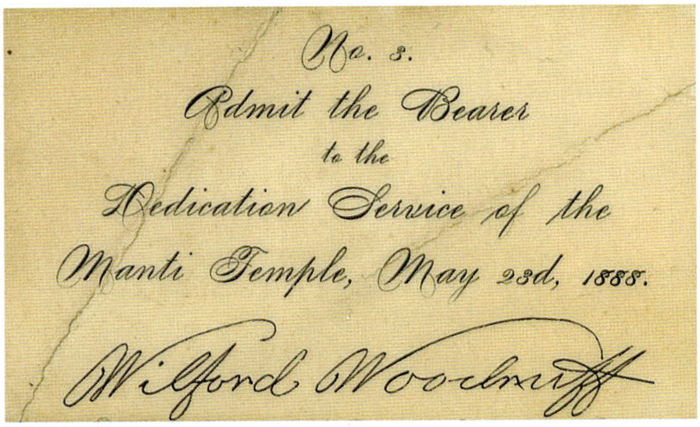

Manti Utah Temple dedication ticket. Courtesy of Church History Library.

On Saturday and Sunday, the roads leading to Manti were clogged with teams and wagons bringing people to the public dedication. Early Monday morning the Saints began to gather on the hill east of the temple from which they would be admitted into the building, "and by 9:30 the grounds were black with people." The doors were opened at 10:00, and the service began one hour later. Elder Lorenzo Snow, next to Wilford Woodruff in seniority, presided. He reminded the congregation that the dedicatory prayer for the Kirtland Temple had been given by revelation. "So the

Manti Utah Temple.
Courtesy of Intellectual
Reserve, Inc.

prayer we are now about to offer up," he testified, "was written and inspired by holy men of God in our day." The prayer referred to existing difficulties and petitioned: "As thou hast in the past overruled the violence of mobs and the cruelty of the wicked for the glory of thy name and the salvation of thy people, we ask thee, Righteous Father, to so control this present persecution that thy purposes may be accomplished in the redemption of thy Zion."[43]

They heard the "most heavenly voices and singing—it sounded to them most angelic, and appeared to be behind and above them, and they turned their heads in the direction of the sound, wondering if there was another choir in some other part of the Temple."

Following the prayer, the choir sang the "Dedication Hymn," with words composed by Charles Walker especially for the occasion:

Righteous God, th'eternal Father,
Lend Thine ear, accept our praise;
While we dedicate this Temple
Reared to Thee in latter days.
Let Thy blessings rest upon it,
Hallow now this sacred shrine,
Fill its courts with joy and gladness,
Holy Father, it is Thine.

Rays of sunshine pierce the prison,
Jesus lighten up the gloom,
Millions hail the joyful tidings,
Vict'ry o'er death, hell and tomb.
Oh what rapture fills the captive!
Christ hath crushed the serpent's head,
And another House erected,
Links the living with the dead.

Oh how anxious souls are waiting,
Eager watching for the day,
When kind friends on earth will save them,
In God's own appointed way.
Let no loved one's spirit linger,
Loose the bands, we have the keys;
Christ hath wrought for all a ransom,
And will grant them sweet release.[44]

Wilford Woodruff, 1888. Courtesy of Church History Library.

Once again, the solemn shout of hosannas accompanied the presentation of yet another temple to the Lord.

Several members of the Twelve addressed the congregation, expressing gratitude for the plan of salvation and for sacred temple ordinances which extend blessings to the millions who died without the opportunity of accepting the gospel on earth. "The erecting of [a] Temple," Elder Franklin D. Richards declared, "was a matter of as much interest and concern to those who had passed behind the veil as to the living." Ever since the site for the Manti Temple had been selected, "they had watched with anxiety for its completion."[45] This service continued until 3:00 p.m.

Similar services convened on the following two days with 1,500 to 1,700 in attendance. In each session the dedicatory prayer and Hosanna Shout were repeated, and other members of the Twelve addressed the congregation. Following each session, those in attendance were given the privilege of walking two by two through the various rooms of the temple, as had been done at Logan. In the evening of the first day, children too young to attend one of the regular dedicatory services were invited to tour the temple.

Remarkable spiritual experiences accompanied these memorable dedicatory services. The Church's *Millennial Star* reported, "On the 21st of May, before the opening exercises commenced, Brother A. C. Smyth, the chorister, seated himself at the organ, and rendered a piece of sacred music, a selection from Mendelssohn, at the conclusion of which, persons sitting near the centre of the hall, and also on the stand at the west end, heard most heavenly voices and singing—it sounded to them most angelic, and appeared to be behind and above them, and they turned their heads in the direction of the sound, wondering if there was another choir in some other part of the Temple."[46]

There was no other choir. Then, several of the Saints beheld departed Church leaders during the services. Typical of several accounts published in the *Millennial Star* were these: "On the 22nd of May, when Brother John W. Taylor was speaking, a bright halo surrounded him, and in that halo the personages of Presidents Brigham Young, John Taylor, and a third personage, whom she believed to be the Prophet Joseph, were seen by Sister Emma G. Bull, of Salt Lake City; also the personage of Brother Jedediah M. Grant was seen by her standing by his son, Brother Heber J. Grant, looking towards him while he was speaking; they were surrounded by a bright halo."[47]

Moses Farnsworth, the temple recorder, noted, "On the 23rd . . . I was sitting at the foot of the east stand, taking notes of the services; I looked up while Brother Heber J. Grant was speaking, and saw a bright halo surrounding him, which swayed to and fro as he moved his body. I laid down my pencil and gazed steadily at him for a few moments."[48]

In summarizing its account, the *Star* affirmed, "The Saints enjoyed a spiritual feast extending through the three days and many shed tears of joy while listening to the testimonies and admonitions of the servants of God. There can be no question but that God has accepted the Manti Temple at the hands of His Saints."[49]

"When we dedicated the Temple at Manti," Elder Franklin D. Richards of the Quorum of the Twelve recalled a few years later, "there were many brethren and sisters that saw the presence of spiritual beings, which could only be discerned by the eyes of the inner man. The Prophets Joseph, Hyrum, Brigham, and various other Apostles that have gone, were seen; and not only so, but the ears of many of the faithful were touched, and they heard the music of the heavenly choir that was there."[50]

Yet another spiritual manifestation occurred the day following the temple's dedication. That night when a pounding rain hit the building, custodian Peter Alstrom ran to close a window. "Opening the door of the sealing room, he was surprised to see, standing above the altar, a personage clothed in white robes, a brilliant light surrounding him and filling the whole room." Upon hearing this, President Wells replied

"There are angels in this place."

"that there are angels in this place we can have no doubt, but it is not given to every one to see them."[51]

In the meantime, while the faithful in Logan and Manti were enjoying the remarkable experiences connected with the dedications of their temples, the Saints in the Salt Lake area were eagerly anticipating the completion of the great temple in that city as well.

Notes

1. Orson Pratt, October 26, 1876, in *Journal of Discourses* (London: Latter-day Saints' Book Depot, 1854–86), 24:25.
2. Orson Pratt, May 20, 1877, in *Journal of Discourses*, 19:19–20.
3. Erastus Snow, November 20, 1881, in St. George Stake Historical Record, MS, Church History Library.
4. Brigham Young, February 14, 1853, in *Journal of Discourses*, 1:277–78.
5. James E. Talmage, *The House of the Lord* (Salt Lake City: Bookcraft, 1962), 110–11.
6. James R. Clark, comp., *Messages of the First Presidency* (Salt Lake City: Bookcraft, 1965), 2:280.
7. Paul L. Anderson, "William Harrison Folsom: Pioneer Architect," *Utah Historical Quarterly* 43 (Summer 1975): 247–52; Laurel B. Andrew, *The Early Temples of the Mormons* (Albany: State University of New York Press, 1978), 175–76. Initially, Joseph A. Young received the assignment to design the Manti Temple but died soon afterward.
8. Truman O. Angell Jr., to John Taylor, May 8, 1878, and William H. Folsom to John Taylor, May 24, 1878, First Presidency (John Taylor) correspondence, 1877–1887, Church History Library.
9. Cache Valley Stake Historical Record, Book A, quoted in Nolan Porter Olsen, *Logan Temple: The First 100 Years* (Providence, UT: the author, 1978), 6–7, and in Melvin A. Larkin, "The History of the L.D.S. Temple in Logan, Utah" (master's thesis, Utah State Agricultural College, 1954), 14.
10. Scott G. Kenney, ed., *Wilford Woodruff's Journal* (Midvale, UT: Signature Books, 1985), 8:247–48, May 8, 1884; Olsen, *Logan Temple*, 10–12; Larkin, "History of the L.D.S. Temple in Logan, Utah," 14–15.
11. Olsen, *Logan Temple*, 24–26.
12. Brigham Young and John Taylor, in *Journal of Discourses*, 19:33–35, May 18, 1877.
13. Quoted in Olsen, *Logan Temple*, 7:374, September 17, 1877.
14. "Washakie: Description of the Lamanitish City in Malad Valley," *Utah Journal*, December 1, 1883; Larkin, "History of the L.D.S. Temple in Logan, Utah," 124.
15. Boyd K. Packer, *The Holy Temple* (Salt Lake City: Bookcraft, 1980), 248.
16. Leonard J. Arrington and Melvin A. Larkin, "The Logan Tabernacle and Temple," *Utah Historical Quarterly* 41 (Summer 1973): 308.
17. C. O. Card, "The Nickel Fund," *Juvenile Instructor*, February 29, 1884, 95.
18. Arrington and Larkin, Logan Tabernacle and Temple," 306.
19. Joseph L. Quayle, "Stories of James Quayle," FamilySearch.org.
20. Olsen, *Logan Temple*, 129–30.
21. Larkin, "History of the L.D.S. Temple in Logan, Utah," 133–35.
22. Quoted in Olsen, *Logan Temple*, 140–41.
23. Franklin D. Richards, in *Journal of Discourses*, 25:231, May 17, 1884.
24. N. B. Lundwall, *Temples of the Most High* (Salt Lake City: Bookcraft, 1947), 108–9.

25. Melvin Clarence Merrill, *Marriner Wood Merrill and His Family* (n.p.: the author, 1937), 78–79.
26. L. John Nuttall diary, MS, L. Tom Perry Special Collections, Harold B. Lee Library, Brigham Young University, May 19, 1884; John Taylor, in *Journal of Discourses*, 25:185–87, May 18, 1884,.
27. Nuttall diary, May 22, 1884.
28. Heber C. Kimball, quoted in *Millennial Star*, August 13, 1888, 521.
29. Daniel Tyler, "Temples," *Contributor*, November 30, 1880, 160; Glen R. Stubbs, "A History of the Manti Temple" (master's thesis, Brigham Young University, 1960), 17–13.
30. Paul L. Anderson, "William Harrison Folsom: Pioneer Architect," *Utah Historical Quarterly* 43 (Summer 1975): 252.
31. Ardis Parshall, "Moroni's Reported Rambles," http://www.keepapitchinin.org/2010/11/18/moronis-purported-rambles/.
32. *Millennial Star*, June 11, 1877, 373.
33. Brian H. Stuy, *Collected Discourses Delivered by President Wilford Woodruff, His Two Counselors, the Twelve Apostles, and Others*, vol. 5 ([Burbank, CA: B.H.S. Publishing, 1992), 5:315.
34. Edward L. Parry, "Autobiography of Edward Lloyd Parry," FamilySearch.org.
35. *Millennial Star*, May 12, 1879, 295.
36. Stubbs, "History of the Manti Temple," 38–42.
37. Thomas Weston Welch, "Early Mormon Woodworking at Its Best: A Study of the Craftsmanship in the First Temples in Utah" (master's thesis, Brigham Young University, 1983), 11.
38. Stubbs, "History of the Manti Temple," 38–42.
39. Welch, "Early Mormon Woodworking," 85.
40. Welch, "Early Mormon Woodworking," 81–85; Stubbs, "History of the Manti Temple," 67.
41. Victor J. Rasmussen, *The Manti Temple* (Manti, UT: Manti Temple Centennial Committee, 1988), 104.
42. Kenney, *Wilford Woodruff's Journal*, 8:496–500, May 13–18, 1888.
43. "The Dedication of the Manti Temple," *Millennial Star* 50 (June 18, 1888), 385–92; for dedicatory prayer see N. B. Lundwall, *Temples of the Most High*, 111–20.
44. "The Dedication of the Manti Temple," 401.
45. Franklin D. Richards, in "The Dedication of the Manti Temple," 403.
46. Moses F. Farnsworth to George Teasdale, July 2, 1888, in "Spiritual Manifestations in the Manti Temple," *Millennial Star*, August 13, 1888, 521–22.
47. Moses F. Farnsworth to George Teasdale, July 2, 1888, in "Spiritual Manifestations in the Manti Temple," *Millennial Star*, August 13, 1888, 521–22.
48. Farnsworth to Teasdale, *Millennial Star*, August 13, 1888, 521–22.
49. "Dedication of the Manti Temple," *Millennial Star*, June 25, 1888, 405.
50. Franklin D. Richards, in *Millennial Star*, June 19, 1893, 431.
51. "A String of Pearls for Those Who Have Intelligence to Appreciate Them," *Young Woman's Journal*, April 1890, 213–14.

5

The Salt Lake Temple Completed

A Mighty Fortress—from on High, by Alan Fullmer.

Even though the construction and dedication of the temples at St. George, Logan, and Manti attracted a great deal of attention and placed substantial demands on the people's energies and resources, the Saints never lost sight of the objective of erecting the great temple at Church headquarters in Salt Lake City. Even during the years when the potentially hostile army was in Utah and the Salt Lake Temple's foundation was covered with dirt, draftsmen in the architect's office were busy planning the exact size and shape for each of the thousands of stones that would be needed for the temple.

Construction Accelerates

As construction resumed during the early 1860s, builders needed to obtain granite from the mountains southeast of the city immediately. Generally, it was not necessary to quarry the rock from the mountainsides because huge granite boulders were strewn

Top left: Four temples dedicated in Utah during the nineteenth century. Courtesy of Lee R. Cowan.

Left and below: Working at the temple quarry, preparing stones for the temple. Courtesy of *Deseret News* and Church History Library.

Drawing by Mahonri Young. Courtesy of *Deseret News* and Church History Library.

thickly along the canyon floor. Using hammers, chisels, and sometimes explosives, the workmen split these boulders into the specified sizes and shapes of stones for the temple. The work moved slowly because there were only a few stonecutters with sufficient skill. These men worked grueling, ten-hour days beginning at 7:00 a.m. but took time for prayer and for spiritual discussions in the evenings. As the work expanded, a village of small cottages sprang up in a grove of trees near the canyon's mouth.

Transporting the granite some twenty miles from the quarry to Temple Square posed a major challenge. Four to six oxen struggling to pull a heavy wagon hauling only a single monstrous stone, or perhaps two medium ones, was a common sight on the streets of Salt Lake City. Some of the individual stones for the temple weighed as much as three tons. Special low-slung wagons were designed to facilitate loading and unloading. The journey from the quarry took three to four days. As a result, progress on the temple seemed to be painfully slow. As late as 1867, the walls were still below ground level. Construction on a canal for transporting stone began, but the necessity of crossing uneven terrain and several canyon streams proved to be an insurmountable barrier. Hence, this project was never completed. A further slowdown occurred in 1868 when workmen were diverted from the temple to help finish the transcontinental railroad. Nevertheless, Church leaders knew that the coming of the railroad would ultimately expedite temple construction in a significant way.

The transcontinental rail line was completed through Ogden in 1869, and the following year a branch line reached Salt Lake City. During the early 1870s, tracks of the Utah Southern Railroad (later part of the Union Pacific) pushed southward toward Utah Valley. Rather than following a direct route, they were swung to the southeast to pass closer to the temple quarry. (Over a century and a quarter later, this exact route would be followed by Salt Lake Valley's Trax light rail system.) In 1873 a narrow-gauge spur was constructed from the main line at Sandy Station to the quarry a few miles to the east. A connection was also made downtown with streetcar

Temple site with derricks.
Courtesy of *Deseret News*
and Church History Library.

tracks from which a rail spur was constructed through the south gate into the temple block. Because these tracks were lightweight, the loaded rail cars had to be pulled by horses the final four blocks along South Temple Street.

A short time later, the tracks along South Temple were replaced with a heavier rail, and steam locomotives took the place of the horses. At the time of President Young's death in 1877, the temple walls were still only twenty feet high, just a little above the level of the first floor. Thus, most of the temple's construction was yet to be accomplished, even though twenty-four years of the forty-year building period had already passed. During the next few years, however, with the problems of transportation resolved, the pace would accelerate considerably.

Derricks were constructed in each of the temple's four corners to lift the heavy stones into place. Unfortunately, there was only one steam-hoisting engine available. It powered the derrick in one corner to lay five courses, or levels, of rock before moving on to the next corner. With the completion of the Logan Temple in 1884, a second engine became available, so construction moved more quickly. The structure was very solid because the builders recalled that President Young had expressed the desire that this temple would stand through the Millennium. Even at their tops, the walls were six feet thick, and the granite blocks were individually and skillfully shaped to fit snugly together. Nearly a century later, Elder Mark E. Petersen attested to the soundness of the temple's construction. He was in the temple when a rather severe earthquake hit, damaging several buildings around the Salt Lake Valley. "As I sat there in that temple I could feel the sway of the quake and that the whole building groaned." Afterward, he recalled, the engineers "could not find one semblance of damage" anywhere in the temple.[1]

Many people contributed to the temple's construction either directly or indirectly. Under the concept of "labor tithing," able-bodied men were asked to donate one day in ten to working on the temple. Wards in the area were assigned in rotation to provide workmen a week at a time. The women assisted by washing and mending clothing for the workmen and by teaching the children of those working on the temple. President Heber C. Kimball had admonished the sisters to give up costly jewelry and fancy hair ornaments in order to donate to the temple fund.[2] Priesthood quorums, as well as individuals with means, hired mechanics to work on the temple. During the 1880s, each ward was expected to maintain one workman in the quarry. "As a boy," President Heber J. Grant recalled many years later, "I paid twenty-five cents regularly to help in the erection of the Salt Lake Temple. Subsequently, as my wages became more, I increased my contribution."[3]

James B. Wilson was typical of the many who contributed to the temple's construction. As a schoolteacher, his monthly salary was meager, so he had almost no cash to pay his tithing. "I finally decided to give the Church one of the two oxen I had in spite of the fact that it would break a wonderful team." Shortly afterward, he happened to pass by the temple block. "I noticed two fine oxen working on a drag which moved the giant blocks about. I was so interested in them that I moved closer

The structure was very solid because the builders recalled that President Young had expressed the desire that this temple would stand through the Millennium. Even at their tops, the walls were six feet thick, and the granite blocks were individually and skillfully shaped to fit snugly together.

for a better view and discovered one of them to be my favorite ox, fattened and in perfect condition. I then fully appreciated the significance of tithing. I was building the temple with my ox."[4]

The temple is "a house of covenants. Here we promise, solemnly and sacredly, to live the gospel of Jesus Christ in its finest expression. We covenant with God our Eternal Father to live those principles which are the bedrock of all true religion."

—President Gordon B. Hinckley

Symbolism of the Temple's Exterior

The Salt Lake Temple's architecture was a blend of the Romanesque (or what some have called the "Round Gothic") with the castellated style of the other early Utah temples at St. George, Logan, and Manti. The Salt Lake Temple's exterior, however, had several unique features. As had been the case in ancient times, the physical arrangement was calculated to teach important lessons. The intent of the temple's design, one architectural historian observed, was "to aid man in his quest to gain entrance back into the presence of God from whence he came."[5]

As has been seen, William Ward, who had a key role in drafting the plans for the temple, testified that the basic concept of the building's design had not come from the architects. At the time of the capstone laying in 1892, he recalled how Brigham Young had instructed Truman O. Angell about what would become the temple's most widely recognized symbolic features: "There will be three towers on the east, representing the President and his two counselors; also three similar towers on the west representing the Presiding Bishop and his two counselors; the towers on the east, the Melchizedek Priesthood, those on the west the Aaronic Priesthood."[6]

As was the case with the Nauvoo Temple, special ornamental stones were an important feature of the Salt Lake Temple's exterior. An earthstone formed the base of each of the temple's fifty buttresses. These were the largest stones in the temple, weighing over six thousand pounds and having on their face a representation of the globe, four feet in diameter. These stones served as a reminder, architect Angell explained, that the gospel message had to go to all the earth.[7] Each buttress had a moonstone about halfway up, and a sunstone near its top. Because the earth is presently in a telestial condition, these three ornamental stones on each buttress might represent the three degrees of glory in ascending order—telestial, terrestrial, and celestial (see 1 Corinthians 15:40–42; Doctrine and Covenants 76:50–113). The starstones on the temple's towers also reminded Latter-day Saints of the telestial kingdom (see Doctrine and Covenants 76:81).

Architectural scholar Richard Oman has suggested another possible interpretation. Referring to Abraham 3:5, he pointed out, "As we move upward into the heavens, the time sequences become longer. Likewise, the temple stones that communicate time begin with a short period of time, the day, and move toward the eternal present, where time almost ceases to move." The earthstones at the temple's base represent our planet, which rotates once every day. Stones about halfway up the building depict the moon's monthly cycle. Sunstones near the top symbolize yet a longer period of time—the year. The depiction of stars even higher on the building's towers suggests even longer periods of revolution.[8]

The constellation of Ursa Major (the Big Dipper), depicted on the west center tower, is positioned so that the two pointer stars at the end of the dipper are actually aligned with Polaris (the North Star) in the heavens. This star appears to be a fixed point in the sky around which other stars revolve; hence, it might be thought of as representing eternity, or the absence of time.

Architect Truman O. Angell suggested another message to be gained from this constellation on the temple—"that through the priesthood of God, the lost might find their way."[9] In the twentieth century, Elder Harold B. Lee referred to this statement in conjunction with the introduction of family home evenings and other priesthood-centered programs and likened it to the increasingly important role being given to the priesthood.[10]

Architectural drawing of earthstones and moonstones. Courtesy of Church History Library.

An interesting feature on the moonstones is often overlooked. Proceeding from right to left, they successively represent the moon's new, first-quarter, full, and third-quarter phases. Because the fifty buttresses cannot be divided evenly by these four phases, at some point the cycle must be interrupted. This was done deliberately to provide a starting point. The break occurs on the north wall. If the date of January 1 is assigned to the new moon immediately after this interruption, dates can also be assigned to each of the succeeding phases. The right buttress on the face of the temple's main east center tower would thus represent April 6, widely associated by Latter-day Saints with the organization of Christ's church. Gilded letters on this same tower identify April 6 as the date of the temple's commencement and completion.[11] The left buttress on this tower includes a representation of the full moon. Because Easter is celebrated on the Sunday following the first full moon after the beginning of spring, this moonstone may be a reminder of the Savior's atoning sacrifice, which was completed with Jesus's resurrection on that first glorious Easter morning.

The buttresses of the east center tower also include cloudstones, which show rays of sunlight penetrating through the clouds. These are representations of the gospel light piercing the dark clouds of superstition and error (Isaiah 60:2–3). They also recall how a cloud of glory filled the ancient temple (1 Kings 8:10) and will rest upon the latter-day temple in the New Jerusalem (Doctrine and Covenants 84:5). On the

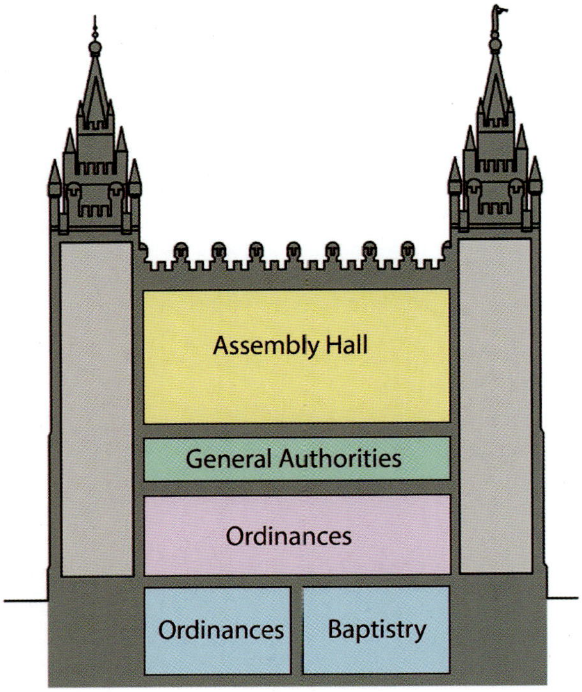

Cross section of the Salt Lake Temple. Courtesy of Lee R. Cowan.

same tower, the keystone at the top of the lower large window depicts clasped hands. These are reminders of the power that comes from brotherly love and fellowship, and of the unity that must exist among those who would build Zion (Galatians 2:9; Moses 7:18; Doctrine and Covenants 38:24–27, 88:133). The hands also suggest the importance of honoring sacred commitments. President Gordon B. Hinckley declared that the temple is "a house of covenants. Here we promise, solemnly and sacredly, to live the gospel of Jesus Christ in its finest expression. We covenant with God our Eternal Father to live those principles which are the bedrock of all true religion."[12] The keystone above the east center tower's upper window depicts God's "all-seeing eye" which watches over both the righteous and the wicked (1 Kings 9:3; Psalm 33:13–14, 18–19; Proverbs 15:3).[13]

The towers were almost completed in 1887 when President Woodruff approved the architect's recommendation that they be finished in stone rather than in wood as originally planned. At this time, even more significant changes were being discussed for the interior of the temple.

The Temple's Interior

The temple's exterior walls were nearing completion in the mid-1880s when Church leaders considered significant changes in the plans for the yet-unconstructed interior. With his responsibilities for the Logan temple finished in 1884, Truman O. Angell Jr. turned his attention to assisting his elderly father in completing drawings for the Salt Lake Temple. Early the following year, he proposed that rather than having two large assembly rooms with elliptical ceilings, as had been the case in Nauvoo, the Salt Lake Temple should follow the pattern that Presidents Young and Taylor had already approved for Logan and Manti. There would be only one assembly room on the upper floor, and it would have balconies under the elliptical windows along each side. The temple's main floor would contain spacious rooms for presenting the endowment, while an intermediate floor would provide smaller council rooms for the use of Church leaders and other priesthood groups. This plan would accommodate three hundred persons in the endowment sessions—more than twice the number that could be served in the basement under the original arrangement. These changes were consistent with President Young's 1860 instructions that the temple would not be designed for general meetings, but rather it would be for the endowments—for the organization and instruction of the priesthood.[14] Thus, even the developing design of the Salt Lake Temple reflected the Saints' unfolding understanding of temple functions.

Truman O. Angell Sr., however, urged President Taylor to finish the temple according to the original plans. No final decision was made prior to the deaths of President Taylor and architect Angell in 1887. Although the general features of the younger Angell's proposal were eventually adopted, none of his plans were followed exactly. The final plans for the temple appear to have been drawn under President Wilford Woodruff's direction by Joseph Don Carlos Young, who became temple architect in early 1888 and architect of the Church in April 1890—just three years before the temple's completion.[15] All the work on the temple's interior was accomplished during these last few years of construction. It seemed appropriate that one of President Young's sons would be responsible for the temple's completion.

Truman Angell Jr. had proposed placing only the first endowment lecture room in the basement and the rest on the temple's main floor which would be divided into four quadrants—the garden room in the southeast, the world room in the southwest, the terrestrial room in the northwest, and the celestial room in the northeast. Architect Young moved the garden room to the basement where it could open on the south directly into a "conservatory of living plants." He also refined the plan by providing that on both floors each room would be a step or two higher than the one preceding it. Patrons therefore followed an upward clockwise progression as they went through the endowment experience. The southeast quadrant of the main floor would be divided into smaller rooms, including the Holy of Holies and sealing rooms.

The first three endowment rooms were to have murals on their walls. Dan Weggeland, a native of Norway who had studied at the Danish Royal Academy of Art in Copenhagen, had painted murals in the first three Utah temples. He encouraged promising young artists to leave the isolation of the Intermountain West and study abroad to expand their talents. He thereby came to be called the "father of Utah art." In 1890 two of these young artists, John Hafen and Lorus Pratt (son of Elder Orson Pratt), asked the Church for financial help, promising to return and paint murals in the temple and render other art services. In June of that year, the First Presidency approved their proposal. They, together with three others—John B. Fairbanks, Edwin Evans, and Herman Haag—were set apart as "art missionaries" and sent to Paris to study at the Julian Academy.

Some have suggested that in the Salt Lake Temple, shafts were provided for elevators and spaces left throughout the building for electric conduits and heating ducts, even before these technologies were known. Truman Angell Sr., however, certainly would have learned about elevators, which were just coming into use at the time of his 1856 mission to Europe. By the early 1860s, electricity was also being used in Utah for the Deseret telegraph. Hence, these technologies were known long before the temple's interior was developed. Still, the west center tower proved to be a convenient location for the elevators, and about half of the buttresses on each side of the temple contained a shaft eleven inches in diameter to facilitate ventilation.[16]

The Impact of Revived Persecution

Before his death in 1868, a prophecy was attributed to Heber C. Kimball that "when [the Salt Lake Temple's] walls reached the square, the powers of evil would rage and the Saints would suffer persecution."[17] This point of construction was reached in 1885 when the main walls of the temple, excluding the towers, were completed.

Three years earlier, Congress had enacted the Edmunds Anti-Bigamy law, which defined "polygamist cohabitation" as a crime, punishable by stiff fines and prison sentences. Thus, the stage was set for the anti-Mormon crusade that raged during the mid-1880s. Dozens of Church members, including many general and local leaders, were imprisoned "for conscience's sake." Others found it necessary to withdraw into "retirement" or to go "on the underground." Between 1885 and 1887, general conferences were held at locations away from Salt Lake City, and members of the First Presidency did not appear in public for several years.

During this time, there were fears that government officials might attempt to confiscate property held by the Church, even the temples. To avert this, President Taylor directed the formation of the independent nonprofit Logan, Manti, and St. George Temple Associations to hold the titles of these sacred buildings and related properties. Similarly, the Salt Lake Literary and Scientific Association received title to property facing the temple block, including the Council House and Deseret Museum.[18] These unique arrangements would continue into the early years of the twentieth century.

The Logan Temple Association served another function as well. In his 1884 dedicatory prayer, President Taylor had petitioned that, consistent with instructions in the Doctrine and Covenants (88:76–80, 117–119), the Logan Temple "may be indeed a house of learning under Thy guidance, direction and inspiration."[19] In that same year, President Taylor suggested that Church leaders in Logan follow the pattern set by the Prophet Joseph Smith in Kirtland and make the temple "a house of learning" as well as "a house of God." Therefore, the association not only received title to the temple but also sponsored monthly lectures in such subjects as theology, civil government, languages, history, natural science, and economics. There was no charge, but only those holding temple recommends could attend. An average of about one hundred persons attended each of these lectures, which convened in the temple recorder's room on the first Saturday afternoon of the month.[20]

Following the passage of the yet harsher Edmunds-Tucker Law in 1887, government officials seized the partially completed Salt Lake Temple, even though the law specifically exempted houses of worship from such action. This stopped work on the building only temporarily. The Church appealed the seizure but was required to pay one dollar per month for the use of the property. This amount was minimal, but the requirement was intended to be humiliating. The Saints' enemies boasted that the Mormons would never be allowed to finish the temple but that the "Gentiles" would complete the building for their own purposes. Eventually, however, the Church's efforts were successful, and by October 1891 the title to Temple Square

Capstone celebration. Courtesy of *Deseret News* and Church History Library.

was regained.[21] These events underscored the difficult circumstances through which the Church and its members had passed.

The Capstone Celebration

During the dark days of persecution, completing the Salt Lake Temple was one bright objective around which the Saints could rally. They took courage as they saw the great temple nearing completion despite tremendous difficulties. Finally, the decision was made to lay the uppermost stone on the temple in connection with the 62nd Annual General Conference in 1892. "As the sixth of April drew near," one observer recorded, "the joy which swept over the hearts of the Saints was visible. . . . It was to them a day of triumph for which they had patiently toiled, many of them the greater part of a lifetime."[22]

On Wednesday morning, April 6, the Saints congregated in the Tabernacle for the concluding conference session. President Woodruff urged the speedy completion

Salt Lake Temple construction workers. Courtesy of *Deseret News* and Church History Library.

of the temple, declaring that "this is the most important work that we have upon our hands."[23] At 11:30 a.m. the meeting closed, and the congregation, which had been seated by quorums, moved out onto the grounds. As a band played "The Capstone March," the people gathered south of the temple. An estimated forty thousand crowded into Temple Square, while an additional ten thousand filled the surrounding streets or watched from windows and the roofs of adjacent buildings. This was the largest group of Saints to be met in one place to that date in the history of the Church. With the flag waving overhead, general and stake authorities took their places on an eight-foot-high stand constructed for the occasion.

Promptly at high noon, President Woodruff stepped to the podium, raised "both hands to heaven," and proclaimed in a loud voice, "Harken [*sic*] all ye House of Israel and All Ye Nations of the Earth, we will now lay the top stone of the Temple of our God!" The official capstone was the upper half of the round ball atop the east center spire. It had been hollowed out to accommodate selected books and other historical memorabilia. President Woodruff pressed a button on the stand and an electrically operated device lowered the capstone slowly and securely. As the stone descended into place, Elder Lorenzo Snow led the Hosanna Shout with thousands of white handkerchiefs waving in unison. From high up on the temple, architect Joseph Don Carlos Young called out, "The capstone is duly laid!" With great emotion the huge throng sang "The Spirit of God." Following this service, the multitude lingered, not wanting to give up the spirit of the occasion.[24]

Later that afternoon, the statue of the angel Moroni was hoisted to its position on top of the capstone. The twelve-and-a-half-foot-tall hammered copper figure had been prepared in Salem, Ohio, from a model by Utah sculptor Cyrus E. Dallin. Dallin was raised in a Latter-day Saint home but was never baptized; however, he later professed that "my 'Angel Moroni' brought me nearer to God than anything I ever did. It seemed to me that I came to know what it means to commune with angels from heaven."[25] Unveiled at a ceremony at 3:00 p.m., the angel Moroni's gold-leafed surface gleamed in the sun. The statue depicted a heavenly herald sounding his trumpet, representing the latter-day fulfillment of John's prophecy of an angel bringing "the everlasting gospel to preach unto them that dwell on the earth, and to every nation, and kindred, and tongue, and people" (Revelation 14:6).

The angel Moroni statue depicted a heavenly herald sounding his trumpet, representing the latter-day fulfillment of John's prophecy of an angel bringing "the everlasting gospel to preach unto them that dwell on the earth, and to every nation, and kindred, and tongue, and people" (Revelation 14:6).

Not all temples have had statues of Moroni. Only one of the Church's previous five temples had an angel on its tower. The Nauvoo Temple featured a weathervane depicting an angel flying in a prone position. This was a common decoration on churches of the time, so whether it was specifically intended to represent Moroni or not is a matter of conjecture. Thus, the Salt Lake Temple was the first to include the familiar vertical figure, which eventually would become a well-known feature of many Latter-day Saint temples. With the statue of Moroni in place, the Salt Lake Temple appeared to be completed, but a great deal of work remained, especially inside the building.

The Final Year of Construction

At the capstone-laying ceremonies on April 6, 1892, Elder Francis M. Lyman of the Quorum of the Twelve issued a challenge to the vast multitude of Saints assembled for the occasion. He spoke to them of President Woodruff's desire to live long enough to dedicate the temple. He proposed a resolution that those present pledge to provide the funds necessary to complete the building so that it might be dedicated just one year later—the fortieth anniversary of the cornerstone laying. This proposition was adopted unanimously. Elder Lyman wanted to head the list of contributors, so he donated a thousand dollars on the spot.[26]

Fundraising efforts received increased emphasis. The first Sunday in May was designated as a special fast day to thank God for his blessings and to ask for his help in completing the temple. (At this time the regular fast day was on the first Thursday of each month; the change to Sunday would not come until 1896.) The money collected on this special fast day went to the temple fund. By October $175,000 was still needed to complete the building, exclusive of furnishings. A special meeting of priesthood leaders convened in the upper assembly room of the nearly completed temple. When the need for funds was explained, those present pledged some $50,000 within a few minutes.[27]

In April 1892, as the art missionaries were completing their second year of study, the First Presidency wrote them, "We would like to get the benefit of the best artistic skill now in the Church in the decoration of this grand building." They also sent dimensions of the needed murals for the first three endowment instruction rooms so the artists could begin their preliminary sketches. By the end of the year, all the art missionaries had completed their studies in Paris and were back home. Before their study abroad, the artists' work had been "unsophisticated with inaccuracies in perspective and proportion." Following their training by the masters, they "painted with great proficiency," being influenced by French Impressionism. In October 1892, Weggeland learned that the First Presidency had approved forming "a committee of our home artists" to assist with the work, noting that only five months remained before dedication. As the art missionaries returned home, they went to work painting the temple murals.

Only two of the three rooms were completed at the time of dedication. In the words of Elder James E. Talmage, walls of the garden room depicted "landscape scenes of rare beauty, . . . the earth beautiful as it was before the Fall." By contrast, the world room murals reflect beasts in "deadly strife," gnarled and misshapen trees, and "seismic disruption"—the present world in its cursed state. However, the first of the three rooms was "finished and furnished in great plainness." Elder Talmage called it "the lower lecture room."[28] In 1915 it would be adorned with a mural painted by F. E. Weberg depicting the organization of the world from swirling masses of matter. It then became known more commonly as the creation room.

The goal of completing the temple within one year was set when most believed that the remaining work would take at least three more years. In fact, as late as March 1893, many still wondered if the temple could be finished by the following month. Nevertheless, those working on the temple made a special effort to complete the project on time. On Thanksgiving Day of 1892, for example, the painters were all at work in the temple. One of the workmen wrote in his diary, "Although sick, I felt strongly impressed to go and do my very best." He also recalled a personal visit by President Woodruff:

> President Woodruff called all of the workmen together. He said he had been told that some of the workmen had stated that it would be impossible to have the temple completed by April 6th. He said when he looked at this body of men he didn't believe a word of it. "Some of you may be sick and weak" (I thought he was talking to me) he continued, "Some of you may give out at night, but you will be here in the morning if you are faithful. You are not here by accident. You were ordained in the Eternal World to perform this work. Brethren I will be here April 6th to dedicate this building."[29]

Following the placing of the capstone, visitors to Salt Lake City were given the opportunity of touring the temple. Unfortunately, many did not show proper appreciation for this privilege or respect for the temple. Some broke off pieces of woodwork or defaced the walls by carving initials and scribbling graffiti. As the construction proceeded at an increasingly feverish pace, the privilege of visiting the temple was soon withdrawn.[30]

The temple was completed and ready for dedication by noon on April 5, 1893, just a few hours ahead of the deadline. Between three and five o'clock that afternoon, the temple was opened for the visit of prominent non-Latter-day Saints of the area. Some six hundred responded to the invitation, including clergy, people in business, federal officials, and their families. They were permitted to pass through every room in the temple from the basement to the roof and to examine any portion of the interior they desired. Qualified guides escorted them and answered their questions. Many expressed appreciation to the Church for this hospitable gesture. This inaugurated the custom of conducting a public open house prior to temple dedications.[31]

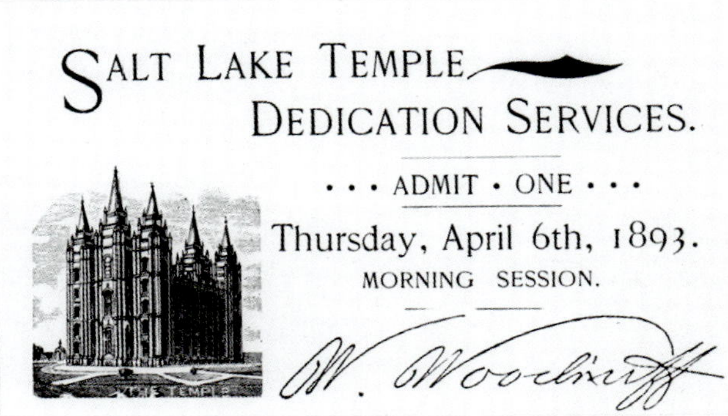

Salt Lake Temple dedication ticket. Courtesy of Church History Library.

The Temple Dedicated

At last, the long-anticipated day was at hand—the dedication of the great temple at Salt Lake City following a forty-year period of construction.[32] Of those who had participated in the 1853 cornerstone-laying ceremonies, only a few were still living—one member of the high priests quorum presidency and three members of the Twelve: Wilford Woodruff, Lorenzo Snow, and Franklin D. Richards. The temple's original architect, Truman Angell Sr., had died in 1887. The supervising architect at the time of dedication, Joseph Don Carlos Young, had been born in 1855, two years after construction had begun.[33] During this period, more than a generation had passed away.

Lorenzo Snow. Courtesy of Church History Library.

In March 1893 the First Presidency called on Latter-day Saints to prepare for the temple's dedication by repenting of their sins, keeping all God's commandments, and seeking forgiveness from one another. "None can for a moment doubt the supreme importance of every member of the congregation being at peace with all his or her brethren and sisters, and at peace with God."[34] At the 63rd Annual General Conference, which convened in the Tabernacle on Tuesday and Wednesday, April 4 and 5, President Woodruff once again spoke of the need for spiritual preparation: "I have a desire in my heart that every one of you, the night before you go into the Temple, before retiring to rest, will go by yourselves in secret prayer, . . . pray that your sins may not only be forgiven, but that you may all have the Spirit of God and the testimony of the Lord

Jesus Christ; that the Spirit of God may be with those who assemble in that Temple."[35] Thus, the dedication was to be a time for personal introspection and reformation.

Only worthy members holding a dedication ticket signed by their local Church leaders were admitted. The Saints entered the temple through the southwest door, descended to the basement, and then walked through the various rooms on each floor before reaching the main upper assembly room. This room could accommodate about 2,250 persons in each dedicatory session.

The first session, Thursday morning April 6, was for general and stake leaders and their families. The venerable President Woodruff, followed by the other General Authorities, led the group into the temple for this first session. This scene was compared to Joshua's leading the children of Israel into the promised land.[36]

A terrible storm arose that day. Rain fell in torrents and the wind blew with savage fury. It was as if the forces of evil were lashing out in violent protest against this act of consecration, President Hinckley reflected a century later. "But all was peace and quiet within the thick granite walls."[37]

The temple's dedication was a spiritual highlight for those who attended. The thirty-one dedicatory sessions, featuring music by special choirs and talks by the General Authorities, were all regarded as part of the Church's annual general conference. In each, the dedicatory prayer was followed by the unique Hosanna Shout, led by Elder Lorenzo Snow. The congregation stood as all present shouted in unison: "Hosanna, Hosanna, Hosanna, to God and the Lamb. Amen, Amen, and Amen," repeated three times. This sacred shout is an expression of joyous praise. The word hosanna literally means "save, we pray." In ancient times, this shout typically was given out of doors and included the waving of leafy tree branches. On the Savior's triumphal entry into Jerusalem, for example, the faithful waved pond fronds as they shouted "Hosanna" in praise to him (John 12:13). In modern times, the shout is accompanied by the waving of white handkerchiefs, as it is typically given indoors. [38]

The temple's dedication was a spiritual highlight for those who attended. The thirty-one dedicatory sessions, featuring music by special choirs and talks by the General Authorities, were all regarded as part of the Church's annual general conference.

The choirs then sang the "Hosanna Anthem," composed by Evan Stephens, the conductor of the Tabernacle Choir, especially for this occasion:

> The House of the Lord is completed. . . . May our off'ring by him be accepted. Amen, Amen. Rejoice, oh, ye Saints, whose patient faith and labor have reared this house wherein today ye stand; rejoice, ye blest departed saintly spirits, behold, your temple, finished, crowns the land. Rejoice, ye souls awaiting your redemption, the work speeds on to set the captive free; thanks be to God for his eternal mercies, thanks be to God for endless liberty.[39]

At a certain point, the choir director signaled the congregation to join in by singing "The Spirit of God." This great hymn had been sung at the dedication of every Latter-day Saint temple, beginning with Kirtland. It reflects temple service with such phrases as "the visions and blessings of old are returning," "the Lord is extending the Saints' understanding," "the knowledge and power of God are expanding; the veil o'er the earth is beginning to burst," and "that we through our faith may begin to inherit the visions and blessings and glories of God." The hymn's chorus specifically reflects the wording of the Hosanna Shout. One Saint who had come from Arizona for the dedication was impressed when the vast congregation "spontaneously" arose as the choir began singing "The Spirit of God," the "melody seemingly enhanced by a heavenly choir." He noted that many commented on the Hosanna Shout being "commingled with the voices of angels."[40]

Andrew Smith Jr., a member of the Tabernacle Choir, described his unusual spiritual experience as the dedicatory prayer was read:

> I concluded to keep my eyes open and look at [the person offering the prayer] instead of closing them as I had done on previous occasions. On reflection I came to the conclusion that I would pay as strict attention to the prayer with my eyes open as I could when I kept them closed. A few moments after the Apostle began to read, a scale seemed to remove from my eyes, and a bright light appeared above his head from behind his shoulders upward. This light remained in that position a few moments and then raised until I could see the face of a personage in the midst of it. It was the countenance of President Brigham Young. . . . There were, in all, about twelve men whom I saw during the dedicatory prayer. When the prayer was concluded and just before the sacred 'Hosannah' shout, I noticed a bright halo of light surrounding several of the brethren, and the speakers during the same services were seemingly encircled by a brightness which appeared to emanate from their own persons.
>
> While President George Q. Cannon was making the concluding remarks during this session, I was overcome and wept for joy. Having bowed my head for a short time I saw nothing for a few moments. On raising it again I saw a brilliant light over the head of each member of the First Presidency while they sat upon the stand.
>
> Whichever way any of the speakers turned while addressing the people, the light followed every movement made by them.
>
> The number of personages seen by me during the services subsequent to the reading of the dedicatory prayer was about twelve, making as near as I can state, about twenty-four in all.[41]

The temple's dedication was obviously an eagerly anticipated highlight in the life of President Woodruff, who regarded it as the fulfillment of prophetic dreams: "Near 50 years ago while in the city of Boston I had a vision of going with the Saints to the Rocky Mountains, building a Temple, and I dedicated it." Furthermore, "two nights in succession before John Taylor's death, President Young gave me the keys of the Temple and told me to go and dedicate it, which I did."[42]

Following the first day's sessions, President Woodruff recorded in his journal, "The spirit and Power of God rested upon us. The spirit of Prophecy and Revelation was upon us and the Hearts of the Saints were melted and many things were unfolded to us."[43] On the following day, President Woodruff told the congregation of a remarkable experience he had had during the night:

> If the veil could be taken from our eyes and we could see into the spirit world, we would see that Joseph Smith, Brigham Young and John Taylor had gathered together every spirit that ever dwelt in the flesh in this Church since its organization. We would also see the faithful apostles and elders of the Nephites who dwelt in the flesh in the days of Jesus Christ. In that assembly we would also see Isaiah and every prophet and apostle that ever prophesied of the great work of God. In the midst of these spirits

> we would see the Son of God, the Savior who presides and guides and controls the preparing of the kingdom of God on the earth and in heaven.
>
> From that body of spirits, when we shout "Hosanna to God and the Lamb!" there is a mighty shout goes up of "Glory to God in the Highest!" that the God of Israel has permitted his people to finish this Temple and prepared it for the great work that lies before the Latter-day Saints. . . .
>
> The spirits on the other side rejoice far more than we do, because they know more of what lies before in the great work of God in this last dispensation than we do.[44]

President George Q. Cannon explained why those in the spirit world would be unusually interested in the dedication of this temple. Because the Saints in the Salt Lake area had come from many nations, he said, "we represent a vast number of the families of the earth," and each individual is actually "the representative of thousands of souls."[45]

President Woodruff's reference that Isaiah was part of the dedication assembly from the other side of the veil is striking and fitting. Over twenty-six hundred years had passed since Isaiah prophesied of a temple in the tops of the mountains that would become an ensign to the nations. It makes sense that Isaiah would be eager to witness the fulfillment of the prophecy and participate in the temple's dedication.

Morning and afternoon dedicatory sessions continued through April 24 (with one evening session on April 7). Approximately seventy thousand attended. Two special "Sunday School services," April 21 and 22, were designed for those too young to attend the regular sessions. About twelve thousand children and their teachers attended these meetings. One of those present on Saturday the 22nd was seven-year-old LeGrand Richards, a future Apostle. He remembered seeing his grandfather Franklin D. Richards among those presiding on the stand.[46]

Benjamin and Emma Bennett, a young couple from Provo, would never forget the temple dedication. As the Friday evening session of April 7 concluded, Emma went into labor. She was rushed into an adjoining room and shortly afterward gave birth to a son. For the next week mother and child were cared for in a home near Temple Square. Then, on Saturday evening, April 15, the little family returned to the temple. In the same room where the baby was born, he was blessed by Joseph F. Smith, second counselor in the First Presidency, and was given the name Joseph Temple Bennett.[47]

On Wednesday, April 19, no regular dedicatory sessions were held, but the General Authorities, stake presidents, and other specially invited brethren gathered for a testimony meeting. The morning session lasted three hours, and the afternoon five. "There was a very heavenly spirit throughout," Elder B. H. Roberts wrote in his journal, "and many were melted to tears." The following afternoon, this same group of 115 men, dressed in white, gathered in the celestial room and united in prayer. Elder Roberts noted that "this prayer circle was the first held in the Salt Lake Temple and the largest held in this dispensation." President Joseph F. Smith, who was voice in the prayer, regarded it as an honor to have been a part of this historic event. Following this experience, the group partook of the sacrament. They then reminisced about Joseph Smith and the early decades of the latter-day work. Of the 115 present, only 36 had witnessed the cornerstone laying for the Salt Lake Temple forty years before; 33 had known the Prophet Joseph Smith, and only 10 had attended meetings in the Kirtland Temple.[48]

The nearly three weeks of inspirational meetings had an impact for good on the Saints. "I believe this Temple Dedication will prove to have a reformatory character among the people," remarked Elder Anthon H. Lund. "The many thousands of Saints will leave these sacred premises with resolves to serve God better than in the past."[49] Elder Roberts confided that he had been moved with a desire to reform and humble himself.[50] Speaking at the special meeting of priesthood leaders on April 19, President Woodruff declared, "Heaven has accepted this people and God has forgiven their sins . . . if they sin no more." He testified that he had felt the influence of the Holy Ghost more powerfully during the dedicatory services than at any other time in his life, excepting the occasion when the Prophet Joseph gave his final charge to the Twelve.[51] Elder Roberts described the dedication as "a Pentecostal time for me" because "the spirit of the Lord has been near."[52]

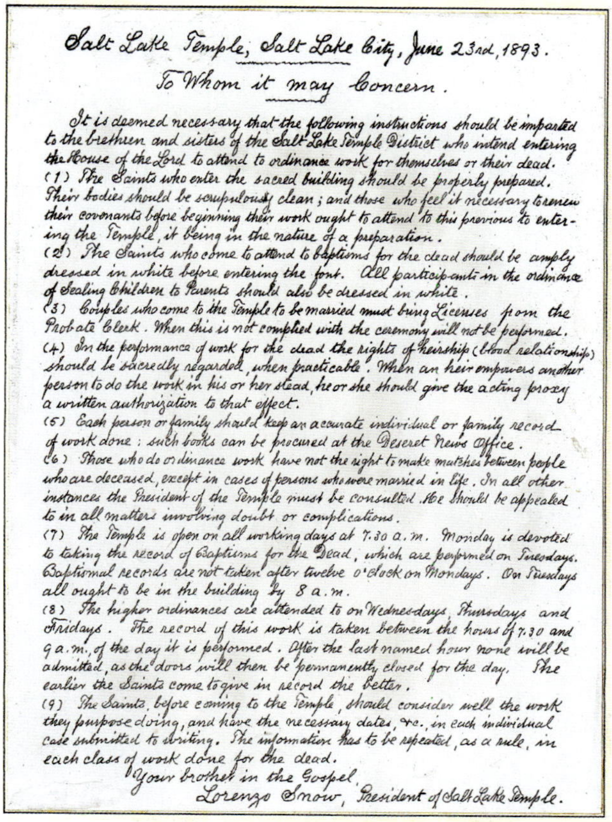
Salt Lake Temple, Salt Lake City, June 23rd, 1893.

To Whom it may Concern.

It is deemed necessary that the following instructions should be imparted to the brethren and sisters of the Salt Lake Temple District who intend entering the House of the Lord to attend to ordinance work for themselves or their dead.

(1) The Saints who enter the sacred building should be properly prepared. Their bodies should be scrupulously clean; and those who feel it necessary to renew their covenants before beginning their work ought to attend to this previous to entering the Temple, it being in the nature of a preparation.

(2) The Saints who come to attend to baptisms for the dead should be amply dressed in white before entering the font. All participants in the ordinance of Sealing Children to Parents should also be dressed in white.

(3) Couples who come to the Temple to be married must bring Licenses from the Probate Clerk. When this is not complied with the ceremony will not be performed.

(4) In the performance of work for the dead the rights of heirship (blood relationship) should be sacredly regarded, when practicable. When an heir empowers another person to do the work in his or her stead, he or she should give the acting proxy a written authorization to that effect.

(5) Each person or family should keep an accurate individual or family record of work done: such books can be procured at the Deseret News Office.

(6) Those who do ordinance work have not the right to make matches between people who are deceased, except in cases of persons who were married in life. In all other instances the President of the Temple must be consulted. He should be appealed to in all matters involving doubt or complications.

(7) The Temple is open on all working days at 7.30 a.m. Monday is devoted to taking the record of Baptisms for the Dead, which are performed on Tuesdays. Baptismal records are not taken after twelve o'clock on Mondays. On Tuesdays all ought to be in the building by 8 a.m.

(8) The higher ordinances are attended to on Wednesdays, Thursdays and Fridays. The record of this work is taken between the hours of 7.30 and 9 a.m., of the day it is performed. After the last named hour none will be admitted, as the doors will then be permanently closed for the day. The earlier the Saints come to give in record the better.

(9) The Saints, before coming to the Temple, should consider well the work they purpose doing, and have the necessary dates, &c., in each individual case submitted to writing. The information has to be repeated, as a rule, in each class of work done for the dead.

Your brother in the Gospel,
Lorenzo Snow, President of Salt Lake Temple.

Above: Instructions from Lorenzo Snow as the Salt Lake Temple opened. Courtesy of Church History Library.

Below: Salt Lake Temple Annex. Courtesy of Church History Library.

Betsy and James Madsen were sealed in the Salt Lake Temple in 1893, one of the first couples married in the new temple. Courtesy of Jena Madsen Stinger.

The Great Temple Enters Service

Lorenzo Snow, nearly eighty years of age and at the time serving as President of the Quorum of the Twelve, was named to be the first president of the Salt Lake Temple. He was provided an apartment in the temple where he could live and personally supervise the sacred activities.

An annex stood about one hundred feet north of the temple proper. Designed by Joseph Don Carlos Young, its architecture was described as Byzantine or Moorish. It was built of cream-colored oolite stone from the Manti quarry. Thus, the architecture and material of the annex were different from the temple itself. Ground was broken on May 1, 1892, and it was dedicated the following year at the same time as the temple. Hence, it was built during the intense last year of temple construction. The annex included a large entry area where patrons presented their temple recommends and where the recorder noted and distributed names of persons for whom ordinances were to be performed. It also included an assembly room seating three hundred where meetings were held for those preparing to enter the temple and where instructions were given to temple workers.[53]

The first ordinances were performed in the Salt Lake Temple on May 23, 1893. Its opening resulted in a more than 50 percent increase in the number of endowments performed for the dead each year. Almost immediately, the temple faced a problem of overcrowding. Temple authorities instructed, "Overcrowding should be especially avoided when work of a sacred character is being performed; otherwise the solemnity which ought always to be attached to it is liable to be depreciated. Conditions in the temple should never contribute to physical discomfort or mental perturbation." To solve the problem, each stake in the area was assigned certain days when its members were invited to attend the temple.[54] This practice of assigning "stake temple days" would become common during the twentieth century. Interestingly, Emma Ray Riggs and David O. McKay, who would become President of the Church

Cutaway model of the Salt Lake Temple before its renovation in the 2020s. Courtesy of Clinton D. Christensen.

a half century later, were sealed in the Salt Lake Temple on January 2, 1901, the first couple to be sealed there during the twentieth century.[55] Because of its location at Church headquarters, the Salt Lake Temple included some features not found in other temples. Between the endowment rooms and the main assembly room is an intermediate floor with a series of rooms for the use of the General Authorities. Especially important is the council room for the First Presidency and Quorum of the Twelve Apostles. In the front of the room are seats for members of the presidency. Facing them in a semicircle are the chairs occupied by members of the Twelve. This group reaches key decisions following prayerful consideration during their weekly meetings in this special room within the temple. These decisions include such matters as ordaining and setting apart new Presidents of the Church, appointing other General Authorities, creating new Church units, and approving programs. Notable examples have included the 1952 decision to build temples overseas, the determination in 1976 to add what we now know as sections 137 and 138 to the standard works, and the 1978 revelation extending the priesthood to all worthy men (Official Declaration 2). Elder Spencer W. Kimball later described the spirit of the key weekly meetings held in this sacred place:

> When in a Thursday temple meeting, after prayer and fasting, important decisions are made, new missions and new stakes are created, new patterns and policies initiated, the news is taken for granted and possibly thought of as mere human calculations. But to those who sit in the intimate circles and hear the prayers of the prophet and the testimony of [this] man of God; to those who see the astuteness of his deliberations and the sagacity of his decisions and pronouncements, to them he is verily a prophet. To hear him conclude important new developments with such

> solemn expressions as "the Lord is pleased"; "that move is right"; "our Heavenly Father has spoken," is to know positively.[56]

Another and even more sacred place is located adjacent to the celestial room. Elder James E. Talmage suggested that this "inner room or Holy of Holies of the Temple" corresponds to the most sacred areas of the ancient tabernacle and temple. This room is of circular design, with a domed ceiling containing panels of jeweled glass which admits indirect light of varying colors and hues. On the wall opposite the room's entrance is a stained glass window depicting the Father and the Son opening the dispensation of the fullness of times as they instructed the youthful prophet Joseph Smith in the Sacred Grove. Elder Talmage explained that this room is reserved "for the higher ordinances in the priesthood relating to the exaltation of both living and dead."[57]

Elder Boyd K. Packer wrote, "Hidden away in the central part of the temple is the Holy of Holies, where the President of the Church may retire when burdened down with heavy decisions to seek an interview with Him whose Church it is. The prophet holds the keys, the spiritual keys and the very literal key to this one door in that sacred edifice."[58]

"Hidden away in the central part of the temple is the Holy of Holies, where the President of the Church may retire when burdened down with heavy decisions to seek an interview with Him whose Church it is."

Temple Square, Salt Lake City, 1899, by William Henry Jackson/Detroit Photographic. Courtesy of Wikimedia Commons.

Lorenzo Snow's Experience

A remarkable experience five years after the temple's dedication confirmed that the Lord truly regarded this as his house. President Woodruff had instructed that following his death the First Presidency should be reorganized immediately rather than waiting two or three years as had been done in the past. Upon learning of President Woodruff's death, Elder Lorenzo Snow, the senior Apostle who would become the next President of the Church, went immediately to the Salt Lake Temple. He dressed in his temple robes and knelt at the sacred altar in the Holy of Holies, where he poured out his heart to the Lord: "I have not sought this responsibility but if it be Thy will, I now present myself before Thee for Thy guidance and instruction. I ask that Thou show me what Thou wouldst have me do." After finishing his prayer, he expected that there might be some special manifestation from the Lord. He waited and waited but there was no reply, no voice, no manifestation.[59]

After finishing his prayer, he expected that there might be some special manifestation from the Lord. He waited and waited but there was no reply, no voice, no manifestation. Disappointed, he left the sacred room and walked through the celestial room out into the large hallway. Here he received a glorious manifestation.

Disappointed, he left the sacred room and walked through the celestial room out into the large hallway. Here he received a glorious manifestation, which he later described to his granddaughter Allie Young Pond. Her experience was described in an article written by LeRoi Snow, son of President Snow:

> One evening while I was visiting grandpa Snow in his room in the Salt Lake Temple, I remained until the door keepers had gone and the night-watchmen had not yet come in, so grandpa said he would take me to the main front entrance and let me out that way. He got his bunch of keys from his dresser. After we left his room and while we were still in the large corridor leading into the celestial room, I was walking several steps ahead of grandpa when he stopped me and said: "Wait a moment, Allie, I want to tell you something. It was right here that the Lord Jesus Christ appeared to me at the time of the death of President Woodruff. He instructed me to go right ahead and reorganize the First Presidency of the Church at once and not wait as had been done after the death of the previous presidents, and that I was to succeed President Woodruff."
>
> Then grandpa came a step nearer and held out his left hand and said: "He stood right here, about three feet above the floor. It looked as though He stood on a plate of solid gold."
>
> Grandpa told me what a glorious personage the Savior is and described His hands, feet, countenance and beautiful white robes, all of which were of such a glory of whiteness and brightness that he could hardly gaze upon Him.
>
> Then he came another step nearer and put his right hand on my head and said: "Now granddaughter, I want you to remember that this is the testimony of your grandfather, that he told you with his own lips that he actually saw the Savior, here in the Temple, and talked with Him face to face."[60]

Not only has the Salt Lake Temple played a unique and significant role in Church governance, but a variety of other factors continued to focus attention on it. With the growth in automobile travel and tourism, the six-towered temple became perhaps the most widely recognized symbol of the restored Church. Furthermore, after the Missionary Home was opened on the adjoining block to the east in 1925, for many years most outgoing missionaries received their endowment in this temple as part of their weeklong orientation (at least until the Missionary Training Center was established at Provo in 1976). Also, a disproportionately large number of Church members over the years have chosen the Salt Lake Temple for their eternal marriages. Thus, as the Church moved into the twentieth century, the Salt Lake Temple has not only taught gospel truths through its richly symbolic exterior but also offered insights and inspiration through the saving ordinances it provides for the living and the dead. In many ways, the Salt Lake Temple has played a key part as God's kingdom rolled forth to fill the whole earth, and therefore it would continue to occupy an important place in the hearts of Latter-day Saints worldwide.

Salt Lake Temple, Courtesy of Intellectual Reserve, Inc.

Notes

1. Mark E. Petersen, *Syllabus of the Ninth Annual Priesthood Genealogy Seminar* (Provo, UT: BYU Press, 1974), 510.
2. Heber C. Kimball, in *Journal of Discourses* (London: Latter-day Saints' Book Depot, 1854–86), 10:165–66.
3. Heber J. Grant, message in *Genealogical and Historical Magazine of Arizona*, April 1942, 3–4.
4. *The Scoutmaster's Minute* (Salt Lake City: Young Men's Mutual Improvement Association General Board, 1948), 10.
5. C. Mark Hamilton, The *Salt Lake Temple: Monument to a People* (Salt Lake City: University Service Corporation, 1983), 147.
6. "Who Designed the Salt Lake Temple?" *Deseret News Weekly*, April 15, 1892.
7. Truman O. Angell Sr., "A Descriptive Statement of the Temple Now Being Erected in Salt Lake City," *Millennial Star*, May 5, 1874, 273–75.
8. Richard G. Oman, "Exterior Symbolism of the Salt Lake Temple: Reflecting the Faith that Called the Place into Being," *BYU Studies* 36, no. 4 (1996–97): 32–34.
9. Truman O. Angell Sr., "The Temple," *Deseret News*, August 17, 1854.
10. Harold B. Lee, in Conference Report, October 1964, 86.
11. Hamilton, *Salt Lake Temple*, 142–43.
12. Gordon B. Hinckley, "The Salt Lake Temple," *Ensign*, March 1993, 6.

13. Duncan M. McAllister, *Description of the Great Temple* (Salt Lake City: Bureau of Information, 1912), 7–10; James H. Anderson, "The Salt Lake Temple," *Contributor*, April 1893, 276.
14. Brigham Young, in *Journal of Discourses*, 8:203, October 8, 1860.
15. Truman O. Angell Jr. to John Taylor, April 28, 1885, and Angell Sr., to Taylor, March 11, 1885, in Hamilton, *Salt Lake Temple*, 54–57.
16. Paul C. Richards, "The Salt Lake Temple Infrastructure: Studying It Out in Their Minds," *BYU Studies* 36, no. 2 (1996–97), 202–25.
17. Orson F. Whitney, *Life of Heber C. Kimball* (Salt Lake City: Bookcraft, 1967), 397.
18. Leonard J. Arrington, *Great Basin Kingdom* (Cambridge, MA: Harvard University Press, 1958), 362–64.
19. N. B. Lundwall, *Temples of the Most High* (Salt Lake City: Bookcraft, 1947), 100–101.
20. Leonard J. Arrington and Wayne K. Hinton, "The Logan Tabernacle and Temple," *Utah Historical Quarterly* 41 (Summer 1973): 312–13; Melvin A. Larkin, "The History of the L.D.S. Temple in Logan, Utah" (master's thesis, Utah State Agricultural College, 1954), 143–155.
21. Anderson, "Salt Lake Temple," 269–70.
22. Anderson, "Salt Lake Temple," 270.
23. Anderson, "Salt Lake Temple," 271.
24. Scott G. Kenney, ed., *Wilford Woodruff's Journal* (Midvale, UT: Signature Books, 1985), 9:192–94, April 6, 1892; compare James E. Talmage, *House of the Lord* (Salt Lake City: Bookcraft, 1962), 149–52.
25. Levi Edgar Young, "The Angel Moroni and Cyrus Dallin," *Improvement Era*, April 1953, 234; see also J. Michael Hunter, "I Saw Another Angel Fly," *Ensign*, January 2000, 30.
26. Anderson, "Salt Lake Temple," 274.
27. Kenney, *Wilford Woodruff's Journal*, 9:222, October 10, 1892.
28. James E. Talmage, *The House of the Lord* (Salt Lake City: Bookcraft, 1962), 185-87.
29. William Hurst diary, as cited in Joseph Heinerman, *Temple Manifestations* (Manti, UT: Mountain Valley Publishers, 1974), 116.
30. Anderson, "Salt Lake Temple," 282.
31. McAllister, "Temples of the Latter-day Saints: Purposes for Which They Are Erected," *Liahona, the Elder's Journal*, February 22, 1927, 417; John R. Winder, "Temples and Temple Work," *Young Woman's Journal*, February 1903, 51.
32. For a description of these events, see Richard Neitzel Holzapfel, *Every Stone a Sermon* (Salt Lake City: Bookcraft, 1992), especially chapter 9.
33. Anderson, "Salt Lake Temple," 279.
34. First Presidency circular letter, March 18, 1893, in James R. Clark, comp., *Messages of the First Presidency*, 6 vols. (Salt Lake City: Bookcraft, 1965–75), 3:241–44.
35. Anderson, "Salt Lake Temple," 292.
36. James E. Talmage, *House of the Lord*, 159.
37. Conference Report, April 1993, 92.
38. See Lael Woodbury, "Origin and Uses of the Sacred Hosanna Shout," in *Sperry Lecture Series 1975* (Provo, UT: BYU Press, 1975), 18–22.
39. "Hosanna Anthem," in *The Choirbook* (Salt Lake City: The Church of Jesus Christ of Latter-day Saints, 1995), 69–71; duplicated phrases have not been repeated.
40. Frank T. Pomeroy, "Temples of Our Lord, Ancient and Modern," *Genealogical and Historical Magazine of Arizona* 2 (April 1925), 34.
41. "Temple Manifestations," *Contributor*, December 1894, 116–17, quoted in Matthew B. Brown and Paul Thomas Smith, *Symbols in Stone: Symbolism on the Early Temples of the Restoration.* (American Fork, UT: Covenant Communications, 1997), 143–44.
42. Kenney, *Wilford Woodruff's Journal*, 9:279, 1893 summary.
43. Kenney, *Wilford Woodruff's Journal*, 9:246, April 6, 1893.
44. Quoted in *Saviors on Mount Zion* (Salt Lake City: Deseret Sunday School Union, 1950), 142–43.

45. George Q. Cannon, as quoted in *Our Lineage* (Salt Lake City: Genealogical Society of Utah, 1934), 20.
46. Lucile C. Tate, *LeGrand Richards: Beloved Apostle* (Salt Lake City: Bookcraft, 1982), 10–11.
47. Anderson, "Salt Lake Temple," 301.
48. Brigham H. Roberts journals, 1890–1893, entries for April 19 and 20, MS 1430, box 3, folder 6, in the Special Collections of the Harold B. Lee Library at Brigham Young University, 1893; Anthon H. Lund journal, April 20, 1893, Church History Library.
49. Lund journal, April 18, 1893.
50. Roberts journal, April 21, 1893.
51. Quoted in Lund journal, April 19, 1893.
52. Roberts journal, April 24, 1893.
53. Hamilton, *Salt Lake Temple*, 182.
54. *Deseret News Weekly*, August 19, 1893, 267.
55. Francis M. Gibbons, *David O. McKay, Apostle to the World, Prophet of God* (Salt Lake City: Deseret Book, 1986), 56.
56. Spencer W. Kimball, ". . . To His Servants the Prophets," *Instructor*, August 1960, 257.
57. Talmage, *House of the Lord*, 193–94.
58. Boyd K. Packer, *The Holy Temple* (Salt Lake City: Bookcraft, 1980), 4.
59. LeRoi C. Snow, "An Experience of My Father's," *Improvement Era*, September 1933, 677, 679.
60. Snow, "An Experience of My Father's," 677, 679.

6

Improving Existing Temples

The Logan, St. George, Manti, and Salt Lake Temples

Logan from on High, by Alan Fullmer.

No new temples were built in Utah during the first half of the twentieth century, but improvements were made, including many changes that attracted visitors. With the increase in travel, especially by automobile during the early twentieth century, Temple Square in Salt Lake City became a popular destination. During the 1920s approximately 200,000 people visited Temple Square each year, and by the 1960s that total had increased tenfold. Visitors marveled at the acoustics of the domed Tabernacle and gained a greater appreciation for the faith of the Latter-day Saints as they learned about the ceremonies with eternal significance and blessing that are offered in the temple. As a result, the six-towered temple became perhaps the most widely recognized symbol of the restored Church and gospel of Jesus Christ. Different kinds of progress were also taking place at other Utah temples.

Baptizing Children

Today the Saints usually think of baptisms for the dead as the only use for a baptismal font in temples, yet that has not been the case throughout the Church's history. Tens of thousands of baptisms for the living occurred for children around ages eight and nine from the 1880s to 1970s.[1] A major reason for this practice was that the temple held one of the only fonts in the area. This changed as fonts were added to tabernacles in the 1950s and then became a standard addition to newly built stake centers in the 1960s.

According to Church records, children were baptized routinely in the St. George, Logan, Manti, Mesa, and Cardston Temples. Baptisms for the living were not performed in the Salt Lake Temple, but they were done nearby in a special font built in the Salt Lake Tabernacle.[2] The first baptisms occurred in the St. George Temple in 1882. They stopped in the St. George and Logan Temples in the mid-1950s, but they continued in Manti until 1972 and in the Mesa Temple until 1973.[3]

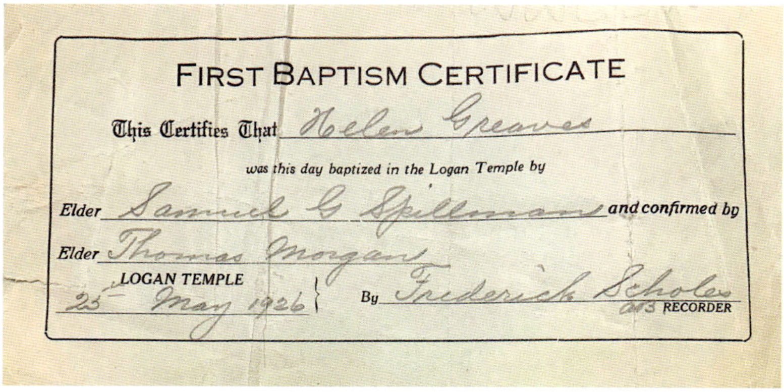
FIRST BAPTISM CERTIFICATE

This Certifies That Helen Greaves

was this day baptized in the Logan Temple by

Elder Samuel G Spillman and confirmed by

Elder Thomas Morgan

LOGAN TEMPLE

25 May 1926 By Frederick Scholes RECORDER

Logan Temple baptismal certificate of Helen Greaves. Courtesy of Jay Burrup.

The first child baptized in the Logan Temple was Rachael Roberts, who was baptized June 3, 1884, just weeks after the Logan Temple was dedicated. All ordinances for the almost twenty-four thousand children baptized in the Logan Temple were performed by ordinance workers. Usually, the baptisms occurred on Monday, Friday, and Saturday, with Saturdays having up to sixty children a day.[4] Sometimes a parent would attend, but the ordinance was not the family experience it is today. Helen Greaves is one example. As an eight-year-old, she and other children her age in the Preston, Idaho, area boarded a bus and were driven to the Logan Temple in 1926. None of their

Logan Temple with annex, by C. R. Savage. Courtesy of Church History Library.

parents came on the trip, and just a few ward members were chaperones.[5] However, the opportunity to go into the temple was a special experience for the children. In Manti, Marjorie Mae Tuttle shared with her family that following her baptism in 1936 all the children were permitted to go climb one of the beautiful spiral staircases and see part of the temple.[6] Almost thirteen thousand children were baptized in the Manti Temple in its first fifty years of operation.[7]

While children are no longer baptized in temples, this practice gives an additional perspective on the use of temples in their first decades. Today, a temple baptismal font is most busy on Saturdays and after school hours as the youth keep the font occupied with the work for redeeming the dead. Many youth bring their own family temple names and are focused on performing ordinances for deceased ancestors. However, President Russell M. Nelson has taught that we should "begin with the end in mind," referencing our goal in getting to the temple. What could have been better for the children of the Church of yesteryear than to begin their journey along the covenant path by being baptized in the temple, laying the foundation for their return for higher temple ordinances!

An Annex

Beginning at Logan and Manti, the one-story annex built on the temples' north side was an important addition. For example, in Logan the "extension," as it was called, measured eighty by thirty-six feet and was twenty-three feet high. Just inside the annex's entrance was a desk where those coming to the temple confirmed their worthiness by presenting their temple recommend. Typically, these structures provided offices for the temple presidency and recorder, a chapel where groups could meet before entering the temple, and dressing rooms with lockers where patrons could change into white clothing in preparation for participating in temple service. An annex was not originally a part of the St. George Temple, but one was built north of the temple during the later 1880s or early 1890s, with access to the temple through one of the entrances in the foundation. Initially it was just a small structure to enclose the water tank and boiler, outdoor supplies, and the custodian's office. In 1902 a new and larger annex replaced it.

An annex was not originally a part of the St. George Temple, but one was built north of the temple during the later 1880s or early 1890s.

These annexes were improved over the years. Facilities such as a cafeteria, a place where babies and children could be cared for while waiting to participate in sealings, or cloak rooms were added. As the number of patrons coming to the temples increased, dressing rooms needed to be enlarged. In more recent decades, many of these functions have been incorporated into the temples themselves, so a separate annex structure was no longer needed.

Other improvements were within the temples. During 1916 a thorough refurbishing of the Logan Temple included painting or washing all walls, replacing worn wooden floors with new hardwood, and installing new carpets produced by area Relief Societies. Because illumination with electricity was extremely rare when this temple was built, oil lamps or tallow candles were still being used. Therefore, the temple was wired according to "the most modern and approved methods" and fitted with "electroliers" in its rooms.[8] Doors were cut in the temple's six-foot-thick stone walls on the first floor so that rooms in the towers, previously less accessible, could be used. A remodeling in St. George the following year created two new sealing rooms to the north and south of the celestial room.

Temples Preserved from Destruction

The first three Utah temples all had incidents that could have resulted in the destruction of the buildings. It was later discovered that when the St. George Temple's tower was struck by lightning in 1878, one of the roof planks had smoldered but fortunately did not ignite. Had it done so, the tar-covered roof would have quickly burned, leading to the destruction of the wooden interior structure below.

On Tuesday evening, December 4, 1917, a short circuit sparked a fire in the utility room under the main stairway in the Logan Temple. Furniture polish stored in the room accelerated the fire which raced up the stairway to the upper floor where most of the damage occurred. The stairway was destroyed; carpets, furnishings, art glass windows, and paintings were ruined. There was also smoke damage throughout the building. Volunteers quickly cleaned the temple. The spiral main staircase was replaced with one having square turns at a cost of forty thousand dollars. Relief Society women produced new carpeting, and the temple reopened after only three months, on March 1, 1918.[9]

Then, on Sunday, August 26, 1928, people in Manti heard a deafening clap of thunder. Within moments, somebody exclaimed, "The temple's been struck by lightning and is burning. Pass the word!" The east tower had been hit. Men carried hoses connected to the temple's water supply up one of the famed circular staircases to the roof, but the pressure was insufficient. Not until the hoses were connected with the town's water system could water be put on the flames. Several witnesses gratefully observed that "it was the slowest burning fire they had ever seen," and fortunately it was extinguished quickly and damage was minimal. Broken windows were soon replaced, and other damage repaired. Of course, an adequate fire suppression system and lightning rods were also promptly installed.[10]

About three months later, early Tuesday morning, November 20, the furnace was lit in the St. George Temple annex. A short time later, the custodian and night watchman smelled smoke, rushed into the furnace room, and saw flames in a pile of wood and coal. The fire was still small and could have been put out quickly, but volunteer firemen had to pull the firehose on a two-wheel cart several blocks to the temple. By this time the flames had gained headway, and the entire annex was destroyed. Much of the furniture and valuable temple records were safely removed from the burning building. For a time, the temple itself was threatened, but the valiant efforts of the volunteer brigade kept the flames from spreading, so there was just some smoke damage.

> The first three Utah temples all had incidents that could have resulted in the destruction of the buildings.

Important Improvements at St. George and Manti

The need to rebuild the annex provided the occasion for the First Presidency to consider also making significant changes within the temple itself. Rather than the lower main assembly hall only being divided by temporary curtains or screens for presenting the endowment, permanent creation, garden, world, terrestrial, and celestial rooms would be created in this area. The temple was closed for over a year during 1937 and 1938 while the new rooms were constructed. Joseph A. F. Averett and Peter W. Kemp were commissioned to paint murals for the first three of these new ordinance rooms. At this time, an elevator was also installed; only one structural timber needed to be removed to create the shaft.[11]

Because the original murals in the Manti Temple were painted directly on the walls in the 1880s, by 1944 the plaster had deteriorated to the point that the murals were severely delaminated. The creation room mural by C. C. A. Christensen could

Manti Temple murals in the world room by Minerva Teichert. Courtesy of Intellectual Reserve, Inc. A striking feature in this room is this large Native American chief painted on the west wall.

be touched up and saved, but the two others needed to be redone. Plaster in the garden and world rooms was replaced, and high-quality sail canvas was applied to the walls. In 1945 Joseph Everett began painting a new mural in the garden room, but unfortunately he died before the work was finished. During 1946 and 1947, Robert L. Shepherd, another noted Latter-day Saint artist, completed the room by painting forest and lake scenes. Murals in the world room were painted in 1947–49 by Minerva Teichert, noted for her art depicting Book of Mormon, western American, and other religious scenes. She depicted the building of the Tower of Babel on the east wall; the Crusades and Columbus's voyage to America on the north wall; Abraham, Joseph, Moses, and the Pilgrims on the south wall; and the establishment of Zion in North America on the west wall. A striking feature in this room is a large Native American chief painted on the west wall.[12]

Murals in the world room, painted in 1949 by Minerva Teichert, depict on the north wall a scene of pilgrimage and on the south wall Joseph being sold into Egypt by his brothers. Courtesy of Intellectual Reserve, Inc.

Expansion of the Salt Lake Temple during the 1960s

Construction directly related to the Salt Lake Temple followed ten years of planning by the First Presidency and the Church Building Committee. In addition to a larger and more functional new annex, there would be a sealing room addition constructed against the north side of the temple; these would total 120,000 square feet of floor space, bringing the temple's total to 253,000. President David O. McKay explained that these improvements would "make it possible for more work to be done by more members of the Church with greater dispatch and comfort."[13] Specifically, a

Church architect Edward O. Anderson. Courtesy of FamilySearch.

surprisingly large number of Latter-day Saints selected the Salt Lake Temple as the site for their marriages. Even though there were eleven other temples in service during 1960, nearly 39 percent of all temple marriages were performed in Salt Lake. This created the need for more sealing rooms and accommodations for wedding parties.

Edward O. Anderson was the architect for this project. He was serving as Church Temple Architect and had already designed the Los Angeles and Swiss Temples. He received his training at the Carnegie Institute of Technology (now Carnegie Mellon University) in Pennsylvania.[14]

The temple closed on June 29, 1962, so construction could commence that summer.[15] During the next month, the Jensen Construction Company of Salt Lake City won the $2,258,000 contract. Additional contracts for mechanical and electrical work brought the total to about three million dollars. The size of this project was underscored by the fact that at the same time a contract was awarded to build the Oakland Temple for a comparable three and one-half million dollars.[16]

The first step was to excavate along the Salt Lake Temple's south and east sides for foundations, passageways, and other facilities.

In August the first step was to excavate along the Salt Lake Temple's south and east sides for foundations, passageways, and other facilities. During the next several months, this digging exposed the temple's foundations to view for the first time in about a century. This included the temple's southeast cornerstone, which had been put into place in 1853. As excavations went deeper, they revealed that there were also footings of rough-hewn sandstone sixteen feet wide at their base beneath the finished blocks of the main granite foundation.[17] While this work was going forward, an intruder eluded the night watchman and set off an explosive early on the morning of November 14, 1962, breaking windows and damaging one of the temple's main east front doors.[18] Needed repairs were quickly made, and the work went forward without any delay.

Because some people raised concerns about building an addition on the iconic Salt Lake Temple, steps were taken to make the addition as well as the nearby annex blend in with the existing structure. Anderson designed them with features to match the temple's original architecture, and they were to be faced with granite from the same quarry in Little Cottonwood Canyon. Even inside the temple itself, improvements in heating, air-conditioning, and fire protection were made while not marring the temple's interior decorations and architecture. To further protect the temple's surface and structure, the addition would be completely freestanding with a few-inch gap, connected to the temple only by a thin diaphragm of lead-covered copper to allow for independent expansion with changes in temperature. The addition would have a large sealing room and waiting rooms for adults and for children on the ground floor, while there would be five smaller sealing rooms and the sealing office on the upper level. A window in the temple's celestial room was transformed into a door to provide access.[19]

Because using blasting powder tends to shatter the stone, granite being removed to form the Church's genealogy records storage vaults could not be used for the temple project. Workmen therefore cut stone blocks from the quarry by using methods like those employed a century earlier. Holes were drilled in a line, and wooden pegs were tapped in until the stone split along this line. A total of fifty thousand square feet of granite would cover the surfaces of the temple annex and sealing room addition, and only the highest grade would be used. A wire saw with silicon carbide cut the stones to their precise dimensions. Arched stones had to be cut by hand. Such skilled craftsmen were scarce, but the architect was grateful that there were still some who could match the quality of the original artisans.[20]

The temple's walls had to be cleaned so they would match the new construction. Crews used a mixture of water and black slag sand from Kennecott to remove the century's worth of patina, changing the temple from its existing dark gray appearance to a much lighter shade. Workmen also replaced damaged mortar and declared the building to be in good condition for its age.[21]

Meanwhile, work on the new Bureau of Information was nearing its conclusion. Significant modifications were made for it to serve as the temporary temple annex. A

Granite and sandstone foundations of Salt Lake Temple. Courtesy of *Deseret News* and Church History Library.

Salt Lake Temple annex project. Courtesy of *Deseret News* and Church History Library.

level wooden floor was constructed above the sloping floor of a downstairs theater. Additional plumbing was added in the basement dressing room areas. A kitchen and cafeteria were created on the main floor. Administrative offices and a chapel were also located on this level. Patrons entered through the east entrance, where the recommend desk was located. They received proxy names in the main rotunda before descending an escalator to the dressing rooms in the basement. Here, temple president Willard R. Smith explained, patrons would "engage in ordinances preparatory to entering the temple for endowment work." They then walked southeast through an underground passageway to the west end of the temple's basement. These facilities were dedicated by President David O. McKay on Thursday, March 7, 1963, at an inspiring service held in the bureau's theater. Work inside the temple took about two more months to complete. Then, at a meeting in the temple's terrestrial room on Tuesday, May 21, 1963, President McKay dedicated the improvements made during the past ten months, paying tribute to the pioneer builders of the temple and describing its refurbished interior as "fitting as well as beautiful." The temple reopened for ordinance work on Monday, May 27.[22] For the next year and a half, while ordinance work was taking place inside the temple, heavy construction was going forward just outside.

The wall around the northern half of Temple Square had been removed to the Bureau of Information and temple annex sites to provide access for construction equipment.[23] By late 1964 these projects had progressed to the point that the wall could be restored.[24] Two sections of wall on either side of the east gate were replaced by a matching high wrought iron fence, allowing a better view of the new addition and annex as well as the landscaping, which was being restored around the newly constructed facilities.[25]

By 1966 the new temple annex was ready to receive temple patrons. Temple workers moved out of the temporary annex on March 19, and patrons began using the new facilities two days later. Temple president Howard S. McDonald gratefully noted that twenty-eight hundred rather than eighteen hundred patrons could come each day, encouraging more people to attend the temple.[26] With the departure of the temple workers, the Bureau of Information, then coming to be called a visitors' center, could be transformed to fulfill its intended function. This reconstruction required over a year.[27] After the new visitors' center had entered service, all these newly constructed facilities were dedicated on October 22, 1967, by Hugh B. Brown, first counselor in the First Presidency, at a meeting in the four-hundred-seat chapel of the new annex. This was fully a year and a half after temple patrons had begun using the new annex and sealing room addition.[28]

By 1966 the new temple annex was ready to receive temple patrons.

Even though the underground parking plaza was opened near the end of 1964, the Church Office Building was not constructed until the 1970s. In 1967 the part of this site directly across the street from the Salt Lake Temple became an outdoor theater with four thousand seats facing the temple. A musical production entitled *Promised Valley* depicted the hopes, tragedies, and triumphs of the pioneers. The object was to share an appealing gospel message with at least some of the estimated twenty-five thousand visitors who came to Temple Square every day during the summer season. With a musical score composed by Crawford Gates, the musical was produced under the direction of the dance, drama, and music committees of the Young Men's and Young Women's Mutual Improvement Associations; members of the cast and orchestra all were volunteers. This production was presented on Monday through Saturday evenings during the months of July and August. During most of the play, the temple was dark, but, as the climaxing note of the finale sounded, the lofty

Volunteers in new temple recorder office. Courtesy of *Deseret News* and Church History Library.

temple spires were suddenly and dramatically illuminated in front of the amazed and appreciative audience.[29]

Finishing Touches

When the new temple annex opened, patrons at first entered directly into the foyer through a door in the north wall of Temple Square. In 1970, however, to accommodate the large number of people coming to the temple and to improve security, a covered entrance ramp and spacious waiting room were constructed at the east end of the annex. This, then, became the usual way to enter the temple.[30]

A second visitors' center opened on Temple Square in 1978. The original Bureau of Information building was razed, and the new South Visitors' Center took its place. These new facilities were dedicated by President Spencer W. Kimball on June 1, 1978 (the very day he received the momentous revelation extending priesthood and temple blessings to all worthy people; see Official Declaration 2). Speaking at the dedication, Elder Gordon B. Hinckley of the Quorum of the Twelve cited Brigham Young's prophetic statement to the struggling pioneers that this area "would become the great highway of nations, and that kings and emperors, and the noble and wise of the earth would visit us here." Elder Hinckley then noted, "It is of singular importance that the beautiful visitors' center to the north of this square, as large as it is, has become inadequate to accommodate the crowds of visitors who come every day of the year. They include some of the rulers of the earth, and the learned, the noble and the wise."[31] While the North Visitors' Center presented exhibits on a variety of topics, the new South Visitors' Center focused on temple service and the history of the Salt Lake Temple.

These improvements around the temple enriched its message to the world, continuing to fulfill Isaiah's words, "Many people shall go and say, Come ye, and let us go up to the mountain of the Lord, to the house of the God of Jacob; and he will teach us of his ways, and we will walk in his paths" (Isaiah 2:3). Enhancements to Utah's historic temples during the first six decades of the twentieth century anticipated a whole new and more efficient concept seen in two temples built in the state during the early 1970s.

Notes

1. For additional information, see the Special Collections section of the Family History Library. Only active temple recommend holders can use these microfilm collections by appointment in the Family History Library.
2. Salt Lake Tabernacle records, "Baptisms for the Living, 1907–1960," Family History Library. Baptisms continued after this period under the direction of the Salt Lake Stake, who used the font for stake baptisms into the early twenty-first century.

3. St. George Temple records, "Baptisms for the Living, 1882–1956," Family History Library; Logan Temple records, "Baptisms for the Living, 1884–1957," Family History Library; Manti Temple records, "Baptisms for the Living, 1888–1972," Family History Library; Arizona Temple records, "Baptisms for the Living, 1928–1973," Family History Library.
4. Logan Temple records, "Baptisms for the Living, 1884–1957," Family History Library.
5. Jay Burrup, email message to Clint Christensen, August 25, 2022, in author's possession.
6. Jeff Thompson, email message to Clint Christensen, August 19, 2022, in private possession.
7. "Manti Temple: Golden Jubilee, 1888–1938," Church History Library.
8. Edna L. Smith, "Improvements in the Logan Temple," *Improvement Era*, March 1916, 458–59.
9. Nolan P. Olsen, *Logan Temple: The First 100 Years* (Providence, UT: Keith W. Watkins and Sons, 1978), 176.
10. Victor J. Rasmussen, *The Manti Temple* (Provo, UT: Community Press, 1988), 66–67.
11. Blaine M. Yorgason, Richard A. Schmutz, and Douglas D. Alder, *All That Was Promised: The St. George Temple and the Unfolding of the Restoration* (Salt Lake City: Deseret Book, 2013), 325–31.
12. Doris R. Dant, "Minerva Teichert's Manti Temple Murals," *Brigham Young University Studies* 38, no. 3 (Summer 1999): 7–28.
13. "Extensive Renovation Begins on S. L. Temple," *Church News*, August 18, 1962, 3.
14. "Edward O. Anderson Builder of Temples," *Church News*, May 14, 1966, 3.
15. "Salt Lake Temple Notice," *Church News*, June 23, 1962, 2.
16. "Contracts Awarded for Oakland, S. L. Temples," *Church News*, July 21, 1963, 3.
17. "Digging Uncovers S. L. Footings," *Church News*, September 8, 1962, 4; "Excavations Expose Depth of Temple Footings," *Church News*, March 30, 1963, 6.
18. "Detonation of Plastic Explosive Damages Front Door of Salt Lake Temple," *Church News*, November 17, 1962, 4.
19. "Granite Set in Place on Temple Addition," *Church News*, October 19, 1963, 3; "Copper Roof Placed on Temple Annex," *Church News*, November 23, 1963, 4.
20. Scott, "New Granite for Temple Square," *Church* News, March 9, 1963, 8–9.
21. Scott, "Salt Lake Temple Looks 100 Years Brighter," *Church News*, January 5, 1963, 8–9.
22. Henry A. Smith, "President McKay Officiates at Special Rites in Salt Lake Temple," *Church News*, May 25, 1963, 3.
23. "Pioneer-Made Masonry Exposed as Power Shovels Level Historic Wall," *Church News*, February 9, 1963, 14.
24. "Wall to Be Restored at Temple Square," *Church* News, July 4, 1964, 3; "Veteran Mason at Work on New Wall," *Church* News, October 17, 1964, 3; Scott, "Temple Wall Gets New Look," *Church News*, December 12, 1964, 12.
25. "Old Wall Removed: Better View of Temple Afforded," *Church News*, January 23, 1965, 13.
26. Scott, "New S. L. Temple Annex Opens," *Church News*, March 19, 1966, 7; "New Annex Aids Work at Temple," *Church News*, April 30, 1966, 12.
27. "General Authorities Tour Visitors' Center," *Church News*, April 22, 1967, 8–9; Joseph Lundstrom, "General Authorities Inspect New Visitors' Center Facility," *Church* News, January 27, 1968, 3.
28. "Temple Annex Dedicated," *Church News*, October 28, 1967, 3.
29. "Temple as Backdrop," *Church News*, April 29, 1967, 6.
30. "A New Main Entrance to S. L. Temple," *Church News*, December 13, 1969, 6.
31. "New Visitors Center Opens," *Church News*, June 10, 1978, 3, 8–9.

7 The Efficient Ogden and Provo Temples

Provo Utah Temple. *Sunrise from on High*, by Alan Fullmer.

Utah's first four temples were dedicated within a space of only sixteen years. Then more than three-quarters of a century would pass before the next of these holy houses would go into service. During this time, the Saints in Ogden and Provo anxiously looked forward to the time when they might have their own temples.

Years of Anticipation

In Ogden

During the early twentieth century, Saints in the Ogden area typically attended the Salt Lake Temple but longed to have their own. On December 12, 1920, Church Patriarch Hyrum G. Smith told attendees at the North Weber Stake conference that Ogden would have a temple "in the near future."[1] The Joseph Clark family offered the Church a site on the hill above Tyler and 30th Streets (where the St. Benedict's Hospital now stands) with the understanding that a temple would be built there someday.

Early on Sunday morning, May 15, 1921, President Heber J. Grant, his counselor Anthony W. Ivins, and local Church leaders inspected this and a downtown site, but the prophet concluded that the time was not right to build a temple in Ogden.[2] President Grant, however, indicated that Church funds were committed to other projects, so "there was no telling when a temple would be built in Ogden."[3] Nevertheless, he conceded, "if all the members of the Church would pay an honest tithing we would build all the temples we need."[4] The Great Depression of the 1930s and World War II during the 1940s put off Ogden's hopes further.

During the 1950s the Ogden area was part of the Logan Temple district. Stakes typically chartered evening bus trips to Cache Valley for a tempe session, but travel was especially dangerous during winter conditions in Sardine Canyon. By that time David O. McKay, who had grown up in nearby Huntsville and served as principal of Ogden's Weber Stake Academy, had become President of the Church. Church members in Ogden naturally wondered if chances for an Ogden Temple were greater. One stake president, Lawrence Olpin of the Lorin Farr Stake, even offered to donate his property to become a temple site. The First Presidency "decided to express appreciation to President Olpin for his offer, and to tell him that we [still] have no plans to build a temple in Ogden."[5]

Utah temples up to the 1970s. Courtesy of Lee R. Cowan.

In Provo

A similar anticipation existed in Provo. For decades residents had referred to what would become the southwest corner of Brigham Young University's upper campus, which overlooked the town to the south, as "Temple Hill." This tradition stemmed from a prophecy believed to have been made by Brigham Young himself sometime in the late 1860s. After he and his party "ascended to the summit of this beautiful hill," Brigham reportedly declared, "You are now standing on holy ground, and the day will come when a magnificent temple will be erected here to our God."[6]

At the turn of the twentieth century, however, BYU officials dramatically expanded the campus atop this hill by erecting a building in honor of Karl G. Maeser, the school's first permanent principal. At its 1911 dedication, Elder John Henry Smith—a member of the Quorum of the Twelve—noted that although the grounds had been "rendered sacred to many of us from our earliest childhood in the thought that a temple someday would be erected upon this hill," the building would instead become a "temple of learning." Following the dedication of the Maeser Building, the idea of a temple on what had become the BYU campus faded. Still, members of the Church remained hopeful that a house of the Lord would be built somewhere nearby.

"You are now standing on holy ground, and the day will come when a magnificent temple will be erected here to our God."

With proposals during the 1940s and '50s for teaching languages to missionaries at Brigham Young University, the idea of a temple in Provo revived. In 1952, BYU president Ernest L. Wilkinson wrote to the First Presidency. He treasured Brigham Young's prophecy that a temple would be built on Temple Hill, now occupied by the BYU campus. He concluded that with the construction of a temple on or next to the campus, "all of the missionaries' training could be accomplished here."[7] The need for a temple nearby was further affirmed as university enrollment soared from 4,510 in 1950 to 10,305 in 1960 and the first student stake was organized in 1956; however, another decade would pass before these ideas became a reality.

About this same time, Ben E. Lewis, who was serving as president of the East Sharon Stake just northeast of the BYU campus, had the following experience:

> One day I had a call from one of our Bishops in the Oak Hills area, saying one of the members of his Ward, a Brother Leichty who owned a sizable piece of property in the Ward, had come to him and told him of a dream he had the night before in which he had witnessed the construction of a Temple on his property, and that if the Church wanted to build a Temple there he would donate his land for that purpose. This call came just three days before we were having our quarterly Stake Conference to which a General Authority had been assigned to come. Back in those days we had two conference sessions, one in the morning and one in the afternoon. In between these sessions we would take the General Authority to one of our homes for dinner. It was our turn to host the General Authority for the Sunday dinner which was held in the family room of our home which sat on a hill overlooking the valley. The room had large pane glass windows, and we could look from that room and see the location of the Leichty property. This provided an opportunity for me to put in a "plug" for a temple in Provo. When I brought the General Authority into our family room I took him over to the window where we could look out and see the Leichty property, and told him about Brother Leichty's dream, and that he had expressed his willingness to

> donate the property to the Church if they wanted to build a temple on it. The General Authority turned to me and said, "Brother Ben, if the Church ever decides to build a Temple in Provo, we will let you know." That took care of that. Barbara called, "It's time to sit down for dinner."[8]

The Decision to Build Two New Temples

As early as the 1950s, President David O. McKay had discussed the possibility of constructing new temples on the Wasatch Front, but other building projects—such as hundreds of chapels, the large Los Angeles Temple, and the first three overseas temples—had consumed available Church funds. But by the later 1960s, this situation had improved.[9]

A new Church Building Committee came into being on July 1, 1965. It was formed to give stability and order to the Church's massive post–World War II building program. Mark B. Garff, a Salt Lake construction company owner, became chairman, and Fred A. Baker, vice president of Ogden's Commercial Security Bank, became vice chairman with responsibility for budgets and finances. Emil B. Fetzer became Church architect and a member of the committee. One of his duties was to inspect temples periodically "to ascertain that they would always be in proper condition to be worthy houses of the Lord. This entailed the responsibility to make certain that all necessary and required repairs, modifications and up-grading were promptly and properly accomplished." He personally reported the results of these inspections to

Church Building Committee in 1965. Left to right: Emil B. Fetzer, Allan M. Acomb, Julian S. Cannon, Mark B. Garff (chairman seated), Fred A. Baker, Victor Laughlin, Horace A. Christiansen, Ray Engebretsen. Courtesy of FamilySearch.

the First Presidency. In 1967 he informed them that the Logan and Manti Temples were "drastically and urgently in need of extensive upgrading, reconditioning, remodeling and refurbishing." Furthermore, their compliance with building codes had been "grandfathered," meaning that if anything at all was done to the building, the whole structure would need to be rebuilt and brought up to the latest codes. He estimated that these repairs would require the temples to be closed for at least two years.[10] Another problem was that the Logan, Manti, and especially Salt Lake Temples were seriously overcrowded. In the light of this information, Church leaders considered what would be the best course to follow.

Noting that BYU students traveled to Manti in great numbers, Garff suggested the possibility of building "a small temple in Provo and one in Ogden." President McKay directed him to investigate the matter further and then make a report. On Tuesday, August 8, 1967, leaders of the Building Committee met with the First Presidency. Garff indicated that the overcrowding in the Logan and Manti Temples was "becoming so acute that it becomes necessary either to remodel those temples or build new ones." He recommended building new ones "if for no other reason than economics," because "remodeling the old temples would cost nearly twice as much as building the new ones." Baker pointed out that the Salt Lake Temple's workload in 1966 was two and a half times as great as it had been in 1950, so this temple particularly would need to be remodeled to expand its capacity if the other temples were not built.

Architect Fetzer presented various options. The Presidency approved the concept of building temples in Ogden and Provo and directed Garff and the Building Committee "to go forward and make provisions for the location of the new temples, prepare their plans, and so far as possible have the same plan for both temples."[11] Brother Fetzer felt sure that even before he made his report on the Logan and Manti Temples, "the First Presidency clearly had in mind to build the new Temples in Ogden and in Provo."[12]

When President McKay approved the temples, he felt some reluctance about the costs and of announcing two temples at one time. Consequently, he gave "absolute guidelines" to the Church Building Committee. Fred Baker recalled the prophet saying there would be no solemn assembly room, no multiple towers, no excess footage, and "no angel Moroni."[13] Further, President McKay emphasized that these temples would be working temples and practical. Indeed, they were quite simple in style compared to their predecessor the Oakland Temple, which finished before them in 1964, and the Washington D.C. Temple, which followed them in 1974.

When President McKay approved the temples, he felt some reluctance about the costs of two temples at one time. He emphasized that these temples would be working temples and practical.

The Amazing Announcement

Without any delay, presidencies of the twenty-eight stakes in the Provo area were invited to a special meeting, which would be held on Monday morning, August 14, 1967. A similar meeting was held that afternoon with the twenty-five stake presidencies in Ogden. Presiding at these gatherings were Hugh B. Brown and N. Eldon

Tanner, counselors to David O. McKay in the First Presidency. Also in attendance were Mark B. Garff and Fred A. Baker of the Church Building Committee.

The Presidency explained that 52 percent of all temple work was being done in the Salt Lake, Logan, and Manti Temples, which consequently were seriously overcrowded. Rather than expending funds to enlarge these temples, Church leaders concluded to build two new ones in Ogden and Provo to reduce the amount of travel required of the Saints. In each location, a committee of stake presidents was appointed to recommend a specific temple site to the First Presidency, who would make the final decision. Sites for both temples were announced within two weeks.

Essential Preparations

Sites for the New Temples

Although other sites were considered, the site chosen for the Ogden Temple was Tabernacle Square in downtown. The Church had owned this ten-acre block bounded by Washington and Grant Avenues and 21st and 22nd Streets since pioneer times. When Brigham Young laid out the town, he had designated this block as the spiritual center for the community. Ground was broken at the southeast corner of the block for the original Weber Stake Tabernacle in 1855, and after delays caused by the Utah War, it was completed and dedicated in 1859. The third ward built its meetinghouse and amusement hall on the southwest corner, and the stake Relief Society also erected its building on the block. A new Ogden Tabernacle was dedicated on the north side of the block in 1956.

The Provo committee discussed several possibilities. One was the downtown park adjacent to the Provo Tabernacle, but it was substantially smaller than the corresponding property in Ogden—less than two acres. There was not enough room for a temple building or for parking. They also felt the temple should be within walking distance of Brigham Young University so students could participate conveniently.

The committee visited other sites but kept returning to the seventeen acres BYU had by then bought from the Leichty brothers just below the mouth of Rock Canyon. The advantage of this site was that it was close to BYU and on a hill, where it could be seen from many different places in the valley; those who came to the temple could look out and get a panoramic view of the valley, Utah Lake, and the Oquirrh Mountains beyond. The First Presidency approved the committee's recommendation and directed the architect to proceed with the plans.[14]

Designing the New Temples

Significant innovations in presenting the endowment during the 1950s would impact the Ogden and Provo Temples. With the rapid growth in the Church around the world after World War II, President David O. McKay recognized the need to build more but less costly temples. The Church Building Committee sought ideas from Latter-day Saint architects about how to accomplish this. Harold W. Burton realized that it would be necessary to reduce the size of these sacred structures without diminishing their "functional capacity." His experience in the motion picture industry in Southern California led him to a possible solution. "It was my opinion that if the first four temple ordinance rooms could be combined, and with picture projection substituted for mural paintings to create a proper setting pertaining to the creation, the garden, and the world, very substantial reduction in the size of the Temple could be effected." Although some felt this idea was "too revolutionary," it was adopted for the Swiss Temple.[15] Using modern motion picture equipment made it possible to present the endowment in a single ordinance room, in more than one language, and with far fewer than the usual number of temple workers. This landmark decision brought a fundamental change in the design of temples.

Joseph F. Merrill (center) and Gordon B. Hinckley producing a Church film. Courtesy of Church History Library.

The new temple film was produced by Gordon B. Hinckley, secretary of the missionary committee (not yet a General Authority), who worked closely with President McKay. "It was a charge of enormous significance," his biographer declared. "The ramifications of this project were enormous, as they would extend far beyond the temple in Switzerland." In the fifth-floor room of the Salt Lake Temple where Elder Talmage had completed his monumental book *Jesus the Christ*, Brother Hinckley spent many evenings, Saturdays, and some Sunday mornings outlining ideas. With President McKay, he spent considerable time reviewing the temple ceremonies and praying for divine guidance. President McKay later remarked, "There is no other man in the church who has done so much in assisting to carry this new temple plan to the Saints of the world as has Brother Hinckley."[16] Elder Harold B. Lee insisted that "there was no difference" between the endowment instruction given formerly "and that which was later given in temples except as to the method." He believed that the use of films to present the "teachings of the holy endowment" had come "under inspiration to our President."[17]

The use of films to present the teachings of the holy endowment had come "under inspiration to our President."

The Swiss Temple—dedicated in 1955—set the pattern for the New Zealand and London Temples, which opened three years later. Originally, each of these newer temples had only one presentation room, meaning that a new session could begin only every two hours. The Oakland Temple—dedicated in 1964—had two large endowment rooms, enabling a new session to start every hour or so. Designs for the new Ogden and Provo Temples would bring even greater improvements.

> "I was in shock. I never had the slightest inkling nor gave it any thought that I would ever be given an assignment to design a Temple. Yet, it had indeed happened."

Announcement

At the August 14, 1967, meetings where the Ogden and Provo Temples were announced, Church leaders explained that these new temples "will be of the smaller type," following the pattern developed for the first overseas temples, "but so designed to have a high capacity."[18] Building both temples from the same basic plan would expedite construction and economize. Efficiency and convenience were prime concerns.

A few days after this meeting, officials of the Church Building Committee were summoned to visit with President David O. McKay and his counselors in his Hotel Utah apartment. After some preliminary discussion about the new temples, President McKay turned to Emil B. Fetzer, the Church architect, and declared, "Brother Fetzer, I would like you to design the new Temples for Ogden and for Provo. Rather than building huge monumental buildings as has been the custom of the past, I would like these two Temples to be functional and economical with temple quality. In the coming years, many Temples will be built. Of necessity, these Temples must be functional in design and cost so that they may accomplish their sacred purposes and be blessings to the Church membership."[19]

As Brother Fetzer and the others left the meeting and walked down the hall to the elevator, he recalled, "I was in shock. I never had the slightest inkling nor gave it any thought that I would ever be given an assignment to design a Temple. Yet, it had indeed happened. The Prophet of the Lord had given me the assignment to design not one but two Temples. This was a major emotional high point to last a lifetime and longer—an exciting moment to cherish and remember forever."[20]

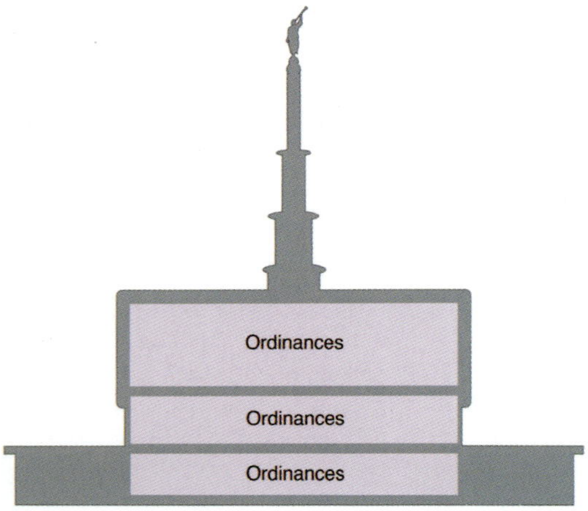

Cross section of Ogden and Provo Temples. Courtesy of Lee R. Cowan.

Emil Fetzer worked closely with Mark B. Garff and Fred A. Baker of the Church Building Committee. In the new temples, they originally understood that they would present the endowment in the traditional way. At a meeting with the First Presidency on October 29, however, Baker was told that the Presidency had approved the use of films in North America as well as overseas, and that the new temples should use films rather than having companies progress from room to room. This surprised him. Architect Fetzer was not at this meeting because he was in Southern California on business.

The following day, Fetzer and Baker needed to fly to Europe on Building Committee matters. They met in the Kennedy airport in New York before boarding a Pan American DC-8 jet for the overnight transatlantic flight. After dinner, Baker shared the First Presidency's instructions with Fetzer, and they proceeded to discuss

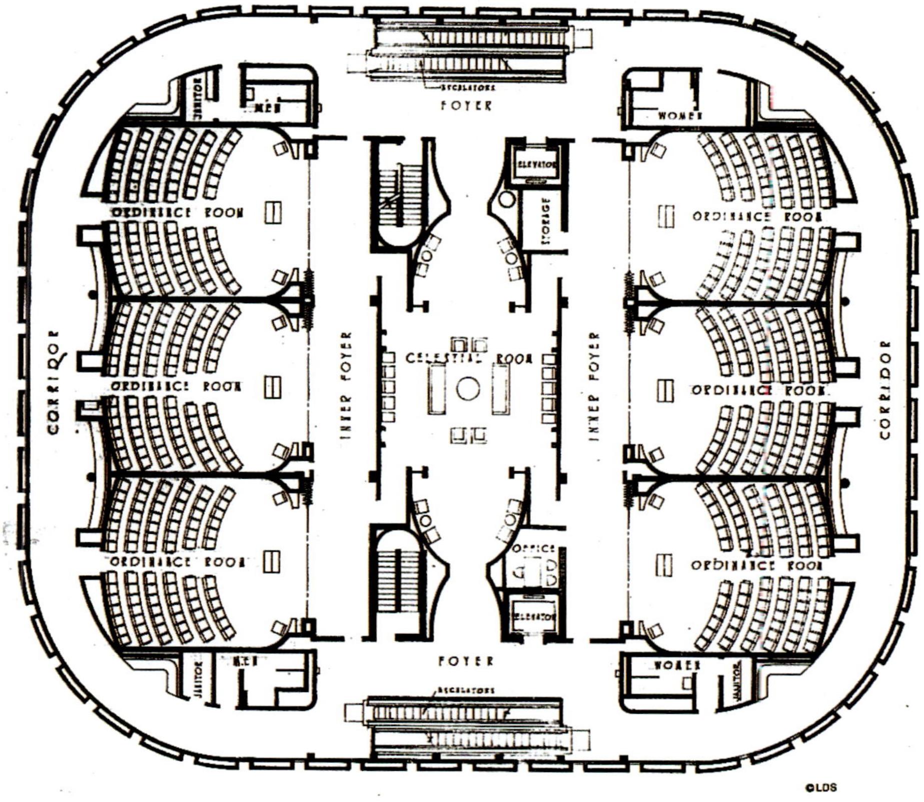

Ordinance rooms surrounding the celestial room in the Provo Temple. Courtesy of Intellectual Reserve, Inc.

the "grand assignment" to design the two temples. As they attempted to work at their seats, a stewardess offered them the use of a table in the galley where they could spread out their papers. Brother Fetzer recalled,

> After we had discussed Temple design for some time, all of a sudden I felt as though I were walking through a Temple Building. I described to Brother Baker what I was seeing in my mind as I was walking through the Temple—the Temple recommend desk in the main entrance foyer, the inner foyer, the offices and ancillary spaces and facilities on the ground floor. On the second floor I saw and described the chapel and sealing rooms. However, the most important of all that I was seeing was the unusual plan configuration of the third floor. There was a large, beautiful, center room surrounded by a cluster of six [endowment presentation] rooms which completely surrounded the celestial room. A broad, circular hallway went completely around the six rooms with access to them from this hallway. It was a wonderful concept and a very unique and distinctive plan arrangement.

Before they knew it, it was daylight, and the plane was landing in Frankfurt. They had been discussing the temple "all night long."[21]

Fetzer later reported that the idea for the outside hallway came from a park in Copenhagen, which was completely surrounded by a roadway in the form of an elongated ellipse. He called this a "Danish ellipse," and "a modification of this idea was adapted to be exactly what I needed to accommodate the rooms and corridors of the

Before they knew it, it was daylight, and the plane was landing in Frankfurt. They had been discussing plans for the temple all night long.

upper two floors."[22] Still, he insisted, this "unique and fundamental modification of Temple design concept was more than my own thinking. It was a direct inspiration given to me by the Holy Spirit."[23]

Mark B. Garff explained that "most monumental structures have been designed with first emphasis on the outside appearance, with the interior fit to the outside design." In contrast to this pattern, he noted that Emil Fetzer "gave first consideration and emphasis to the needs of the interior and then designed the exterior to enclose the areas." Hence, the outside walls of the temple's main upper portion followed the rounded course of the third-floor hallway"[24] and illustrated the architectural maxim "form follows function."

To make the temples as functional as possible, Fetzer consulted with numerous individuals. To facilitate movement from floor to floor, he provided not only elevators, but escalators, which were "never before planned in temples."

The main floor of the 115,000-square-foot temples would be rectangular, while the upper two floors would have elliptical corners. "Since the second floor is recessed below the third floor and since gold glass windows of the second floor are continuous full height panels," Architect Fetzer explained, "it gives an appearance that the third floor is floating above the Temple base." He continued, "This is the effect that I desired—that the sacred ordinance rooms and the celestial room would appear to be above and separated from the mundane and worldly aspects of life."[25]

To make the temples as functional as possible, Fetzer consulted with temple presidents and workers, members of the Genealogical Society, the Building Committee, other Latter-day Saint architects, and General Authorities. To facilitate movement from floor to floor, he provided not only elevators, but escalators, which were "never before planned in temples." Fetzer explained that the continuous hallways around the perimeter of the second and third floors would make it impossible to get lost; all people needed to do was keep walking and they would be brought back to the starting point.[26]

The exterior of each temple was of white cast stone, gold anodized aluminum grilles, and bronze glass panels. A spire in the center of the building, golden in color, reached a height of about 185 feet. Over the years, various symbolic meanings have been read into the temple's design. Upon looking at the rounded corners and gold-colored towers, many local Church members believed the temples were designed to symbolize the cloud and pillar of fire that led the ancient Israelites during their wanderings in the desert. However, Fred Baker, who worked closely with Emil Fetzer in designing the temple, recalled, "We didn't have any symbolism in mind. . . . The truth is that we were so focused on what happened inside the temple, it never entered our mind" that there should be any symbolism outside.[27]

Fundraising

The First Presidency asked members in each temple district to contribute one million dollars, less than one-fourth of the total cost for erecting their temple. General Church funds would pay the balance. The Presidency asked local leaders to give this priority and let their "other building projects go for the time being and raise this money as fast as possible."[28] The stake presidencies received this challenge "with great enthusiasm,"[29] anticipating that the Saints would be eager to assume a major share of the construction cost.

Church members responded willingly and enthusiastically. A bishop in the Ogden area brought up the ward's quota in priesthood meeting, and by the time Sunday School was over only three hours later, the entire amount had been contributed.

In the Spanish Fork Stake, fundraising was well underway for a total of $320,000 needed for a new stake center and for a new chapel in Salem. With the announcement of a temple, these plans were temporarily set aside. "It seemed that every heart was touched," stake president Joseph Toronto gratefully noted. The stake's share for the temple was fifty-six thousand dollars, but "we raised over seventy-five thousand dollars, the easiest money we ever collected because of the great willingness of both young and old to sacrifice," President Toronto affirmed. "For example, children would say, 'Grandpa, we can't have an ice cream cone, go to the movie, or go on that vacation. We are sacrificing to build the temple.' There were many sacrifices from our faithful members. The Saints not only paid their allotments for the temple in record time, but also their allotments for stake and ward buildings. And tithing increased also."[30]

The Church organized the "Youth Build a Temple" program (YBAT), and many young people were eager to help build their temple. A ward in Harrisville, for example, was assessed $3,461 as its share. The bishop was eager to get his youth involved:

President Hugh B. Brown at Ogden Temple and Provo Temple groundbreakings. Courtesy of *Deseret News* and Church History Library.

"The girls scraped and painted old barns, tended children, bottled fruit, and did ironing. The boys did everything from washing cars to laying sewer pipes. And the money was raised."[31] In both Ogden and Provo the Saints contributed substantially more than they were asked.

Construction of the Temples

President Hugh B. Brown, first counselor in the First Presidency, presided at the groundbreaking ceremony for the Ogden Temple on September 8, 1969, President McKay's ninety-sixth birthday. He conducted the same inaugural ceremony in Provo just one week later. He praised the Saints for their willingness to contribute funds for the temple. In Provo, he recounted his own contributions to the Church both in time and money and then concluded that "the Church owes me not one cent. I have received more than I have ever given." President Brown concluded with his testimony and then reaffirmed, "The Lord owes me nothing, I owe him everything."[32]

Above: Richard and Dawn Cowan at the Provo Temple groundbreaking. Courtesy of Richard Cowan.

On each occasion, after President Brown officially turned the first shovel of dirt, the other General Authorities followed. Next the stake presidents and then the

Above and left: Early construction progress of Ogden Temple. Courtesy of *Deseret News* and Church History Library.

bishops in the temple districts had their turns. Finally, others who were present were able to participate by wielding the gold-colored shovels to turn over some of the soil.

The final set of plans for each temple filled 135 large pages. Several construction companies were invited to study these plans and submit a formal bid. "Contractors were selected based on their past construction performances and on the size of projects that they had successfully completed commensurate to the size, cost, scope and finish of the Temples," Emil B. Fetzer explained. "Due to the sacred character of the Temples, selected contractors were required to be Temple worthy members of the Church."[33] The Okland Construction Company received the contract for the Ogden Temple, and the Hogan & Tingey Construction Company won the contract to build the similar Provo Temple—each costing just over $4,275,000. Builders were asked to rush their work "against an early deadline."[34]

Because the stainless-steel baptismal fonts were so large, they needed to be put into place in the temple basement before the concrete for the main floor was poured overhead. Wrapped in heavy plastic, the font was protected from damage as

Presidents N. Eldon Tanner and Joseph Fielding Smith (top left) at Ogden Temple cornerstone ceremony and President Harold B. Lee (top right) at Provo Temple cornerstone ceremony. Courtesy of *Deseret News* and Church History Library.

construction then proceeded all around it. By the end of 1970, the outer walls of the ground floor were completed, and structural steel for the upper floors was in place.[35]

When temples were built of large hewn stones, placing the cornerstone had marked the beginning of construction, such as at Kirtland, Nauvoo, and Salt Lake City. When reinforced concrete became the norm, as was the case with Ogden and Provo, cornerstone laying became purely symbolic and was conducted during construction after the walls surrounding the cornerstone area were sufficiently completed. President N. Eldon Tanner, second counselor in the First Presidency, officially placed the Ogden Temple's cornerstone on September 9, 1970—just one year after groundbreaking. Church President Joseph Fielding Smith presided at Provo's cornerstone laying on May 21, 1971. More than six thousand interested spectators gathered at each of these ceremonies. At each temple, the cornerstone box contained historical memorabilia including copies of the scriptures, photos of Church leaders, copies of current Church magazines and of local newspapers, and photos of temple construction to that point.

When the 118-foot spires were put into place during the summer of 1971, the exterior appeared to be finished. The spire was anchored to a steel base and was sheathed by four tiers of fiberglass. A metal spike or lightning rod topped the last four feet of the spire.

Provo Temple open house. Courtesy of *Deseret News* and Church History Library.

Open House and Dedication

Keith Wilcox, president of the Weber Heights Stake, chaired the Ogden Temple dedication committee. He would later help design the Washington D.C. Temple and serve as the Ogden Temple's third president and as a General Authority Seventy from 1984 to 1989. He insisted that construction of the temple had raised the spiritual level of the entire community. The public open house, which operated from December 16 to 30, 1971, attracted over 150,000 visitors. After first seeing exhibits and watching an introductory video in the adjacent tabernacle, they proceeded to the temple.

During the Provo open house, January 10 to 29, 1972, the 246,201 visitors started their experience in a large, heated tent set up in front of the temple. An enclosed passageway to the front door not only sheltered them from the winter weather but

First Presidency at Ogden Temple dedication: Harold B. Lee, Joseph Fielding Smith, and N. Eldon Tanner. Courtesy of *Deseret News* and Church History Library.

also ensured that their shoes were clean and dry by the time they reached the temple. Some traveled hundreds of miles to the event; youth groups in chartered buses came from as far as St. George.

Those participating in the open houses felt a special spirit as they visited the temple. The Church's *New Era* magazine published a number of responses from the youth and young adult readers: "I had such a wonderful feeling while inside the temple, I didn't want to leave"; "After coming 600 miles to see the house of the Lord, then having the experience, I realized it was worth traveling around the world for"; "The whole temple seemed to be a part of heaven"; "The spirit there was unbelievable, and it is not even dedicated yet"; "I think it has caused me to have a new outlook on life. Now I look forward to the future instead of fearing it"; "This was the most completely peaceful twenty minutes that I have ever experienced." Some were particularly impressed with the sealing rooms: "When I saw the sealing rooms, I knew that I truly wanted a temple marriage"; "The mirrors give such a beautiful representation of eternity."[36]

President Joseph Fielding Smith dedicated the Ogden Temple in six sessions, two each day from Tuesday, January 18, through Thursday, January 20, 1972. Overflow groups were accommodated in the nearby Ogden Tabernacle. In his opening remarks, President Smith declared, "May I remind you that when we dedicate a house of the Lord, what we really do is dedicate ourselves to the Lord's service with a covenant that we shall use the house in the way that He intended."[37]

Only two sessions were required for the dedication of the Provo Temple on Wednesday, February 9, because several large auditoriums in nine buildings on the BYU campus carried the proceedings by means of closed-circuit television. One of these was the recently opened 23,000-seat Marriott Center. Because this venue was typically filled with cheering crowds at basketball games, witnessing throngs leaving the dedication sessions in reverent silence was an unusual and impressive experience.

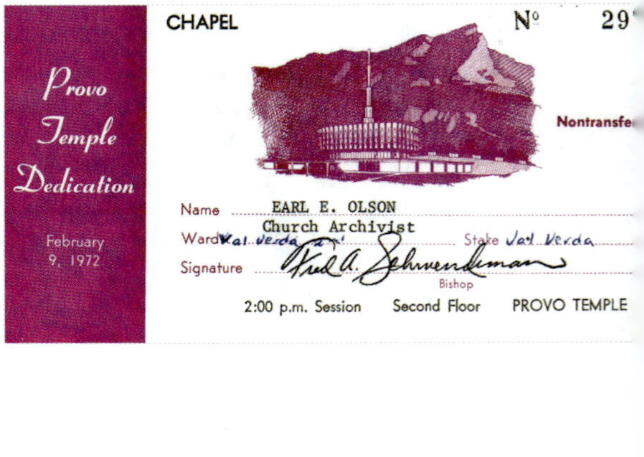

Top: Ogden Temple dedication ticket. Bottom: Provo Temple dedication ticket. Courtesy of Church History Library.

President Joseph Fielding Smith shared the same prepared message in each of the two sessions. In Provo he noted that his grandfather, Hyrum Smith, had been born on this date in 1800 and that it was fitting that this anniversary was being marked by the dedication of another temple "wherein those keys and powers, held jointly by him and the Prophet Joseph Smith, may be used for the salvation and exaltation of many of our Father's children." President Smith testified that the decision to build these temples had come through inspiration. He affirmed that "in this holy house we are entitled to receive revelation and guidance from on high. The Lord is anxious to reveal His mind and His will to us, and to give us counsel and direction and doctrine as rapidly as we are able to receive them."[38]

President Smith had his first counselor, Harold B. Lee, read the dedicatory prayer in each session. The prayer in Provo specifically petitioned, "Let that great temple of learning—the Brigham Young University . . . be prospered to the full. Let Thy enlightening power rest upon those who teach and those who are taught. . . . May those who teach and study in all academic fields have their souls enlightened with spiritual knowledge, so they will turn to Thy house for blessings and knowledge and learning that surpass all that may be found elsewhere." Looking to the future, President Smith acknowledged that "we look forward to the day, O our God, when Thou wilt reveal unto Thy servants where other temples shall be built, in all the nations where Thy saints increase in numbers and serve Thee in righteousness."[39] The Ogden and Provo Temples were the fourteenth and fifteenth operating temples in the Church. In less than three decades, the total would exceed one hundred.

Impact of the New Temples

When Fred Baker of the Building Committee took the initial reports of activity in the Ogden Temple to Church headquarters, he found the senior leadership to be stunned; they couldn't believe that the "little temple in Ogden" was outperforming the "flagship temple" in Salt Lake City. With the coming of these two new temples, this sacred work surged. Between 1971 and 1975, in the area bounded by Logan on the north and Manti on the south, the number of ordinances soared by about 140 percent. Because the activity in the Logan, Salt Lake, and Manti Temples was not diminished significantly, most of this increase came from the two new temples. For the next quarter of a century, the Provo Temple led the Church in the total number of endowments performed for the dead, even when the estimated 15 percent from Brigham Young University and the nearby Missionary Training Center was subtracted.

Attending the temple was an important activity for these two groups. It was not only part of preparation for missionary service, but it was also significant to the future missionaries personally. Elder Glenn Griffin recalled, "I was quite nervous about the following two years. I will never forget the peace that I felt whenever I walked the grounds of the Provo Temple."[40] A sister missionary, BreeAnna Barney, appreciated

Ogden Utah Temple (center), February 2010. Courtesy of Intellectual Reserve, Inc.

They couldn't believe that the "little temple in Ogden" was outperforming the "flagship temple" in Salt Lake City.

the power she felt as she walked toward the temple with a group of enthusiastic missionaries.[41]

Students at Brigham Young University also appreciated the temple. Clayton Schmoekel thought of it as "a place of refuge" while he was away from home. "Sometimes school can be very difficult, and trials and temptations build up." Attending the temple gave him confidence. "The temple always gives me hope," he gratefully acknowledged.[42] When Rylie Jex left home, she encountered new faces and new challenges. "I was grateful for one steadfast thing in my life amidst all the changes," she reflected.[43] Gladys Ibarra, a student from Florida, similarly remembered, "When I came to BYU my whole world turned upside down—with its beautiful tall mountains, dry climate, snow, and members surrounding me everywhere. I knew I was far away from the tropical paradise I called home. It was a huge and intimidating change in my life, but one of the greatest blessings to me was having a temple nearby. It was the one place where every time I entered I knew where I was, who I was, and I felt peace and at home."[44]

Briana Crook described how driving down University Parkway from Orem, she could "see the Provo Temple lit up, in all its glory welcoming me home."[45] Brooke LeFevre thought of the temple back home as "my temple," but acknowledged that after coming to BYU, the Provo Temple had assumed that role. She was grateful that the temple workers became acquainted with her by name; one time when she came alone without her friend, one kindly worker said, "Oh, don't you worry. We will always be here for you; you are never alone." This simple assurance "brought immediate tears to my eyes," she gratefully reflected.[46]

When Kate Kimball was called to leadership in her campus ward Relief Society, she was overwhelmed. However, she acknowledged, "When I attended the Provo Temple as a willing servant of God, I received promptings which directed me how to best fulfill my calling. I was able to see the sisters in my ward as if through the eyes of God. My love for them grew with each thoughtful visit to the temple."[47]

Returned missionaries linked attending the temple with memories of their earlier experience at the MTC. Young married students looked upon attending the temple together as a powerful means to strengthen their eternal relationship. For many, Friday-evening temple trips became a favorite date night and included dinner in the temple cafeteria before the endowment session. Others found the temple to be a particular strength as they prepared for eternal marriage. Cory Hinds expressed that when he was present as his fiancée received her endowment, he realized, "The joy I felt watching new converts on my mission enter into the waters of baptism did not come close to comparing to the joy I felt as my soon-to-be bride entered into temple covenants with the Lord."[48] Daniel Wahlgren, a new husband, affirmed, "I love the temple and want to share that with my wife. We've only been married a few weeks, but I want our marriage to be a forever and eternal marriage."[49]

For the next quarter of a century, the Provo Temple led the Church in the total number of endowments performed for the dead.

The exteriors of these two temples remained relatively unchanged for over three decades. Then, as part of a project to upgrade the Ogden Temple and enhance its grounds, a statue of Moroni was placed atop the temple's tower on November 18, 2002. A similar statue was placed on the twin Provo Temple a few months later, May 12, 2003. The golden towers of these temples were painted a brilliant white to increase contrast between them and the gold-leafed angelic figures. Because the entrances of both temples were on the west, observers wondered in which direction Moroni would face.[50] Most (but not all) Latter-day Saint temples face east, so ideally, they conjectured, statues of Moroni should face that direction. Because the Second Coming of Jesus Christ has been likened to the dawning of a new day (see Joseph Smith—Matthew 1:26), orienting the herald angel toward the east suggests a call to prepare for the Savior's advent. The Ogden and Provo statues were placed facing east.

The unique design of these two temples would continue to distinguish them among the growing number of these sacred houses worldwide. In the meantime, additional temples had been built in Utah—three larger and one smaller. Three others had been remodeled in significant ways.

Now that the Ogden and Provo Temples were up and running and had taken a considerable load from Logan and Manti, the time had come to look at renovating and refurbishing the first three pioneer temples that were now almost a century old.

Notes

1. "Ogden to Get a Temple Mormons Are Told," *Standard-Examiner* (Ogden, UT), December 13, 1920.
2. *Deseret News*, May 16, 1921; see also *Salt Lake Tribune*, May 17, 1921, in Journal History of The Church of Jesus Christ of Latter-day Saints, May 15, 1921, 1.
3. Doyle L. Green, "Two Temples to Be Dedicated," *Ensign*, January 1972, 6.
4. "First Presidency Inspects Temple Site, *Deseret News*, May 16, 1921, 5.
5. Gregory A. Prince and Wm. Robert Wright, *David O. McKay and the Rise of Modern Mormonism* (Salt Lake City: University of Utah Press, 2005), 269.
6. Benjamin H. Bullock, affidavit, 1952, Church History Library.
7. Ernest L. Wilkinson to the First Presidency, August 7, 1952, Brigham Young University Archives.
8. Ben E. Lewis, "I Remember, 1988–2000," 25-26, L. Tom Perry Special Collections, Harold B. Lee Library, Brigham Young University, Provo, Utah.
9. Prince and Wright, *David O. McKay and the Rise of Modern Mormonism*, 269.
10. Emil B. Fetzer, *Completed Writings of Emil Baer Fetzer* (privately published, 2003), 1, Church History Library, Salt Lake City.
11. Prince and Wright, *David O. McKay and the Rise of Modern Mormonism*, 269.
12. Fetzer, "Sacred Twin Temples," 2.
13. Fred A. Baker, interview by Justin R. Bray and Scott R. Christensen, January 12, 2012, Church History Library.
14. Lewis, "I Remember," 13:27.
15. Harold W. Burton, "Architectural Features of the Oakland Temple of The Church of Jesus Christ of Latter-day Saints," MS 4235, folder 1, Church History Library, 6.
16. David O. McKay, dedication proceedings, New Zealand Temple, April 20–23, 1958, Church History Library, quoted in Richard O. Cowan, *Temples to Dot the Earth* (Springville, UT: Cedar Fort, 2011), 177.
17. Harold B. Lee, "Preparing to Meet the Lord," *Improvement Era*, February 1965, 122.
18. Henry A. Smith, "2 New Temples Planned," *Church News*, August 19, 1967, 4.
19. Emil B. Fetzer, "The Sacred Twin Temples: Ogden Temple Provo Temple," in Emil Fetzer and June Fetzer, *Completed Writings of Emil Baer Fetzer* (n.p., the authors, 2003), 3.
20. Fetzer, "Sacred Twin Temples," 3.
21. Fetzer, "Sacred Twin Temples," 3.
22. Fetzer, "Sacred Twin Temples," 4; see also Doyle L. Green, "Two Temples to Be Dedicated," *Ensign*, January 1972, 6–11.
23. Fetzer, "Sacred Twin Temples," 4.
24. Fetzer, "Sacred Twin Temples," 5.
25. Fetzer, "Sacred Twin Temples," 5.
26. Fetzer, "Sacred Twin Temples," 5.
27. Fred A. Baker, interview by Justin R. Bray and Scott R. Christensen, January 12, 2012, Church History Library.
28. Quoted in Joseph Young Toronto, *Forever and Ever: The Life History of Joseph Young Toronto* (Provo, UT: BYU Press, 1996), 171.
29. Henry A. Smith, "2 New Temples Planned," *Church News*, August 19, 1967, 4.
30. Toronto, *Forever and Ever*, 171.

31. Elaine Cannon, "Their Book of Acts," *New Era*, February 1971, 13.
32. Stephen W. Gibson, "A New Temple Begins," *Church News*, September 20, 1969, 3.
33. Fetzer, "Sacred Twin Temples," 9.
34. "Church in Action: Provo Temple Rises Rapidly," *Church News*, May 2, 1970, 13.
35. "Church in Action," *Church News*, October 17, 1970, 13.
36. "Inside a House of the Lord," *New Era*, April 1972.
37. "New Ogden Temple Dedicated," *Church News*, January 22, 1972, 3.
38. "Hyrum Smith Honored by Pres. Smith," *Church News*, February 12, 1972, 3–4.
39. "Dedication Prayer of Provo Temple," *Church News*, February 12, 1972, 5.
40. Glenn Griffin, statement to Richard O. Cowan, September 14, 2012.
41. BreeAnna Barney, statement to Richard O. Cowan, September 13, 2012.
42. Clayton Schmoekel, statement to Richard O. Cowan, September 13, 2012.
43. Rylie Jex, statement to Richard O. Cowan, September 8, 2012.
44. Gladys Ibarra, statement to Richard O. Cowan, September 6, 2012.
45. Briana Crook, statement to Richard O. Cowan, September 13, 2012.
46. Brooke LeFevre, statement to Richard O. Cowan, September 12, 2012.
47. Kate Kimball, statement to Richard O. Cowan, September 12, 2012.
48. Cory Hinds, statement to Richard O. Cowan, September 6, 2012.
49. Daniel Wahlgren, statement to Richard O. Cowan, September 13, 2012.
50. "Moroni Statue," *Daily Herald* (Provo, UT), May 13, 2003, A1.

HOLINESS TO THE LORD
THE HOUSE OF THE LORD
THE CHURCH OF JESUS CHRIST OF LATTER-DAY SAINTS
ST. GEORGE TEMPLE
COMMENCED
DEDICATED

8 Renovating Temples

The St. George, Logan, and Manti Temples

St. George Temple. *Afterglow*, by Alan Fullmer.

St. George Temple. Courtesy of *Deseret News* and Church History Library.

With the success of the new Ogden and Provo Temples, Church leaders decided to renovate and refurbish its older temples in the 1970s and '80s. These included the Arizona Temple at Mesa, the Hawaii Temple at Laie, and three in Utah—St. George, Logan, and Manti. The impact of the decisions to change Logan and Manti had repercussions for decades and influenced how the Church approached renovating temples.

Other Temples Refitted

St. George Temple

On March 2, 1974, the St. George Temple closed for more than a year and a half. A new annex included a chapel, offices, cafeteria, laundry, dressing rooms with 906 lockers for patrons, and a beautifully landscaped main entrance. New electrical, heating, plumbing, air-conditioning, and fire prevention systems were installed in the temple itself.

St. George Temple assembly room. Courtesy of *Deseret News* and Church History Library.

The three endowment rooms located side by side across the west end of the temple were remodeled to use films in presenting the ordinance. Because these rooms could be used simultaneously, architect Emil B. Fetzer was perplexed by the problem of providing access from the basement dressing rooms in the annex on the north to each of these three new rooms without needing to pass through one of the others.

One evening Fetzer was working late in the Architect's Office on the twenty-eighth floor of the Church Office Building, prayerfully pondering possible solutions but "could not seem to arrive at a satisfactory plan." He left the office "with the problem firmly in mind." There wasn't much traffic at this late hour. He later recalled what happened as he drove under the arches of the famed Eagle Gate: "I heard a voice that was clear and distinct, but it was not a spoken sound, rather a transmission of thought into my mind. . . . 'If you move the fire tower stairway out away from the west wall of the temple, a lobby space will be created.'" With this inspiration, he was able to design an addition on the west side of the temple with stairways and elevators to reach the three endowment rooms on the ground level as well as facilities on higher

The Logan Temple baptistry pre-1970 renovation. Courtesy of Nolan Olsen.

floors in the temple. He affirmed that this was "an incredibly marvelous, simple, logical and crucial revelation for needed help."[1] After receiving most of the endowment presentation in one of these three rooms, patrons would enter a central room for final instructions before concluding the endowment by proceeding into the beautiful celestial room. In these last two rooms, the arched ceiling of the temple's lower assembly hall can still be seen. Four new sealing rooms brought the total to twelve.

The large assembly room occupying the upper half of the temple has remained almost completely unchanged since the structure was built. Only a sprinkler system for fire prevention was added. Windows still have the original wavy glass brought around Cape Horn to Los Angeles in 1871. Even electric lights remained absent from this room.

This renovation greatly enlarged the St. George Temple's capacity, enabling it to double the number of ordinances performed. President Spencer W. Kimball rededicated the temple in six sessions on Wednesday and Thursday, October 15–16, 1975.

Logan Temple

As discussed in chapter 6, the First Presidency decided to use funds to build the Ogden and Provo Temples instead of tackling the need to remodel the Logan and Manti Temples. However, by the 1970s the time had come to look at some urgent improvements for the venerable temples. Particularly, the Logan Temple was in a critical condition, according to Fetzer. There were challenges with the outer walls

Renovation of Logan Temple. Courtesy of Nolan Olsen.

showing signs of buckling, and the footings and basement walls needed concrete to stabilize them because of trenching that had previously been done near the footings for some mechanical needs.

Members of the Building Committee had also gone through the temple and worried about the congestion and flow of the temple with the multiple narrow stairways that Truman Angell Jr. had created for the progression from room to room. The floors changed for the endowment a few feet with every room, which also made remodeling more difficult for the structure. There were also electrical and mechanical needs. From such a long list of issues, Emil Fetzer concluded that the temple needed to be completely renovated.[2]

Fetzer proposed to the First Presidency in February 1975 the "complete removal of the building interior" and a new plan for the baptismal department, new ordinance rooms, eleven sealing rooms, and administrative offices that he projected would cost five million dollars. Indeed, the renovation was more than the cost of a new temple. Fetzer said, "The First Presidency realized that it was very necessary and urgent that something be done to the Logan Temple, but they appeared astonished and rather dismayed by this drastic and somewhat extreme proposal."[3] He didn't hear back from the First Presidency for six months, after which they gave their approval.

One interior part of the temple was going to remain, and that was the priesthood assembly room on the top floor of the temple.

But as the renovation continued, the floor supporting the assembly room had "dangerous structural problems," including a split in the main structural beam. Fetzer feared that if the assembly room was not replaced then there was a risk the floor could collapse. He admitted this plan was not popular with the community: "I had to swallow twice and be very brave to be responsible for such drastic and irreversible decisions. Some of the older Logan Temple patrons and workers, remembering the history and sacred, wonderful times spent in the Logan Temple, complained bitterly against and roundly condemned my proposals for removing the entire Temple interior for this Temple."

Ultimately, Fetzer focused on a spiritual reason for his alterations to the pioneer temple. The new design allowed for a doubling of temple ordinances. He wrote, "This capability of having so many more Endowments performed in a given time, must be considered of incalculable worth to the work in Our Heavenly Father's Kingdom. The inspired concepts and designs of my architectural work and decisions were emphatically and unequivocally sustained and upheld by the First Presidency of the Church."[4] Fetzer stated that the ordinance work was the "important and real worth and purposes of the Temple."[5]

The temple closed October 2, 1976, for remodeling. Because of the temple's age, utilities and mechanical systems needed to be updated. The original interior was completely removed, so only the four-foot-thick exterior stone walls remained. The dark gray silica limestone in these walls was so hard that two men working with jackhammers needed a week to cut a doorway through. Inside this shell, four new endowment rooms, simply decorated in different colors and using the filmed presentation, surrounded the beautiful celestial room on the main floor. There were eleven sealing rooms, and the large priesthood room filled the upper floor. On the north, the "extension" was replaced by a new annex with offices, a chapel, nursery, cafeteria, laundry, and dressing rooms. Stone from interior walls was used to construct an exterior elevator shaft. The main walls were cleaned and repaired. Total floor area became about 104,000 square feet. The Okland Construction Company completed this extensive project. Landscaping included eleven varieties of trees and twenty-six varieties of shrubs.[6]

Original Logan Temple assembly room. Courtesy of Intellectual Reserve, Inc.

Reed Bullen, the newly appointed temple president, was grateful for "an old traditional temple on a scenic site overlooking Cache Valley with a new temple on the inside that will be highly functional."[7] However, not all were pleased with the changes. According to architect Paul L. Anderson, the mayor's office in Logan wrote a letter to the First Presidency "accusing the Church of destroying Logan's religious heritage." Before the renovation in 1975, the Logan Temple had been placed on the National Register of Historic Places, but after the remodel the Utah State Historical Society considered removing it from the historic register.[8] The feeling was that the pioneer murals, handiwork, and craftsmanship had been replaced by inserting a 1970s-style Ogden or Provo Temple decor into the shell of the pioneer temple. Some of the pulpits, door frames, baptismal font oxen, and stained glass were salvaged by the Church's Historic Sites division of the Historical Department under the direction of Florence Jacobsen and Paul Anderson. The salvaged pieces were later used in the new Museum of Church History and Art in Salt Lake City built in the 1980s, and also in the Manti renovation.[9] While some physical interior pieces of the temple's history were preserved, the fact remained that the Architect's Office did not show a sensitivity toward the pioneer craftsmanship and heritage of the temple, which deeply hurt some members of the Cache Valley community.

Detail, Logan Temple. Courtesy of Intellectual Reserve, Inc.

Open House and Dedication

At the VIP open house, Monday, February 5, 1979, Elder O. Leslie Stone of the Seventy, executive director of temples, explained that "a new temple has been built inside the walls of the old" and that the temple's capacity had been expanded 75 percent.[10] The four-week public open house extended from February 6 through March 3. President Bullen believed that this opportunity to visit the temple during the open house "may be a chance of a lifetime in this area."[11] A temporary visitors'

Open house invitation. Courtesy of Church History Library.

Logan Temple. *Dawning of a New Day,* by Alan Fullmer.

center, staffed by members of local stake seventies quorums, was set up in a nearby ward chapel; it featured films on temple work in general and the Logan Temple in particular. Some 213,184 persons visited the temple, more than twice the number anticipated. On February 19, Presidents' Day, a record 19,205 toured the temple, and lines extended as much as seven blocks. Bus groups came from as far away as Boise, Idaho; Richfield, Utah; and Star Valley, Wyoming.[12]

There were nine rededication sessions, three each day Tuesday through Thursday, March 13–15, 1979. President Spencer W. Kimball spoke at and offered the dedicatory prayer in each of these sessions in the large priesthood room, and about 1,250 attended. Another 450 watched by closed-circuit television in other parts of the temple. The proceedings were carried to two overflow locations outside of the temple; 1,700 persons were seated in the Logan Tabernacle, and 350 watched in the nearby ward chapel. President Kimball dedicated the temple as "a lifting symbol of God the Eternal Father and His Son Jesus Christ" and declared that it "stands in all its majesty as a monument to the faith and devotion of our pioneer fathers." He reported that up to that time, more than 18 percent of all ordinances worldwide had been performed in the Logan Temple. Following the rededication, ordinances were resumed and immediately were increased by over one-third compared to the years just before the reconstruction.

A Movement toward Historic Preservation

As the United States of America prepared for its bicentennial in 1976, interest increased in society about what should be done to preserve the historic buildings in the country. In the past many vital heritage sites like Mount Vernon were almost destroyed. In fact, at one point in the 1830s, part of Independence Hall in Philadelphia was torn down, until French general Lafayette implored the people, saying, "Here is the birthplace of freedom in all the world," which stopped the project.[13] As a new country, the United States was working to establish ways to honor the old while building the new. The National Register of Historic Places was one way for communities to honor past buildings and bring visibility to their history. Some of the oldest and largest structures in the western United States were the temples in Utah, and as they reached their centennials and faced renovation projects, would the Manti Temple face the same drastic change as the interior of the Logan Temple?

First Presidency at Logan Temple dedication, left to right: N. Eldon Tanner, Spencer W. Kimball, and Marion G. Romney. Courtesy of *Deseret News* and Church History Library.

As part of the Church's desire to preserve its history, in 1973, President Harold B. Lee appointed Florence Jacobsen to be the curator for the Church's Historic Sites. Jacobsen, who had just finished serving as the Young Women General President, was well respected and had a fine eye for preservation. In the years to come, she and her team from the Historical Department demonstrated how historic sites like the Joseph Smith home in Palmyra, New York, could be rebuilt and decorated with artifacts and furniture from the 1820s, capturing the historical time period of the First Vision. Back when Jacobsen was Young Women General President, she had kept the Lion House from being torn down when the Church Office Building was constructed, and she later oversaw its renovation along with the Beehive House.[14] The Historical Department could be a valuable resource in preserving Utah's temples, if they were allowed to work with the Architect's Office and the Building Department.[15]

Manti Temple

Emil Fetzer proposed in 1978 that the Manti Temple receive a "complete upgrading and refurbishing."[16] By 1982 plans were ready to undergo the remodel.

Finished celestial room, Manti Temple. Courtesy of Historic LDS Architecture.

The decision to have the Historic Sites division directly involved in a temple project was unprecedented.

However, area Saints were worried that this project "might drastically change the temple" as had happened in Logan.[17] In response, President Gordon B. Hinckley, the newest member of the First Presidency, turned to Jacobsen, placing her in charge of the interior design and refurbishing of the temple. The decision to have the Historic Sites division directly involved in a temple project was unprecedented. Her team worked closely with Jim McCrae of the Building Department, who was appointed as the liaison by Emil Fetzer to work with the Historical Department.[18]

Since the Manti Temple had been dedicated during the height of persecution by the federal government during the days of plural marriage and when the Church was in considerable debt, the temple had been sparsely furnished in the 1880s. Under the direction of Jacobsen, the temple's interior was refurbished to reflect the Eastlake Victorian design popular at the time of the temple's construction and to decorate it more fully as the Saints might have desired at the time.

Manti Temple open house. Courtesy of *Deseret News* and Church History Library

Jacobsen's team located a small part of the original celestial room rug that had 26 colors of thread and a beautiful floral pattern in a Manti home. The rug piece was sent to a manufacturer in England that still had nineteenth-century equipment and was able to reproduce the carpet. Jacobsen also included the community in the temple project. She reached out to several sisters to help with one of the sealing rooms. Sixty-four sisters spent months preparing intricate needlepoint upholstery for one sealing room, and a donated Persian rug adorned another.[19]

Unlike the white color scheme used in the Jordan River, Ogden, and Provo Temples, Jacobsen employed a gray-green wallpaper in the main hallway of the Manti Temple, using antique furniture and wainscotting that matched the original woodwork. Initially skeptical of the interior plan, the employees of the Building Department eventually respected Jacobsen's choices. Additionally, at the open house one local resident shook Jacobsen's hand and said, "You didn't change a thing," which she felt was a supreme compliment. This showed that the temple still maintained its pioneer heritage in the eyes of the community.

The Manti Temple did still have some major changes, though not nearly to the scale of the Logan Temple. Improvements included the addition of a new kitchen and cafeteria, new dressing rooms, a children's nursery, and three sealing rooms in the annex. A separate baptistry entry door was cut through the temple's south wall to accommodate youth coming to participate in baptisms for the dead. Completely new air-conditioning, heating, electrical, and plumbing systems were installed. Stone used to remodel the exterior of the annex came from the same nearby quarry as the original temple.

> "This building was not constructed to be a work of art or museum piece, but to accommodate the work and purposes of the Lord."

One major issue of concern, raised by temple president Wilbur W. Cox on behalf of the Manti Temple community, was maintaining the live endowment ceremony instead of installing the film as was now common in other temples. Fetzer noted the First Presidency reviewed the request and asked for his opinion. He reported back to the Brethren that due to the rural nature of the temple district, there would not be a significant difference in how many endowments were performed between the live endowment and the film. The First Presidency was sensitive to the interest of the local members and directed that Brother Fetzer accommodate the flow of the temple endowment to support the live presentation. This important decision allowed the Manti Temple to have a unique and special feeling for those who visited the temple to worship in the ensuing decades. Only Manti and the Salt Lake Temple would continue to do the live presentation until their renovations in the 2020s.

During a brief open house, Thursday–Saturday, June 6–8, 1985, a total of 40,308 persons toured the refurbished temple. President Gordon B. Hinckley, second counselor in the First Presidency, rededicated it in nine sessions, Friday–Sunday, June 14–16. At the opening of the first session, he commented about his feelings on seeing the restored temple: "I could scarcely hold back the tears. Something happens to me when I go into these [historic] temples. I see the magnificence of the workmanship wrought with rudimentary tools. I have been in most of the great buildings of the world—palaces of kings and houses of parliament—and in none of those places have I had the kind of feeling I get in coming into these early pioneer houses of God."[20] The rededicatory prayer affirmed, "With great care, its beauty so carefully crafted by its original builders, has been brought back." Still, President Hinckley noted, "This building was not constructed to be a work of art or museum piece, but to accommodate the work and purposes of the Lord."[21]

Notes

1. Blaine M. Yorgason, Richard A. Schmutz, and Douglas D. Alder, *All That Was Promised: The St. George Temple and the Unfolding of the Restoration* (Salt Lake City: Deseret Book, 2013), 336.
2. Emil B. Fetzer, *Completed Writings of Emil Baer Fetzer* (privately published, 2003), 215–16, Church History Library, Salt Lake City; Fred A. Baker, interview, January 12, 2012.
3. Fetzer, *Completed Writings*, 216.
4. Fetzer, *Completed Writings*, 221.
5. Fetzer, *Completed Writings*, 225.
6. "Logan Temple to Close," *Church News*, September 18, 1976, 3; "Temple Renovation Is Almost Complete," *Church News*, October 14, 1978, 3.
7. "Temple Renovation," 3.
8. Paul L. Anderson, interview by Jessie Embry, February 13 and 28, 2015, 9, Church History Library.

9. Anderson, interview, 11.
10. Lynne Hollstein, "Tours Begin in Logan Temple," *Church* News, February 10, 1979, 3.
11. "Temple Renovation," 3.
12. "Temple Tours in Logan Begin," *Church News*, February 3, 1979, 3, 8–9; "213,184 Guests Tour Remodeled Logan Temple," *Church News*, March 10, 1979, 3.
13. Anderson, interview, 6.
14. Kenneth Mays, "Remembering an interview—Florence Smith Jacobsen, granddaughter of two LDS Church Presidents," *Deseret News*, March 15, 2017.
15. Andersen, interview, 10–12; Florence S. Jacobsen interview by Mary L. Olsen, 2010-2012, Church History Library.
16. Fetzer, *Completed Writings*, 229.
17. Rasmussen, *Manti Temple*, 76.
18. Anderson, interview, 31. See also Anderson, "Preserving the Manti Temple," *Journal of Mormon History* 46 (April 2020): 113-122. Peggy Fletcher Stack, "Former Mormon Women's Leader Florence Jacobsen Dies at 103, but Her Hand in Preserving Historic Sites Lives On," *Salt Lake Tribune*, March 29, 2017.
19. Andersen, interview, 50.
20. "Glistening 'New' at 97, Manti Temple Rededicated," *Church News,* June 23, 1985, 3, 11; "Manti Temple Restored to Like-New Status," *Church News,* June 9, 1985, 8–9.
21. "Sanpete Valley Saints Eagerly Await Manti Temple Rededication," *Ensign,* June 1985, 72; "Manti Temple Rededicated," *Ensign*, August 1985, 73–74.

9

Larger Temples during the Later Twentieth Century

The Jordan River Utah, Bountiful Utah, and Mount Timpanogos Utah Temples

Jordan River Utah Temple. *Evening Glow*, by Alan Fullmer.

The last two decades of the twentieth century witnessed significant developments in temple building. While many smaller temples were being built worldwide, these decades saw the construction of three large temples in Utah.

Even with the Provo and Ogden Temples, the increasing number of faithful Latter-day Saints in the area had created serious overcrowding in the Salt Lake Temple. There had also been a general quickening in the pace of temple work in Utah County with the Provo Temple. President Spencer W. Kimball pointed out that of the 53,337,080 endowments which had been performed for the dead since they had started in the nineteenth century, 33 percent, or 17,540,332, had been done during just the previous six years, from 1972 to 1977.[1]

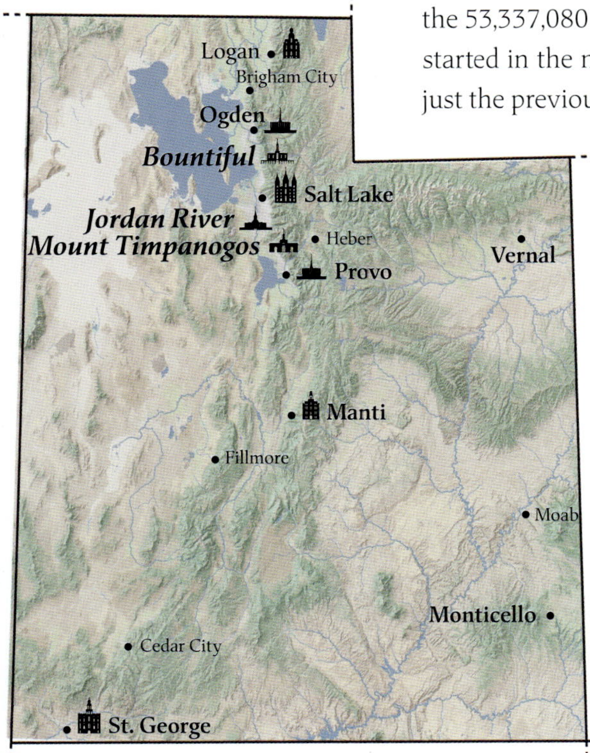

Utah's large temples up through the 1990s. Courtesy of Lee R. Cowan.

The Jordan River Utah Temple

Fred A. Baker, managing director of the Church Building Committee (later the Building Department), had received many calls and opportunities to see land that members were offering for temple sites, but something was different about his meeting in 1977 with Alma and Helen Holt in South Jordan, Utah. Since the time Alma was young, his family would leave the farm and fields every month and go to town, visiting Temple Square while in Salt Lake City. Over the years, Alma and his five sisters—Ida, Essie, Leah, Naomi, and Ann—spoke privately about how they felt part of the family property should be given to the Church for a temple. Yet at the time no one predicted a second temple would be built in the Salt Lake Valley in the 1980s.

When Brother Baker explained to Alma Holt that the Church could not guarantee the site would be used for a temple and that it would likely be used for a meetinghouse, Holt felt discouraged but responded to Baker and asked if he would explain their story directly to the prophet. After hearing about the property in their weekly meeting, President Kimball directed that a thank-you note be sent to Holt but then later asked Baker privately if the First Presidency could visit the Holts' land.

Fred Baker arranged for a car to take Spencer W. Kimball, Marion G. Romney, and N. Eldon Tanner to the Holt property. Baker gave special instructions to the driver that when they pulled up near the flood-irrigated furrows and uneven ground, "Don't you let the Presidency walk out in that alfalfa field, because they'll fall immediately." Fortunately, the First Presidency was fine, and two weeks later, President Kimball entrusted Fred A. Baker and Emil Fetzer to begin designing a temple to be known as the Jordan River Temple. The impressions of the Holt family had been realized.

The donated Holt property was a fifteen-acre parcel on a gentle knoll located on 1300 West at about 10200 South in the city of South Jordan. It would also have

Jordan River Utah Temple site, 1978. Courtesy of *Deseret News* and Church History Library.

access to Redwood Road, a major north–south traffic artery just to the west; property for this connecting road had been donated by the family of T. Udell Bailey.[2] The geographical area to be served by the new temple was the smallest in the Church, comprising only the south half of the Salt Lake Valley.

President Kimball called a meeting in the fall of 1977 for all the stake presidents in the Salt Lake Valley to meet in the solemn assembly room of the Salt Lake Temple on a Sunday morning at 8:00 a.m. There, he surprised most in the room by announcing the building of a second temple in the valley, particularly that the temple would be built on the west side. He also requested that all funds for the temple be raised by the members.[3]

The sacrifices started by the Holt family in giving their property were just the beginning. Saints young and old gave toward the building of the new temple, far surpassing the cost for the temple. There were many examples of sacrifice, particularly in less affluent areas. One young man with a wife and three children was earning a hundred dollars per week; he went without lunch so he could contribute one dollar per day to the temple. A stake president explained plans for raising funds for the temple in stake conference; following the meeting, three widows, all with limited means, independently wrote out checks for a thousand dollars without knowing about what the others were giving. A four-year-old boy gave his bishop a brown sack filled with money, insisting, "This is all I own, and I want to give it to the Church for the new temple." After another family had discussed what they might do for the temple, their eleven-year-old daughter who was "seriously ill with a rare blood disease" went to her room and brought back a jar filled with coins totaling nearly a hundred dollars; she gave it to her father and said, "This is all the money I have, and I would like it all to go to the temple."[4]

The ordinance rooms would seat 124, giving it the largest capacity of any temple in the Church.

The temple was designed by Church architect Emil B. Fetzer, who had designed the Ogden and Provo Temples a decade earlier. Like the earlier two temples, the Jordan River Temple would have six ordinance rooms surrounding the celestial room. Despite this similarity, Fetzer explained that the new temple would have "its own unique personality." It would incorporate "refinements" learned from building temples during the last ten years. It would be about 25 percent larger; the ordinance rooms would seat 124, giving it the largest capacity of any temple in the Church. There would be a 300-seat chapel and seventeen sealing rooms.[5] Its 148,236 square feet of floor space would make it the fourth largest temple in physical size, after only the Salt Lake, Los Angeles, and Washington D.C. Temples. The temple would face east, but all four sides would have a "front" appearance. Parking for 680 cars would be on the side and in the back. The extensive use of stained glass with nighttime illumination would make it a prominent landmark, easily seen from many parts of the valley and from aircraft approaching the Salt Lake International Airport. President Kimball noted that Brigham Young had prophesied that the time would come "when the whole valley will be one community from hill to hill"; he said that "this thought intrigues us" and that "we hope this temple will look out over that [whole] community."[6]

Fetzer explained that all the construction companies selected to submit bids had excellent reputations, had completed "beautiful projects," and had the capacity to erect the temple.[7] When bids were opened on May 23, 1979, the Layton Construction Company of Salt Lake City had the lowest bid of $12,548,000 and received the contract to build the temple.[8]

All temple ceremonies are uplifting, and in every way contribute "to the great preparation that the earth may be made ready to receive her king, the Lord Jesus Christ."

Ground was broken on Saturday, June 9, 1979, under blue, cloudless skies. An estimated ten to fifteen thousand interested spectators were present. The entire First Presidency and many other General Authorities of the Church attended. The Mormon Youth Chorus provided music. President Kimball refuted the prevailing notion that "the condition of human souls is eternally and irrevocably fixed by divine decree immediately after death." He insisted that those who died without the opportunity to be baptized may still qualify for redemption by having the needed baptism performed by proxy in their behalf. He explained that "other essential ordinances have to be performed for the dead who cannot do it for themselves" and that "temples are the God-appointed places for such sacred work." He affirmed that all temple ceremonies are uplifting, including commitments to live high standards of morality and chastity, charity, and benevolence, to devote talents and material means to the cause of truth, and in every way contribute "to the great preparation that the earth may be made ready to receive her king, the Lord Jesus Christ. With the making of each covenant and the assuming of each obligation," he taught, "a promised blessing is pronounced contingent on faithfulness."[9]

President Ezra Taft Benson of the Quorum of the Twelve Apostles insisted that the temple would be a visible witness that "God intended that the family be eternal," that he "has not left man to grope in darkness," and that "the power of God can stay the power of evil." He testified that "the power of Godliness" associated with temple

By breaking ground with a backhoe instead of a shovel, President Spencer W. Kimball puts a new twist on his motto "lengthen your stride." Courtesy of Deseret News and Church History Library.

ordinances "will thwart the forces of evil if we will be worthy of these sacred blessings. This valley will be preserved, our families protected, our children safeguarded as we live the gospel, visit the temple, and live close to the Lord." He affirmed that the temple "will be a light to all of this area. It will be an inspiration, not only to Latter-day Saints, but to many others as well." Other speakers included Elder O. Leslie Stone of the First Quorum of the Seventy, who was executive director of temples, Church architect Emil B. Fetzer, and Ben E. Lewis, who was chairman of the fundraising committee. In his prayer dedicating the site, President Kimball petitioned that the work for which the temple would be built "be carried out through time and the Millennium to the blessing of millions of thy children."[10]

The service occupied nearly two hours. Rather than using the traditional gold-colored shovels, President Kimball donned a hard hat, took the controls of a huge backhoe, and then, to the approving applause of the crowd, proceeded to move the first bucketful of earth. His counselor President N. Eldon Tanner quipped that the prophet was simply carrying out his oft-stated admonition to "lengthen our stride."[11]

Statue of the Angel Moroni

At the time the Jordan River Temple was being built, the practice of the Church was to place statues of the angel Moroni on its larger temples. The figure to be placed atop the temple's tower was a copy of the angel sculpted by Avard Fairbanks a few years earlier for the Washington D.C. Temple. The original was eighteen feet tall, while the bronze copy for Jordan River (as well as for the Seattle and Mexico City Temples) was fifteen feet in height. Fairbanks was born into an artistic family in Provo, Utah,

Jordan River Utah Temple under construction. Courtesy of *Deseret News* and Church History Library.

in 1897. He was the son of John B. Fairbanks, one of the art missionaries sent to Paris to receive training before painting murals in the Salt Lake Temple. Avard won prizes for his sculpting by the age of twelve. He studied art in New York City and abroad, earning degrees at Yale and at the Universities of Washington and Michigan. After teaching on several campuses, he was serving as dean of fine arts at the University of Utah when he sculpted his angel. He stated that he wanted his sculpture of Moroni to have an "upward reach."[12]

Before the statue of Moroni was elevated to the tower, it was gold-leafed under the direction of Alfred A. Lippold, an immigrant from Germany. He had served as an apprentice "to a master who was a real master." He had completed projects in the Utah State Capitol, Hotel Utah lobby, and new Utah Symphony Hall. "He and a crew of four turned bronze to gold in one day, applying about a thousand two-inch squares of gold leaf." Lippold acknowledged that completing this project on the ground was much easier than when he had worked on figures of Moroni at the Salt Lake and Los Angeles Temples over two hundred feet in the air.[13] The plan was for the angel to be covered with canvas when it was placed on the tower and then be unveiled at the cornerstone laying ceremony as the Tabernacle Choir sang "An Angel from on High."[14] This plan was thwarted, however, when a strong wind blew the shroud off the figure a few days early.

Cornerstone Ceremony

About twelve thousand spectators filled the sloping lawn in front of the temple for the cornerstone ceremony on Saturday afternoon, August 15, 1981, some arriving as much as five hours early. Gordon B. Hinckley, who had been appointed as an additional counselor in the First Presidency just three weeks earlier, testified that temple

Aerial view of Jordan River Utah Temple cornerstone ceremony. Courtesy of *Deseret News* and Church History Library.

work "is an affirmation of our conviction that life continues after death for all of our Father's children." He pointed out that hundreds of hours will be spent serving inside the temple "without gratitude spoken from those for whom it is done." President Benson recalled that the Saints had been commanded to "stand in holy places" to avoid prophesied latter-day difficulties and insisted that "temples have been provided by a benevolent Father in Heaven to protect us from the tribulations." He testified, "The saints in this temple district will be better able to meet any temporal tribulation because of this temple. Faith will increase as a result of the divine power associated with the ordinances of heaven and the assurance of eternal associations." He then reaffirmed his promise made two years earlier at the groundbreaking that the whole valley would be blessed because of the Saints' faithful temple service.[15]

Fetzer observed that because temples were now built of reinforced concrete, cornerstones no longer have any structural function, and that these ceremonies "are held more to install the box of artifacts than to mark a phase of construction." Articles in the hermetically sealed copper box included photographs of the General Authorities and of temple construction, copies of the standard works and other Church books, current issues of the *Deseret News* and other local newspapers, and copies of the *Church News* with articles about the temple. After members of the First Presidency and President Benson had daubed mortar around the plaque that would cover the cornerstone box, "a long line of members including children" had their turn after the ceremony to apply "thin trowels of mortar around the stone."[16]

Open House and Dedication

A total of 568,342 persons visited the temple during its monthlong public open house which extended from September 29 through October 31. Among the special groups welcomed at the temple was a group of airmen from Hill Air Force Base representing several nations; one of them commented, "We have never seen anything like it. Now we understand why your religion is so important to you." Three days during the last week of the open house exceeded 30,000. The 32,146 who came on October 29 was the greatest number ever to come on a single day to any temple open house. The 500,000th visitor was received as an honored guest that day. She was Myrtle Wade Gates of West Jordan, an eighty-one-year-old grandmother who came in a wheelchair and with an oxygen tank. Her home teacher had arranged the visit. "It's the most exciting thing that has ever happened to me," she exclaimed with surprise. "It's really made my day!"[17]

Jordan River Temple dedication ticket. Courtesy of Church History Library.

The Jordan River Temple was dedicated in fifteen sessions, three each day on November 16–20, 1981. Proceedings were carried by closed-circuit television to various rooms in the temple and to the Salt Lake Tabernacle over fifteen miles away on Temple Square downtown. Some 163,000 faithful members eight years of age and above were able to attend. President Kimball, who had undergone brain surgery not long before, attended but did not speak. This was the first time a second temple was built in a valley where one already existed. At the dedication, temple president Donovan H. Van Dam described this as "another marvelous work and a wonder" that nobody had dreamed could come to pass. "With six temples already in Utah, we looked too far-away for such things to happen."[18]

President Tanner, President Kimball's first counselor, encouraged "fathers and mothers to speak to their children about the temple" and to worthily go there in order to "prepare ourselves to meet the Savior." Elder Mark E. Petersen powerfully expounded the necessity of work for the dead, and "his testimony of the Savior brought tears to many eyes." Several in the audience described a "light that seemed to radiate from his face as he spoke." Elder Petersen later told his family of "the strength of the Spirit he had felt."[19]

The dedicatory prayer asked the Lord to accept the temple and petitioned, "Pour out Thy blessings upon it as a house into which Thou wilt come, and in which Thy Spirit will direct all that is done that it may be acceptable unto Thee. Frustrate the designs of the adversary against Thy people and Thy work, and may the efforts of all who fight against Zion come to naught. May the glorious work roll on in majesty and

Jordan River Utah Temple celestial room. Courtesy of Intellectual Reserve, Inc.

power to fill the whole earth, even as the waters cover the mighty deep."[20] In the years since the opening of the Jordan River Utah Temple, it has been one of the busiest temples in the entire Church.

A few years after the temple dedication, Emil Fetzer attended the marriage of one of his relatives and was surprised that the sealer was Alma Holt, who threw his arms around Brother Fetzer "in a brotherly embrace."[21] Both men had been blessed through their experiences seeing the rise of the Jordan River Temple.

The Bountiful Utah Temple

The history of the land for the Bountiful Utah Temple suggests that while God knows the future purposes for his temple sites, not all locations have been ideal or initially showed much promise. In 1897 Israel Barlow purchased from the US government forty acres of land just below the ancient shoreline of Lake Bonneville above Bountiful. For years, the family struggled to dry-farm the land. It would occasionally provide a hay or wheat crop, but for the most part there wasn't enough water for a

View from Bountiful Utah Temple site. Courtesy of John P. Barlow.

successful farm. Yet by the 1970s a nice apricot orchard provided a good crop of fruit. The land was an unlikely bowl up against the mountain without much access.

Then the ravaging rains and flash floods during the unforgettable spring of 1983 caused landslides and damaged homes in Bountiful. To create an earthen dam to protect Holbrook Canyon, Bountiful city approached the Barlow family and removed two hundred thousand cubic yards of soil from the property for the dam. By 1988 a new road called Bountiful Boulevard provided access to the property. Leo Barlow stated it would have cost him a million dollars to create access to the property. Now the Lord was subtly creating the steps so that the property would be ready for a temple.[22]

In 1988 the First Presidency announced the purchase of two possible temple sites, one in Bountiful, Utah, and the other in Bogotá, Colombia. President Benson and his counselors, Gordon B. Hinckley and Thomas S. Monson, had visited the

Bountiful site that had been sold by the Barlow family to Ellis Ivory for development. President Monson later recalled how President Benson looked up to the mountains and out to the lake "in a spirit of contemplation" and then declared, "This site will be so suitable for a beautiful temple of the Lord." The First Presidency explained that "while there are no definite plans for immediate construction, the choice properties were acquired while available." The nine-acre Bountiful site, high on the east bench, afforded "a panoramic view of the valley and the Great Salt Lake." A new road would provide access to the property.[23] The official announcement of temple construction came two years later.

Saturday, May 2, 1992, was sunny but cool when ground was broken for the Bountiful Temple. Approximately 7,500 had gathered at the site, some seated in chairs, others standing, and many seated on the hillside above. A fleet of chartered buses brought them to the site from parking lots down the hill. Another 2,500 watched by closed-circuit television at the Bountiful Regional Center. Associates steadied ninety-two-year-old President Benson as he and his counselors broke ground on the steep, windswept hillside. Three boys and three girls were invited to then have their

Bountiful Utah Temple rendering. Courtesy of Intellectual Reserve, Inc.

Just weeks before passing away, President Ezra Taft Benson helps children at the Bountiful Utah Temple groundbreaking services. Courtesy of Leslie T. Foy and Lorraine MacKay.

turn. In his remarks, President Hinckley explained that "the site and the conception of a temple was the prerogative of the prophet of the Lord," so he wished President Benson could be able to speak to the assembled throng. He insisted that this was "the greatest era of temple building in the history of the world," with as many temples being dedicated in the last seven years as in the entire previous history of the Church. (Of course, this record would be eclipsed by the rapid pace when he himself would become President of the Church just a few years later.) When President Hinckley determined that those seated on the hillside could hear him, he likened this occasion to the time when King Benjamin addressed his vast congregation from a tower.[24]

The twenty-eight stakes from North Salt Lake to Kaysville in south Davis County constituted the Bountiful Temple district, with a membership of 92,000. Elder Marlin K. Jensen and later Elder John E. Fowler, both of the Seventy, served as Presidents of the Utah North Area and chaired the Bountiful Temple committee. Blaine T. Jensen, a Regional Representative of the Twelve, was vice chair. The Okland Construction Company received the contract and was ready to begin construction right away.

The temple measures 195 by 157 feet, and the central tower, surmounted by the golden figure of Moroni, rises to a height of 176 feet. The exterior was finished in Bethel white granite, quarried just a few miles from Sharon, Vermont, where the Prophet Joseph Smith was born. The temple's architect was Allen B. Erekson, who also served as project administrator for temples and special projects. He explained that the temple was not "tied to any style of architecture, but has some features similar to the Salt Lake Temple, while other details have been gathered from various sources." He noted that "symbolic details" representing the sun, moon, and stars were included on the temple's exterior as a reminder of the three degrees of glory.

Bountiful Utah Temple. *Winter Meets Fall*, by Alan Fullmer.

A unique feature of the Bountiful Utah Temple is ample underground parking, made necessary by the lack of space on the hillside site. With a floor area just over a hundred thousand square feet, the temple has four 90-seat endowment-presentation rooms, the celestial room, and eight sealing rooms on the second floor, offices and dressing rooms on the main floor, and a baptistry and cafeteria in the basement.

Erekson explained that the temple's interior lighting, colors, furnishings, and artwork were designed to have "a level of elegance that doesn't distract from the Spirit." Those entering on the temple's lower level find "rich warm colors" that become "progressively lighter" and more "elegant" higher in the building. The art glass windows also have "an ascending feel," with varied colors providing privacy near the bottom and clearer glass admitting more light higher up. Beveled crystal glass near the top acts as a prism, casting a rainbow of colors into the celestial room. The windows have the motif of Jacob's ladder, increasing in detail as it rises. The stunning chandeliers came from the Czech Republic. All this was accomplished under the planning

Bountiful Utah Temple dedication tickets. Courtesy of Church History Library.

and supervision of Lawrence W. Wyss, manager of interior design for the Church's temples.[25]

Open House and Dedication

By the fall of 1994, construction was complete and the temple was ready for its six-week open house. On November 3 and 4, Church leaders greeted members of the press, community leaders, and other special guests. Temples "are to us the most sacred precincts in the whole world" and "the center of our worship," explained Elder James E. Faust of the Quorum of the Twelve, because in them we undertake "to seal and bind on earth that which is to be sealed in heaven." Elder John E. Fowler of the Seventy noted that faithful Latter-day Saints "make great efforts to be sealed in a temple" because they are "places to contemplate the importance of marriage and family, reflect on challenges, and to find peace." Newly appointed temple president Harold C. Yancey observed that "the temple is placed so many people can see it. It will be a great blessing," not just to Latter-day Saints but to the entire community, and "all can point to it with pride as a place of beauty."

The public open house was from November 5 through December 17. Visitors described the temple as having "reverent grandeur," being "elegant without ostentation." The temple's "natural cherrywood moldings and attractive furniture" created a "welcoming, almost homey atmosphere." The chandelier in the brides' dressing room seemed like "a bouquet of glass, a celebration of the importance of temple marriage." In the two-story-high celestial room the huge chandelier was like "a fountain of crystal in frozen cascade." Still, spiritual feelings impressed visitors most.[26] By the time the open house concluded, more than 870,000 people had visited the temple with the help of 45,000 volunteers.

The temple was then closed so it could be made ready for dedication. Elder Fowler explained that the temple was "scrubbed from ceiling to carpet . . . to be absolutely spotless as we present this holy house to the Lord." Ruth Yancey, the new temple matron, reported that the people were also getting ready and were eager to help. "They have made children's clothing and quilts for the nursery and have donated altar covers with beautiful crocheting. They are ready to serve and willingly give of their time," she gratefully acknowledged.[27]

Dedication of the Bountiful Utah Temple extended over an entire week. The cornerstone ceremony took place early on the first day, at 7:00 a.m., even before sunrise. Sunday, January 8, 1995, was a chilly winter day. As the group of Church leaders and their wives walked down a wooden ramp to the southeast corner of the temple, an outside choir appropriately sang "High on the Mountain Top." Choir members were grateful to be warmed by the Spirit. President Gordon B. Hinckley quipped, "Let's get the mud in place before it freezes." The plaque was then sealed in place over the cornerstone box containing historical artifacts.[28]

Four dedicatory sessions were held each day in the temple's celestial room from Sunday through Saturday, January 8–14. President Howard W. Hunter spoke and offered the dedicatory prayer in the first session. "We thank thee that thou did reveal thy priesthood, even the sacred sealing power, by the hand of Elijah the prophet so that in this temple and all thy other holy houses thy faithful Saints may be endowed with power from on high and may enter into those everlasting covenants which open the door to the receipt of all the blessings of Abraham, Isaac, and Jacob and all the holy prophets. The plan of salvation taught in the temple with simplicity yet with power will be as a never-failing beacon of divine light to guide our footsteps and keep them constantly on the pathway of eternal life." The prayer continued, "We plead with thee to make us worthy to inherit the fullness of those blessings found only in thy holy temples—even those blessings which grow out of a continuation of the family unit forever."[29]

WEEK ENDING JANUARY 14, 1995

Church News

Published by the Deseret News, Salt Lake City, Utah

THE CHURCH OF JESUS CHRIST OF LATTER-DAY SAINTS

BOUNTIFUL TEMPLE

Like beacon on a hill, Church's 47th temple is dedicated in Utah

— see pages 3-6

Second of a two-part New Testament map — see pages 8-9

Bountiful Utah Temple dedication, front cover of *Church News*, January 14, 1995. Courtesy of *Church News*.

As President Hunter was offering the prayer, the sun broke through the clouds, bathing the celestial room in brilliant light. President Hunter attended six of the twenty-eight sessions. (He would pass away on March 3, just two months later, after presiding over the Church for only nine months.) Forty-nine General Authorities spoke during the week. To accommodate all who wanted to attend, proceedings were carried by closed-circuit television to other rooms in the temple and to five other buildings—the Salt Lake Tabernacle, the Bountiful Regional Center, and tabernacles in Ogden, Brigham City, and Logan. As each session closed, faithful Saints reverently left the temple as well as the other locations with tears flowing freely and scarcely wanting to talk, being overwhelmed by the impact of what they had just experienced. Attending a temple dedication was "a cherished experience long to be remembered." Others were already in line to enter the following dedicatory session.[30] After the chilly start, weather was fortunately relatively mild. With the multiple sessions and overflow locations, 201,655 Saints were able to attend, the largest number ever to participate in a temple dedication.[31]

Ordinances in the Bountiful Utah Temple commenced at 6:00 a.m. on Tuesday, January 17, three days after the last dedicatory sessions. There were enough anxious Saints present at this early hour to fill three ordinance rooms for the first endowment session.

Groundbreaking services ticket. Courtesy of Mike Anderson.

The Mount Timpanogos Utah Temple

Meanwhile, construction was progressing on a similar temple about fifty miles further south. At the October 1992 general conference, in connection with the sustaining of Church officers, President Gordon B. Hinckley announced plans for "another temple in Utah County to relieve the pressure on the Provo Temple, which is operating far beyond its designed capacity." The exact site was disclosed during the April 1993 general conference six months later. As part of his address honoring the Salt Lake Temple during its centennial, President Hinckley indicated that other temples would be built, including one on "a site in American Fork, Utah, which the Church has owned for many years." Located at 900 East and 700 North, this nearly twenty-acre site had been part of a welfare farm.[32]

Originally purchased in 1953 by the Timpanogos Stake, the eighty-acre farm owned by Adolphus and Thelma Pulley was used as a Church welfare farm to produce hogs, beef, alfalfa, and grains. For almost four decades, the land was used to bless those in need. In 1992 the Church traded most of the acreage for land in Alpine, Utah, and retained twenty-three acres in American Fork for a temple site.[33] Later at the groundbreaking held on Saturday, October 9, 1993, Elder Joseph B. Wirthlin of

Sea of people at Mount Timpanogos Utah Temple groundbreaking services. Courtesy of Mike Anderson.

the Twelve noted that the farm on this property had provided for temporal welfare, but the temple would contribute to the people's spiritual well-being. He believed that the greatness of the 11,750-foot Mount Timpanogos, after which the temple would be named, appropriately represented "the valiancy and the faithfulness" of the Utah Valley Saints.

At the groundbreaking ceremony, an estimated twelve thousand eager persons were in attendance, and music was provided by a 440-voice choir. Responding to questions about why the Church would build another temple in Utah, President Hinckley noted that the Provo Temple was the busiest in the Church, operating at 115 percent of its designed capacity, and that the Jordan River Temple was the second busiest. Even though forty-five temples were operating, 20 percent of all ordinances were performed in just these two temples. He referred to a "lost and found" sign he saw on the grounds and explained that service in the temple brings salvation to bless those who otherwise would be lost, but who are found through family history research and vicarious temple ordinances.

President Thomas S. Monson indicated that he had received a letter from a young boy, Samuel Barnes, who had learned in Primary that pioneer children had helped

Construction of Mount Timpanogos Utah Temple. Courtesy of Church History Library.

build temples. He wrote that he wanted to help with the Mount Timpanogos Utah Temple "and that you can tell me how on Saturday at the groundbreaking services." President Monson responded, "Samuel, I thought maybe today I would try to tell you how you can help with the Mount Timpanogos Temple and in so doing, if everyone else wants to listen in, fine. But this message comes directly to you, Samuel." He recommended that the boy put a picture of the temple in his room where he could see it each evening and morning when he said his prayers, that he look forward to participating in baptisms for the dead in the temple, then later to receiving his endowment before serving as a missionary, and then to kneeling "at a sacred altar with a sweet daughter of our Heavenly Father, an eternal companion, and hear these words, 'I pronounce you husband and wife for time and for all eternity.'"[34]

Construction was about two-thirds complete when a highly visible milestone was reached—placing the statue of the angel Moroni. The American Fork Police Department estimated that twenty thousand people filled the streets surrounding the temple on Monday, July 17, 1995, to see a tall crane lift the thirteen-foot, two-hundred-pound gold-leafed statue of the angel to the top of the temple's tall spire. As the figure came to rest, the crowd broke into applause and spontaneously began singing "The Spirit of God." Steve Studdert, president of the Highland East Stake and vice chair of the temple committee, believed that the presence of such a large crowd "speaks for the interest and faithfulness of the Latter-day Saints in the area. They

President Gordon B. Hinckley conducts cornerstone service. Courtesy of *Church News*.

literally clogged the streets, but it was done in a wonderful spirit." He regarded it as "a moving demonstration of an outpouring of faith that was very touching."[35]

With a floor area of 104,000 square feet on three levels, the temple's plan was like that of the Bountiful Utah Temple, but there were some subtle differences. The Mount Timpanogos Utah Temple's spire was a little taller, reaching a height of 190 feet. The temple was faced with Sierra white granite, and the tower was of a slightly lighter shade. The inside colors were also different, carpeting ranging from mauve to off-white. In the brides' room and celestial room, patterns in the carpet reflected those in the stained glass windows. The grounds were landscaped to reflect the rural setting then characteristic of northern Utah Valley.[36]

By the time the open house ended, some 679,217 visitors had passed through the Mount Timpanogos Utah Temple.

Just a week before the open house was to begin, as President Studdert read the Lord's admonition to "prepare every needful thing" (Doctrine and Covenants 88:119), he was impressed with the need for a last-minute cleaning of the temple's grounds and surroundings. He called on each stake in the temple district to provide one hundred volunteers the next morning. Over four thousand responded, often at a personal sacrifice because of the short notice. Nevertheless, they had smiles on their faces as they spent about four hours weeding, pruning, digging, planting, and hauling off debris from the temple site and the 160-acre grounds of the Utah State Developmental Center across the street. The Center's grounds superintendent smiled when he heard about this project, but he was moved to tears when he was told how many volunteers would be contributing their time to beautify his property as well as that surrounding the temple. President Studdert explained: "We wanted to say to the development center 'thank you for your patience during the last three and a half years of construction' and 'thank you in advance for your patience as hundreds of thousands of people visit your neighborhood [during the open house].' What better way could we show our love for our neighbors than to say to them, 'let us help you where you can't help yourself.'"[37]

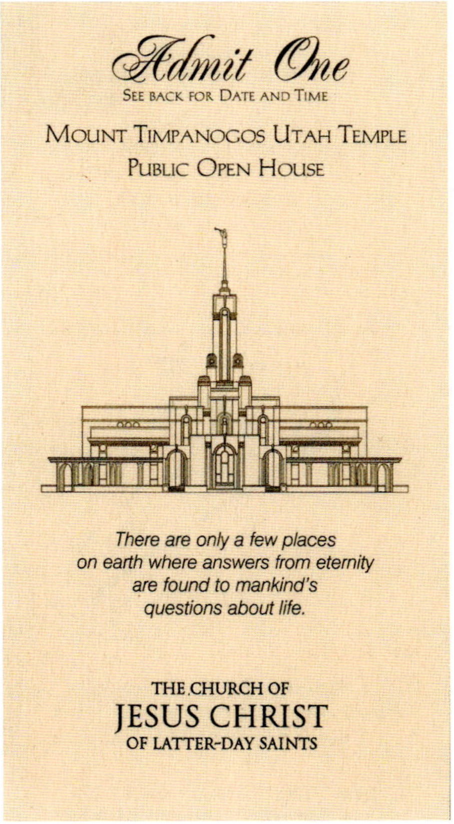

Public open house ticket. Courtesy of Church History Library.

Open House and Dedication

Like the Bountiful Utah Temple, the Mount Timpanogos Utah Temple had a six-week open house, running from August 10 through September 21. Visitors first entered one of several temporary shelters outside of the temple where they viewed a video presentation on the doctrinal purpose of temples. As they were about to enter the temple, many heard a children's chorus singing such numbers as "I Love to See the Temple" or "I Feel My Savior's Love"; all the wards in the temple district had the assignment to provide these groups of young singers in rotation. Visitors then walked quietly through the temple, passing through areas including the baptistry, brides' dressing room, chapel, one of the ordinance rooms, a sealing room,

Children singing at the Mount Timpanogos Utah Temple open house. Courtesy of Church History Library

and the celestial room. Brief recordings explained the function of each area. As guests exited the temple, missionaries were on hand to answer questions.[38]

President Hinckley insisted that the tours should emphasize "the ordinances and covenants of the temple rather than the architecture of the building." This has resulted in "a profound outpouring of the Spirit" and numerous missionary referrals. Developmentally disabled residents of the center across the street were among the first guests; arrangements were made for family members to accompany them as they visited the temple. One sixty-year-old man seemed upset and quite agitated as he entered the temple, and his brother wondered if bringing him to the open house had been a mistake. Suddenly the man, whose speech was usually unintelligible, shouted, "Stop!" Behind the recommend desk was a large painting of the Lord holding a lamb in his arms. The man folded his arms like the Savior's, seemed to calm down, and clearly said, "Jesus." They completed the tour in peace. A man with terminal brain cancer was being pushed in a wheelchair. In the celestial room he stood for several minutes, gazing at the infinite reflections in the opposing mirrors, and then quietly said, "All is well. I am ready to go now." By the time the open house ended, some 679,217 visitors had passed through the Mount Timpanogos Utah Temple. More than 56,000 volunteers had served as guides or supervisors, pushed wheelchairs, answered questions on the grounds, cleaned the building each night, or repaired the padding placed to protect the carpeting. During the open house, one of these volunteers lost his wife of fifty-six years. The day after her funeral he was at his post, saying, "This is where Beth would want me to be. This is my duty."[39]

Right: Mount Timpanogos Utah Temple. *Nightfire*, by Alan Fullmer.

At this time the Mount Timpanogos temple district extended from Alpine to Orem in northern Utah Valley and in the Heber and Vernal areas of northeastern Utah. The forty-three stakes had a membership of 131,000 members.

Winter, Mount Timpanogos Utah Temple. Courtesy of Intellectual Reserve, Inc.

As had been the case at Bountiful, the Mount Timpanogos Utah Temple's dedication filled an entire week. The cornerstone ceremony took place at 8:00 a.m. Sunday morning, October 13, 1996, just as the sun was rising over Mount Timpanogos. As Church leaders emerged from the temple, an 880-voice chorus of young adults, 20 from each stake in the temple district, sang "We Thank Thee, O God, for a Prophet." President Hinckley and then others placed mortar to seal the plaque over the cornerstone box, which contained the accustomed memorabilia plus samples of wall coverings and wood moldings from inside the temple. Three dedicatory sessions were held that day and then four sessions each day through Saturday, October 19. Closed-circuit television carried the proceedings to the American Fork Tabernacle, Salt Lake Tabernacle, and to twelve stake centers in the temple district. Thus, a total of 157,917 faithful Saints were able to attend the dedication.[40]

The dedicatory prayer encapsulated the temple's functions: "Here, in the beautiful font, baptisms will be performed by living proxies in behalf of the dead. Here with repentant hearts we will be made clean before Thee and stand clothed in robes of spotless white. Here we will be instructed in the things of eternity and enter into solemn covenants with Thee. Here at sacred altars we will be joined as husbands and wives, as parents and children under the authority of the eternal Priesthood in bonds of covenants that will endure forever."[41] President Hinckley pronounced the prayer in the first and ten other sessions. His counselors conducted the balance of the twenty-seven sessions. A total of fifty-two General Authorities participated during the week.

Celestial room of Mount Timpanogos Utah Temple. Courtesy of Church History Library.

President Thomas S. Monson had stayed in touch with Samuel Barnes since the time of the groundbreaking, and the young man now thought of him as a good friend. President Monson invited Samuel, now twelve years of age and suffering from incurable Crohn's disease, to attend one of the dedicatory sessions. During the session, President Monson called Samuel to come stand by him at the pulpit. He presented the young man a piece of temple granite and told him that he and Sister Monson prayed for him every day. When Samuel was invited to respond, he stated that "he was thankful that there was a temple close by" and that "he had such a good friend to help him make it through the hard times." Afterward, he told his family that he knew "why so many people went to the temple"; he felt so good in there that "he didn't want to leave." Just a week later, he joined other youth in his ward to do baptisms in the temple. His mother, Deborah, affirmed that Samuel "has taught the family about faith and about answers to prayers."[42]

Ordinances commenced in the Mount Timpanogos Utah Temple on Tuesday, October 22, 1996. Several large temples were now in service in Utah. Before the end of the century, two other and quite different temples would be dedicated—one much smaller, and the other constructed from an existing older building.

Notes

1. "New Temple Planned in Utah," *Church News*, February 4, 1978, 3.
2. "Temple Completion Set for '81," *Church News*, June 3, 1978, 3.
3. *Church News*, June 9, 1979, 2.
4. "Temple Completion Set."
5. "Temple Completion Set."
6. "Temple Contract Awarded," *Church News*, June 2, 1979, 3.
7. John L. Hart, "First Presidency Sets Jordan River Groundbreaking Date," *Church News*, April 28, 1979, 3.
8. "Temple Contract."
9. Dell Van Orden, "Ground Is Broken for Temple," *Church News*, June 16, 1979, 3.
10. Van Orden, "Ground Is Broken."
11. Van Orden, "Ground Is Broken."
12. J. Michael Hunter, "I Saw Another Angel Fly," *Ensign*, January 2000, 30–36.
13. Hart, "Man with a Midas Touch," *Church News*, August 8, 1981, 3, 12.
14. "Temple Statue to Be Unveiled," *Church News*, August 8, 1981, 3.
15. Hart, "1,200 Attend Temple Rites," *Church News*, August 22, 1981, 3, 8–9.
16. Hart, "1,200 Attend Temple Rites."
17. "568,000 People Visit Jordan River Temple," *Church News*, November 7, 1981, 5.
18. Van Orden, "Church Dedicates New Jordan River Temple Near S. L.," *Church News*, November 21, 1981, 3, 5; "About the Cover," *Church News*, November 21, 1981, 2.
19. Peggy Petersen Barton, *Mark E. Petersen: A Biography* (Salt Lake City: Deseret Book, 1985), 180.
20. "Dedicatory Prayer Offers Praise," *Church News*, November 21, 1981, 4–5.
21. Fetzer, *Completed Writings*, 90.
22. John Paul Barlow, Bountiful Utah Temple Site History, 1992, Church History Library.
23. "Sites Are Purchased for Temples in Bountiful, Utah and Bogota, Colombia," *Church News*, May 28, 1988, 2; John L. Hart, "Ground Broken for Bountiful Temple," *Church News*, May 9, 1992.
24. Hart, "Ground Is Broken," 2.
25. "Elegance to Complement the Spirit," *Church News*, November 12, 1994, 6.
26. "Public Invited to Bountiful Temple," *Church News*, November 5, 1994, 3, 7; Hart, "Thousands View Sacred Precincts," *Church News*, November 12, 1994, 3–4.
27. Hart, "Thousands View," 4.
28. Dell Van Orden and John L. Hart, "Winter Chill No Obstacle to Warmth of Dedication of Beacon on a Hill," *Church News*, January 14, 1995, 3, 5.

29. "Magnificent Edifice Consecrated to Lord," *Church News*, January 14, 1995, 4; capitalization and punctuation standardized.
30. Van Orden and Hart, "Winter Chill," 4; Hart and Mike Cannon, "Experience of a Lifetime at Dedication," *Church News*, January 14, 1995, 6.
31. "200,000 Attend Dedicatory Sessions, *Church News*, January 21, 1995, 3.
32. "American Fork Site Selected for New Utah County Temple," *Church News*, April 10, 1993, 3.
33. Mount Timpanogos Utah Temple History, Church History Library.
34. John L. Hart, "Mt. Timpanogos Utah Temple Groundbreaking Another Significant Step in the Greatest Era in Temple Building," *Church News*, October 16, 1993, 3–4.
35. "20,000 See Statue Lifted Atop Mount Timpanogos Temple," *Church News*, July 22, 1995, 3.
36. R. Scott Lloyd, "Thousands Visit Newest Utah Temple, 49th in the Church, during Open House," *Church News*, August 17, 1996, 3–4.
37. Sara Jane Weaver, "4,000 Answer Last-Minute Service Call," *Church News*, August 10, 1996, 3, 11.
38. Lloyd, "Thousands Visit Newest Utah Temple," *Church News*, August 17 1996, 3–4.
39. Lloyd, "Tours of New Temple Touch Hearts, Lives As 500,000 Attend," *Church News*, September 14, 1996, 3–4; Lloyd, "700,000 People View Newest House of God," *Church News,* September 28, 1996, 3–4.
40. Dell Van Orden, "Mount Timpanogos Temple Dedicated: 5,000 Watch President Hinckley Apply Mortar to Cornerstone," *Church News*, October 19, 1996, 3, 5; Weaver, "157,917 Attend Dedication: Many Renew Resolve in Mount Timpanogos Temple," *Church News*, October 26, 1996, 3.
41. "May It Be a Beacon of Peace, Refuge," *Church News*, October 19, 1996, 4
42. Weaver, "157,917 Attend Dedication," 3.

10 Small Temples

The Monticello Utah Temple

Monticello Utah Temple, the first small temple in Utah. *Breaking Storm*, by Alan Fullmer.

Monticello Utah Temple, first small temple in Utah. Courtesy of Lee R. Cowan.

The Monticello Utah Temple, dedicated in 1998, was one of the first small temples erected by the Church at the end of the twentieth century. The story of its construction begins far beyond the Beehive State.

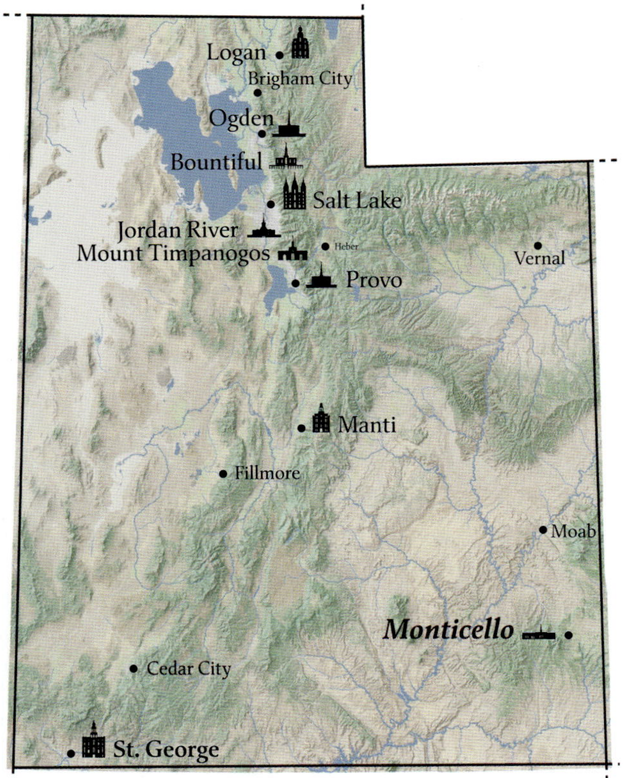

President Hinckley's Inspiration

For at least two decades, President Gordon B. Hinckley had been concerned with making temple blessings more readily available to the Saints scattered globally. "Too many times he had organized stakes in various areas of the world in which few of the brethren interviewed for leadership positions had been to the temple. He found himself wondering if there weren't a way to build smaller, less expensive temples and to build more of them throughout the world."[1] He discussed these concerns with President Harold B. Lee as early as the 1970s.

In June 1997 President Hinckley visited the Latter-day Saint colonies in northern Mexico to participate in the celebration of the centennial of the Church-sponsored academy, or high school, there. He was impressed when he learned that this small group of faithful Latter-day Saints had contributed more than one hundred mission presidents over the years. Meredith I. Romney, president of the Colonia Juārez Stake, met him at the El Paso airport. During the three-hour drive to the colonies, the prophet talked "quite a bit about temples. One of his concerns for the people here was the distance they traveled to attend the temple." President Romney described how stake members typically made a three- to four-day excursion to the temple in Mesa, Arizona. Only a few months earlier, however, a change in the immigration policy had made it impossible for members without passports to attend the Mesa Arizona Temple, a privilege they had previously enjoyed. The complicated and expensive procedure for obtaining passports effectively prevented many Mexican Saints from going to the temple because they could not afford to obtain the needed documents. The prophet indicated that he was concerned about getting temples closer to the members.

President Hinckley noted that a smaller temple could be built more quickly and yet include all the essential facilities needed for temple ordinances.

On Thursday evening, June 5, as President Hinckley arrived at the special fireside on the Academia Juārez campus, "he was impressed at the reverence and respect of the people assembled under the large tent, as everyone was in their seats ten to fifteen minutes early, quietly awaiting his arrival," President Romney noted. "This was also the first opportunity that many people had of seeing and hearing a prophet speak in person."

Elder Eran A. Call of the Seventy spoke first. He reminisced about his experiences growing up in nearby Colonia Dublán and attending the Juārez Stake Academy. He also recounted how the colonies had produced hundreds of missionaries and scores of mission presidents—a record unequaled by any other Church units of their size. This caught President Hinckley's attention, President Romney recalled.[2]

President Hinckley was the principal speaker. After reviewing the history of the colonies and praising the Saints for their faithfulness, the prophet surprised his listeners with an unexpected idea: "This is the greatest era in the history of the Church and in the world for temple building. I would like to see the time come when all of our people throughout the world could get to a temple without too much inconvenience. I think you are about as far away as anybody and I don't quite know what to do about you. There aren't enough of you to justify a temple. Now, if you'd multiply the membership here and get about 20,000 members of the Church here, or 30,000, we'd build a beautiful temple. That's a challenge for you." Many who were in attendance commented that they had never before even contemplated the possibility of a temple in the colonies, so they were electrified by this totally unexpected yet wonderful suggestion. The next morning President Hinckley spoke again at the academy's commencement exercises. Immediately following the meeting, President Meredith Romney again had the privilege of driving him back to the airport in El Paso. "On the way into Mexico, President Hinckley was sitting beside me in the front seat and was quite talkative," President Romney recalled. "However, on the way back he sat in the back seat and seemed to be resting and meditating. He commented several times on how impressed he was with the people at the fireside, the musical numbers presented, and the sweet spirit that was there. He also commented on the graduating class."[3]

"The concept is beautiful. It's a very workable concept."

President Hinckley later described what was going on in his mind during the drive back to the airport: "As we were riding to El Paso, I reflected on what we could do to help these people in the Church colonies in Mexico. They've been so very faithful over the years. They've kept the faith. They've gone on missions in large numbers. These [two small] stakes have produced very many mission presidents who served faithfully and well. They've been the very epitome of faithfulness. And yet, they've had to travel all the way to Mesa, Arizona, to go to a temple. . . . I thought of these things and what could be done. The concept of . . . smaller temples came into my mind. I concluded we didn't need the laundry. We didn't need to rent temple clothing. We didn't need eating facilities. These have been added for the convenience of the people but are not necessary." President Hinckley noted that a smaller temple could be built more quickly and yet include all the essential facilities needed for temple ordinances. After boarding the airplane, he recalled, "I took a piece of paper" and "sketched out the

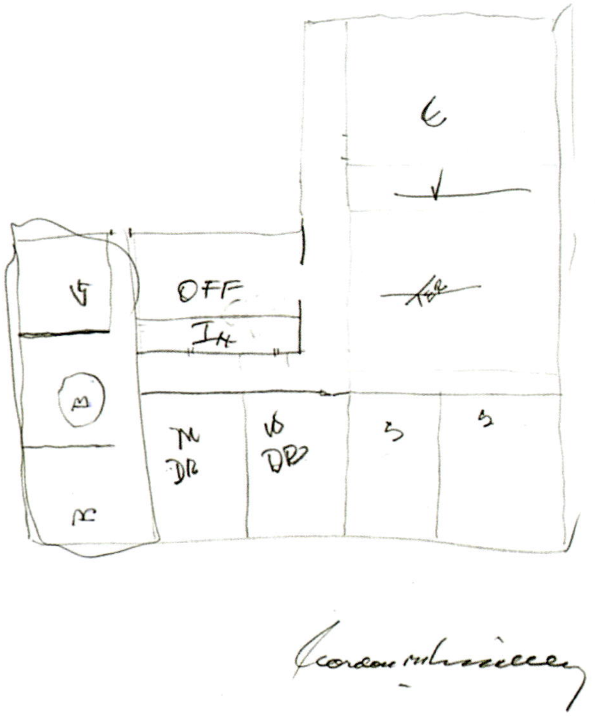

Gordon B. Hinckley's sketch of small temple. Courtesy of Church History Library.

plan, and turned it over to the architects to refine it." He concluded, "The concept is beautiful. It's a very workable concept."[4]

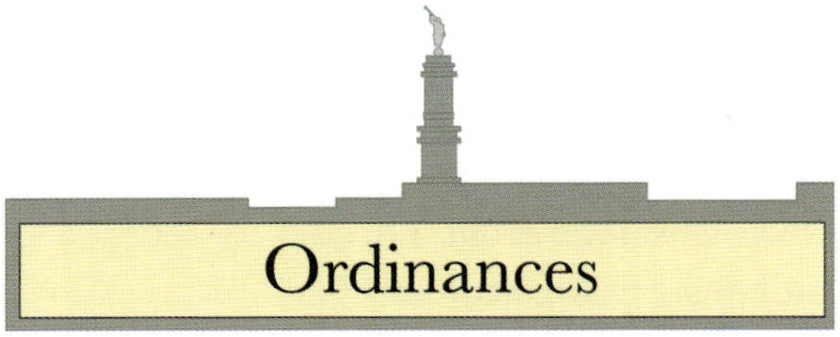

Illustration of smaller temple. Courtesy of Lee R. Cowan.

Later, at a regional conference in Chihuahua City, President Hinckley also spoke of his experience following the visit to Colonia Juārez: "There came to my mind an idea I'd never thought of before. It was inspired of the Lord to build a temple there, a small one, very small, six thousand square feet with facilities." He emphasized, "Every faithful member needs access to the house of the Lord. The gospel is not complete without the ordinances of the temple."[5] Later, in the temple's dedicatory prayer, the prophet specifically used the word *revelation* to describe the source of the small temples concept. "It was here in Northern Mexico, that Thou didst reveal the idea and the plan of a smaller temple, complete in every necessary detail, but suited in size to the needs and circumstances of the Church membership in this area of Thy vineyard. That revelation came of a desire and a prayer to help Thy people of these colonies who have been true and loyal during the century and more that they have lived here. They are deserving of this sacred edifice in which to labor for themselves and their forebears."[6]

"Every faithful member needs access to the house of the Lord. The gospel is not complete without the ordinances of the temple."

The Surprising Announcement

During the October 1997 general conference, in the Saturday evening priesthood session, the construction of these temples was announced publicly for the first time. "There are many areas of the Church that are remote, where the membership is small and not likely to grow very much in the near future," President Hinckley began. "Are those who live in these places to be denied forever the blessings of the temple ordinances? While visiting such an area a few months ago, we prayerfully pondered this question. The answer, we believe, came bright and clear. We will construct small temples in some of these areas, buildings with all of the facilities to administer all of the ordinances." He explained that they would be built "to temple standards, which are much higher than meetinghouse standards. They would accommodate baptisms for the dead, the endowment service, sealings, and all other ordinances to be had in the Lord's house for both the living and the dead." A local man would be called to preside over each of these temples; his first counselor would be the temple recorder, and his second counselor would serve as temple engineer. Because patrons would bring their own temple clothes, no expensive laundry facilities would be needed (except for baptismal clothing). Then came the stunning news: "We are planning such structures immediately in Anchorage, Alaska, in the LDS colonies in northern Mexico, and in Monticello, Utah." Like the Mexican colonies, members in the other two locations had to travel relatively long distances to reach a temple. The nearest temple to

Architectural rendering of small temples announced in October 1997. Note the white angel Moroni called for in early plans. Courtesy of *Church News*.

Monticello, for example, was Manti, a four-hour drive. President Hinckley declared that the Church was determined "to take the temple to the people and afford them every opportunity for the very precious blessings that come of temple worship."[7]

President Jed Ervin Lyman of the Blanding Stake was listening to the priesthood session of general conference on that momentous Saturday evening, October 4, 1997. When he heard that a temple would be built in nearby Monticello, he "almost jumped up and shouted!" He and his members were "just absolutely thrilled."[8]

When the stake president heard that a temple would be built in nearby Monticello, he "almost jumped up and shouted!" He and his members were "just absolutely thrilled."

The Saints in the Monticello Area

The history of the Church in southeastern Utah goes back to 1855, just eight years after Brigham Young and the first pioneers reached the Salt Lake Valley. President Young called a group in the Manti area to take the gospel to Native Americans in the region. These Elk Mountain missionaries built a fort on the Colorado River at the present site of Moab, but after just a few months, an Indian uprising forced them to discontinue their efforts. The next Latter-day Saint activity would not come until nearly a quarter century later. In 1879 President John Taylor appointed a group from the Parowan and Cedar City area to develop a road and establish a colony on the San Juan River in southeastern Utah. During the fall of that year, several families set out, expecting to reach their destination in about six weeks. A major obstacle was the two-thousand-foot Colorado River Gorge. The only way down was through a narrow slot canyon, scarcely wide enough for the wagons. After chiseling a road through this Hole-in-the-Rock, the men locked the wheels of the wagons and attached chains with which they held the wagons back as they skidded down the steep descent. They then needed to float the wagons across the river and build a road up the other side. By this time, bitter winter weather had set in. Building the road through the broken-up country was an ongoing challenge. After six months, they finally reached the location of their future colony, which they named Bluff City. Church historian Andrew Jenson concluded that "these pioneer settlers experienced more hardships than any other colony known in the history of the Church."[9] Many present-day Church members in the area are descendants of these sturdy Hole-in-the-Rock pioneers. Soon other settlements were established, and in 1883 they were organized into the San Juan Stake. At a stake conference in 1894, Elder Brigham Young Jr. of the Quorum of the Twelve spoke on the importance of performing vicarious ordinances on behalf of the dead and prophesied that "in the near future a Temple would be built in this County."[10]

Monticello Utah Temple construction. Courtesy of Robin Ramsay.

Over the years, the Church has continued to grow in southeastern Utah. The name of the San Juan Stake was changed in 1974 to the Monticello Utah Stake. At the time the temple was built, the district also included the Moab, Blanding, and Blanding West Stakes in Utah as well as the Durango Colorado Stake.

Construction of the Monticello Utah Temple

At first Church leaders considered a downtown site but decided to place it adjacent to the north chapel. The 1.33-acre plot was donated by a father and son, Ernest and Paul Sondregger of Monticello. Being on a gentle rise, the temple would be easily visible to those approaching the town from the north on Highway 191.

Since the concept of these small temples was new, Church leaders wanted the temple at Monticello to be built first, as it would be more accessible to Church headquarters and therefore easier to inspect. President Hinckley explained, "We wanted to build one we could get to, that we could observe. This is somewhat new ground we were treading, and we wanted to be able to examine it and see how things fit together."[11]

Church leaders broke ground at Monticello just six weeks after plans for this temple were announced. Elder Ben B. Banks of the Seventy, who was serving as Utah South Area President, presided at the ceremony on November 17, 1997. On this sunny Saturday, an estimated 2,550 persons, about double the number expected, gathered on the site. Many stood on piles of dirt, construction equipment, and truck beds to have a better view. A choir of seminary students from Monticello and Blanding performed "High on the Mountain Top," "We Love Thy House, O Lord," and "Now Let Us Rejoice." Elder Banks affirmed that "We have the opportunity to live in the greatest day in the history of the Church in building temples to our Father in Heaven." Elder Banks's counselors in the Area Presidency who likewise were of the Seventy also spoke; Elder Dennis B. Neuenschwander declared, "Though the temple might be of a smaller dimension, there is no small dimension to what occurs here and what will occur within the walls of the temple. All the essential ordinances of and for the salvation of God's children that are performed in the largest of the temples will be performed also in the smallest of the temples." Elder Neil L. Andersen correctly predicted that this temple "would be the first of a flood of small temples that will dot the earth."[12]

Though it was small, this temple was constructed according to the same higher standards as any other temple.

The 7,000 square feet of floor area was less than half that of a typical meetinghouse. For example, the ward chapel next to the temple had an area of 18,000 square feet. Though it was small, this temple was constructed according to the same higher standards as any other temple. President Hinckley affirmed that the Monticello Utah Temple "contains all the features necessary for the work of the Lord to be done in this holy house. It lacks some features to be found in larger temples, but those are not of an essential nature. All of the essential qualities are there, all of the facilities are here. This is a beautiful building. It has been well constructed. There's been no scrimping anywhere. This building can take its place among the great temples of the Church, smaller, but of the same beauty and the same quality."[13]

The exterior was "Noah's Crème," or off-white marble imported from Turkey. Local members noted that "the hue of the temple seems to change with the weather conditions and time of the day" and that "the color of the marble perfectly complements

Exterior with sunstones. Courtesy of Robin Ramsey.

1

Sunday, 26 July 1998
8:00 A.M.
General Seating

Monticello Utah Temple Cornerstone and Dedication

Ticket Holder's Name

Bishop's Signature

Dedication ticket. Courtesy of the Temple Department.

the color of the local landscape." This exterior surface would also withstand the sandstorms typical of the Four Corners region. Windows featured art glass from Germany.[14]

Placing the figure of the angel Moroni atop the temple was an eagerly anticipated milestone. A crowd of about one thousand gathered on Thursday, May 14, to see the six-foot statue be hoisted to the top of the temple's fifty-foot spire. This was the first time one of the statues designed particularly for the small temples was seen publicly. They were each six feet tall and formed in white acrylic fiberglass. Sculpted by Karl Quilter and reproduced in fiberglass by LaVar Wallgren, the figure depicted a younger angel blowing a trumpet in his right hand and holding out a scroll symbolizing the gospel in his left. It represented the fulfillment of John's vision of a latter-day angel bringing "the everlasting gospel to preach unto them that dwell on the earth, and to every nation, and kindred, and tongue, and people" (Revelation 14:6). The statue was placed under the supervision of project architect Mark Shaffer.[15]

Dedication Events

The Monticello Utah Temple was constructed faster than any other in the Church. It required less than eight months to be completed and to be

Recommend desk in the Monticello Utah Temple. Courtesy of *Deseret News* and Church History Library.

ready for the open house. J. Sperry Eardley, president of the Monticello Utah Stake, affirmed that the temple had been "very well received in the community" of which 30–40 percent were not Latter-day Saints. "Our people are very excited and elated to have a temple in the area."[16]

VIP tours were offered on Wednesday, July 15. Speaking to dignitaries gathered in the chapel next door to the temple, Elder Banks pointed out, "As nice as this chapel is, . . . temples are different. . . . They are built as close to perfection and precision as possible because at the dedication, a temple does become a House of the Lord."[17] Coming to the temple impressed Jim Dyer, a state legislator from neighboring Colorado. He stated that he had "two very touching experiences in the last week." First, as a veteran of Marine service in southeast Asia, he had seen the traveling Vietnam War Memorial on which he saw the names of three friends who had paid the ultimate price in combat. The second experience was his visit to the temple's celestial room. "There was something about that last room that gave me the most peaceful feeling. I don't know what it was, and I don't know how to explain it."[18]

"Temples are different. They are built as close to perfection and precision as possible because, at the dedication, a temple does become a House of the Lord."

During the three-day public open house July 16–18, a total of 20,348 persons viewed the new temple. An interesting problem took place on the last morning of the open house. Thousands of moths covered the lawns, sidewalks, and walls of the temple. At the same time, starlings were creating a mess as they built nests on the meetinghouse next door. As the custodian was removing the moths with a leaf blower, "the starlings swooped in and began to devour the moths in midair," and they were

Monticello Utah Temple interior. Far left: Celestial room. Left: Baptismal font. Courtesy of *Deseret News* and Church History Library.

mostly gone in twenty minutes. Observers were reminded of how seagulls had saved the pioneers' crops in 1848.[19]

The temple was dedicated by President Hinckley in eight sessions on July 26 and 27, 1998. The 8 a.m. cornerstone session was followed by three dedicatory sessions on Sunday and four more on Monday. Proceedings were carried by closed-circuit television to the ward chapel next door and to the stake center downtown. A total of 8,108 were able to attend.

The Sunday morning cornerstone ceremony represented the completion of the temple. Some 1,300 persons gathered outside the temple to witness the proceedings. The cornerstone choir's sixty-six singers came from all five stakes in the temple district. Their eagerness to participate was exemplified by eighteen-year-old Suzanne Eardley of Monticello, who had knee surgery just six days before; "regardless of the surgery, she said she was going to be singing in the choir."[20] As President Hinckley arrived fifteen minutes before the 8 a.m. opening session, the cornerstone choir sang "We Thank Thee, O God, for a Prophet." After President Hinckley and other dignitaries applied mortar to the plaque covering the cornerstone box, others from the congregation—children and adults—took their turns. One of those applying mortar was Agnes Hurst of Blanding, who was ninety-six years old. "I wanted to ask President Hinckley how I did," she later quipped. "I think the temple is one of the

Marjorie Hinckley and Gordon B. Hinckley at the Monticello Utah Temple cornerstone ceremony. Courtesy of Robin Ramsay.

most marvelous things in our area," she asserted. "It was something we had hoped for but never expected in our lifetime."[21]

"This is a very happy day for me," declared President Hinckley at the dedication of the first of the smaller temples he had envisioned while returning from Mexico the year before. "It's taken a long time to fulfill Brigham Young Jr.'s prophetic statement. I'm glad to be in harmony with Brigham Young Jr. The inspiration of the Spirit is strong, clear, and certain that this is where the house of the Lord should be built," the prophet testified. "No one could be happier than I am."[22] In addition to President Hinckley, other speakers during the dedication included second counselor President James E. Faust, Elder Joseph B. Wirthlin of the Quorum of the Twelve, W. Eugene Hansen of the Presidency of the Seventy and executive director of the Temple Department, and all three members of the Utah South Area Presidency.

Lyle G. Adams of Monticello, the new temple's first president, was a great-grandson of one of the original pioneers. "I feel like the Hole-in-the-Rock trip really sanctified him," President Adams insisted, speaking of his ancestor. "It put his descendants on the road to being faithful Latter-day Saints. The blessings [of the temple] are indescribable. The feeling in this whole area is one of deep, deep gratitude." He noted that seven couples had already scheduled weddings in their new temple.[23]

President Jed Ervin Lyman of the Blanding Utah Stake, another grandson of one of the early leaders, had similar feelings: "I had heard all my life that a temple someday would be built in the area, but I didn't know it would happen in my lifetime. Having the temple in the area is pretty overwhelming."[24]

Later Developments

One of the most visible changes at the Monticello Temple occurred less than a year after its dedication. Unfortunately, the white statues of the angel Moroni tended to blend in with the sky on cloudy days and therefore seemed to disappear. This problem would likely be made even worse by the snowy landscape in Anchorage, Alaska. When President Gordon B. Hinckley visited Monticello on July 6, 1998, just before the dedication, he expressed the feeling that the Church should return to the golden statues.[25] Hence, the figure of Moroni delivered in October of that year for the Colonia Juārez Chihuahua Mexico Temple was gold. Then in December, a gold-colored statue was placed on the Anchorage Alaska Temple. Finally, on May 25, 1999, a seven-foot gold-leafed angel was substituted on the Monticello Utah Temple's spire.

The original three small temples (Monticello, Anchorage, and Colonia Juārez) all had a floor area of about 7,000 square feet and included just one room for presenting the endowment; this meant that a new session could begin only every two hours. Only a few weeks after the dedication of the Monticello Utah Temple, construction of a second generation of small temples commenced, beginning in Columbus, Ohio, and Spokane, Washington. Their plan was enlarged to about 11,000 square feet, adding a second ordinance room plus some other facilities, and enlarging the dressing room area; now sessions could begin about every hour and a quarter. With the announcement of these temples, as well as temples in such locations as the Minneapolis–St. Paul, Detroit, and Edmonton areas, it was apparent that these smaller structures would also be built in some larger centers of Church population. A third generation of these smaller temples, beginning with Columbia River, Washington, in 2001, enlarged the plan to about 16,000 square feet, further enhancing their efficiency. In light of this experience, two of the original three small temples were enlarged; only the Colonia Juārez Temple would remain unchanged.

Changing the angel Moroni statues on the Monticello Utah Temple (from white to gold). Courtesy of Robin Ramsey.

The Monticello Utah Temple was closed during most of 2002 for its renovation. A new celestial room was constructed on the north end of the temple, allowing a second endowment room to be created in the area of the former celestial room. The temple's floor area was enlarged to 11,225 square feet. The two-room sequence of presenting the endowment, originally developed for the St. Louis and Vernal Temples, was instituted at Monticello, allowing sessions to begin more frequently. When these changes were completed, there was another public open house, November 2–9, and the temple was rededicated November 17, 2002, once again by President Hinckley.

The first three small temples: (1) Larger Monticello Utah Temple. Courtesy of Intellectual Reserve, Inc.

(2) Anchorage Alaska Temple. Courtesy of Intellectual Reserve, Inc.

(3) Colonia Juárez Chihuahua Mexico Temple. Courtesy of Intellectual Reserve, Inc.

Legacy of the Monticello Utah Temple

President Gordon B. Hinckley announced the goal of having one hundred temples in service by the end of the year 2000. This goal was more than met—on December 17, 2000, the Church's 102nd temple was dedicated, in Porto Alegre, Brazil. Thirty-four, exactly one-third of all the Church's existing temples and almost all of the small variety, had been dedicated during that year alone. Within a decade of Monticello's dedication, over sixty of these smaller temples (having an area of less than 20,000 square feet) would be constructed. They would be found on nearly every continent.

Within a decade of Monticello's dedication, over sixty of these smaller temples would be constructed. They would be found on nearly every continent.

The Saints regarded some of these smaller temples as specific fulfillments of prophecy. Speaking at a conference at Grants Pass, Oregon, in 1924, for example, Elder Melvin J. Ballard of the Quorum of the Twelve declared that a temple would be built one day in the Rogue River Valley.[26] A small temple was dedicated at nearby Medford in 2000. Then when a chapel was dedicated in the Columbus area in 1991, the stake president emphasized the importance of temple attendance (at that time, requiring an overnight drive to Washington, D.C.), and prayed, "Help us to realize that as we attend more regularly, the temple could move closer, even to our doorsteps."[27] Another small temple, also dedicated in 2000, was built next door to this chapel.

Thus, the pattern of smaller temples, first seen in Monticello, Utah, spread to bless Latter-day Saints all over the world.

Monticello Utah Temple sign (right) and entrance (below). Courtesy of Intellectual Reserve, Inc. and Robin Ramsay.

Notes

1. Sheri L. Dew, *Gordon B. Hinckley: Go Forward with Faith* (Salt Lake City: Deseret Book, 1996), 325.
2. Meredith Romney, interview by Richard O. Cowan, November 17, 2006, in author's possession.
3. Meredith Romney, interview by Richard O. Cowan, November 17, 2006, in author's possession.
4. Dell Van Orden, "Inspiration Came for Smaller Temples on Trip to Mexico," *Church News*, August 1, 1998, 3 and 12.
5. Based on notes taken by Mona Cluff, wife of Chihuahua Mission president, at Chihuahua regional conference, March 13, 1998, typescript in Virginia H. Romney, "History of the Colonia Juarez Chihuahua Temple," (1999), 1:54–55, notes in author's possession.
6. Gordon B. Hinckley, "This Is a Day Long Looked Forward To," *Church News*, March 13, 1999, 7.
7. Gordon B. Hinckley, in Conference Report, October 1997, 68–69.
8. Dell Van Orden, "President Hinckley Dedicates the First of Smaller Temples," *Church News*, August 1, 1998, 3, 11.
9. Andrew Jenson, *Encyclopedic History of the Church* (Salt Lake City: Deseret News, 1941), 772–73.
10. San Juan Stake general minutes, November 25, 1894, Church History Library.
11. Van Orden, "Inspiration," 3, 12.
12. R. Scott Lloyd, "Ground Broken for the First of Church's New 'Small' Temples," *Church News*, November 22, 1997, 3.
13. Van Orden, "Inspiration," 12.
14. Chad S. Hawkins, *The First 100 Temples* (Salt Lake City: Deseret Book, 2001), 146.
15. Bill Boyle, "Statue of Angel Moroni Placed on Top of Temple," *Church News*, May 23, 1998, 4.
16. Van Orden, "President Hinckley Dedicates the First," 12.
17. Lloyd, "Monticello Temple Opens Doors to Public," *Church News*, July 18, 1998, 3
18. Lloyd, "20,000 Tour New Temple Prior to Its Dedication," *Church News*, July 25, 1998, 12.
19. R. Scott Lloyd, "20,000 Tour New Temple Prior to Its Dedication," *Church News*, July 25, 1998.
20. Van Orden, "President Hinckley Dedicates the First," 3, 11.
21. Van Orden, "President Hinckley Dedicates the First," 11.
22. Van Orden, "President Hinckley Dedicates the First," 3; Hawkins, *First 100 Temples*, 148.
23. Van Orden, "President Hinckley Dedicates the First," 11.
24. Van Orden, "President Hinckley Dedicates the First," 11.
25. Mark Shaffer, quoted in Virginia H. Romney and Richard O. Cowan, *The Colonia Juārez Temple: A Prophet's Vision* (Provo, UT: Religious Studies Center, Brigham Young University, 2009), 60.
26. "Promise Fulfilled," *Church News*, November 6, 1999, 16.
27. Hawkins, *First 100 Temples*, 164.

11 From Tabernacles to Temples

The Vernal Utah and Provo City Center Temples

Vernal Sunrise Aerial, by Alan Fullmer.

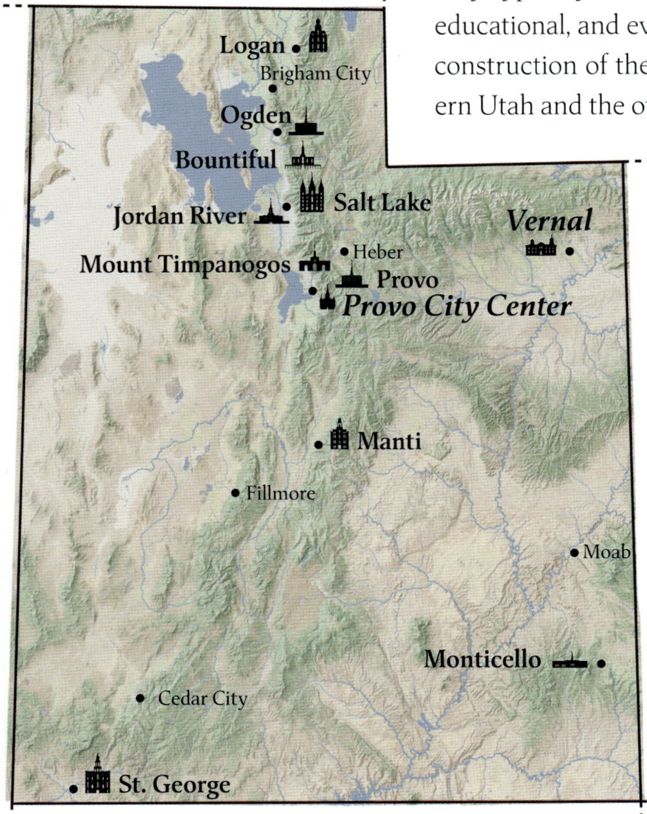

Utah temples as of 2000, including the Vernal Utah and Provo City Center Temples. Courtesy of Lee R. Cowan.

Two of Utah's temples are different from all others. They were constructed within the shells of earlier tabernacles and thus do not have the appearance of most other temples. Tabernacles were imposing buildings constructed in earlier decades at the heart of several Latter-day Saint communities to accommodate stake or multi-stake conferences and administration. In addition to their primary religious function, they typically also served as community centers, providing the setting for cultural, educational, and even political gatherings. Rather different circumstances led to the construction of these two unique temples, one located at Vernal in rural northeastern Utah and the other at Provo on the densely populated Wasatch Front.

The Vernal Utah Temple

The Saints in Northeastern Utah and Their Tabernacle

After the pioneers reached the Salt Lake Valley, three decades would pass before Latter-day Saint settlement commenced in the relatively isolated Uintah Basin of northeastern Utah. The first Church-sponsored colonists arrived in the basin in 1877 and began establishing small settlements in Ashley Valley. The winters were often quite harsh. Snows piled up, many animals froze to death, and food supplies were scarce. The settlements barely survived, and such hardships contributed to the rugged heritage of devoted determination among the Uintah Basin Saints.

Still, the settlements continued to grow. By 1887 the Latter-day Saint population in the area had passed one thousand and the Uintah Stake was organized with headquarters at Ashley Center (renamed Vernal when the post office was established there and incorporated in 1897). When areas of the Uintah Indian Reservation to the west were opened for non–Native American settlement in 1905, one of the last land rushes in the nation resulted as newcomers flocked to homestead.

For about a decade, stake leaders had been planning an adequate venue for conferences and other meetings.[1] In 1897 the tabernacle site selection committee chose a lot at the edge of town where it could be seen from the adjacent highway. The Church purchased the site from the Jacob Workman family for four hundred dollars; the family then donated the money to the building fund. Stake president Samuel Bennion asked T. T. Davies, an architect from Provo, to design the building. Within thirty days he provided preliminary plans for a building over one hundred feet long.

William H. Siddoway, a member of the high council, became the building overseer. Most of the labor was contributed by volunteers who put in full days on their farms or places of employment and then worked on the tabernacle at night, on weekends, or other free days. Excavation for the foundations was accomplished by horse-drawn

Dedication of the Uintah Stake Tabernacle, 1907. Courtesy of Church History Library.

scrapers and by men with picks and axes. The sandstone foundation blocks, quarried north of town, had to be large enough to support the brick walls, but small enough to be hauled in by wagon. Most blocks measured six by three by two and one-half feet. To provide structural support, workmen created large arches in the foundation under the building's north, west, and south entrances. All the lumber for heavy beams and finished woodwork was native pine brought from the surrounding mountains.

The bricks had to be laid three to five layers across so the walls would be stable and would support the roof. The bricks were of local red clay and were fired in the kilns of Abnar and Nick Swain. They donated one-fourth of the bricks outright and provided the rest at half their normal rate. Aaronic Priesthood young men were the hod carriers who took bricks and mortar up ramps in the scaffolding to the brick layers.

As the walls were nearing completion, William Cook of Vernal, who had been a builder of Brigham Young's Gardo House, drew the plans for finishing the building. Some beams for roof trusses were spliced without nails. The octagonal tower above the west facade was surmounted by a tin dome like those on the Kirtland and Nauvoo

Temples. Inside, the stand was on the east with entrances and a U-shaped balcony on the other three sides. The pine pillars supporting the balcony were painted to look like marble, and the pine pews were finished to have the appearance of oak. The seating capacity was about 1,800. The total cash outlay for the building was $37,058.15 (nearly a million dollars in the twenty-first century).[2]

In 1907 Church President Joseph F. Smith traveled to Vernal by train and buggy to dedicate the tabernacle as part of the two-day stake quarterly conference. An overflow congregation gathered reverently into the tabernacle on Saturday morning, August 24, for the opening session. The local newspaper reported, "No former religious gathering in the county has even approached this one. There were people present from all parts of the valley . . . to witness the ceremonies."[3] President Joseph F. Smith was the concluding speaker in the afternoon session. He commended the Saints for their sacrifice in building the tabernacle and then offered the prayer dedicating it to the Lord.

The conference continued the following day. During the Sunday morning session, President Smith spoke particularly to the youth, encouraging them to look forward to and prepare for temple marriages. He added that he "would not be surprised if the day would come when a temple would be built in your own midst here."[4] Probably none present realized how literally his prophetic words would be fulfilled.

For the next three-quarters of a century, the tabernacle was used mostly for stake quarterly conferences and other church meetings. In 1924 a sixty-foot lumber rear addition was added to house seminary classes. The tabernacle also served a variety of other functions including high school and seminary graduations, Easter and Christmas pageants, weddings, funerals, and musical performances.

Still, by the 1970s the need for the tabernacle was lessening. Newer stake centers nearby could accommodate more people for conferences. They also had classrooms for the Church's growing instructional programs, as well as cultural halls to serve dance, drama, athletic, and other activities—all facilities which the tabernacle lacked. Furthermore, the tabernacle's heating system was not adequate for the Uintah Basin's cold winters, and there were no functioning restrooms, nor air-conditioning. In all, the Church had erected about a hundred tabernacles, but as they increasingly could not accommodate the Church's expanding programs, the majority had been torn down.[5] The Saints in Vernal naturally wondered about the future of their own historic and beloved tabernacle.

On June 20, 1983, the Vernal Utah Stake was divided to form the Vernal Utah Glines and Vernal Utah Uintah Stakes. The Glines stake received jurisdiction over the tabernacle, but this was the last stake conference held there. When the adjoining stake center was remodeled, heat and water were permanently cut off from the tabernacle, and the Church Physical Facilities department considered the building now to be unsafe, discouraging further meetings there. The property was even briefly put up for sale, but no suitable buyers appeared. By now all the stakes in the area had their own stake centers and thus did not need the old tabernacle.[6]

The Unexpected Announcement

Between 1984 and 1986, President Gayle McKeachnie and his counselors in the Glines stake presidency confidentially submitted proposals to general Church leaders about the possibility of building a temple within the walls of the old tabernacle. At this time the nearest temple was in Provo, so people in the Vernal area had to travel over 150 miles to get there. Because the roads through the mountains were often icy during the winter, travel on them was quite dangerous. The First Presidency ultimately rejected the proposal for a temple and asked for other ideas for the building. However, the stake presidency decided to bide their time.[7]

Stake leaders again considered renovating the tabernacle in 1988, but the million-dollar cost was too great for the building's projected limited use. Four years later, Laird Hartman succeeded McKeachnie as president of the Glines stake. When the stake presidency began receiving requests from various groups to use the tabernacle for activities they believed were not appropriate for a dedicated building, they were prompted once again to raise the question of the tabernacle's future.

On Friday, November 5, 1993, President Hartman received a startling phone call from the Presiding Bishopric indicating that Presidents Hinckley and Monson, counselors to Church President Benson, would come to Vernal one week later to consider what should be done with the tabernacle and inviting him to show them through the building. Following the tour on November 12, President Hinckley quipped, "I don't know what we are going to do with this beautiful old building. It's kind of like me—its bolts are getting old and rusty."[8] Only twelve days later (fittingly, the day before Thanksgiving), President Hinckley called President Hartman stating that "after much prayer and consideration," the First Presidency was "impressed to renovate the tabernacle into a temple" and wanted to know if the stake president felt that "the people in the area would support that decision." President Hartman assured him that "the great majority of people would rejoice in this decision and that we would support it with all our hearts."[9] Church leaders asked him not to discuss this matter with anybody. All the other stake presidents in the area received the news a month and a half later in a meeting at Church headquarters on January 16. This would be the first time an older building would be rebuilt into a temple, and at that time it would be the only temple constructed of red brick rather than the more traditional off-white building materials.

Finally, in a letter to the Uintah Basin area Saints dated February 9, 1994, the First Presidency announced the following:

> Dear Brothers and Sisters,
>
> As you are aware, there has been much discussion over a period of many years concerning what to do with the old Uintah Tabernacle in Vernal. The building has not been occupied for a long period and is in serious disrepair.
>
> There is much sentiment attached to the building. However, extensive engineering and architectural study has indicated that it would be extremely costly to restore and that no ecclesiastical need exists for it.

Under this proposal the temple needs of the faithful Saints in the area will be met and the exterior of the old building will be preserved as a memorial to the faithful people who built it with much sacrifice almost a century ago.

> After giving prayerful consideration to the matter and following extensive study, we have concluded to use the shell of the building, restoring its original outside appearance, and creating within it, a beautiful temple. Additional needed space will be gained by excavating the area around the east end of the Tabernacle. By so doing the original aspect of the historic structure will be preserved.
>
> Under this proposal the temple needs of the faithful Saints in the area will be met and the exterior of the old building will be preserved as a memorial to the faithful people who built it with much sacrifice almost a century ago.
>
> We have discussed this proposal with the stake presidents of the area who have expressed their endorsement of it. We hope that it will be warmly received by members of the Church and the entire community.[10]

This letter was read in meetings throughout the area on Sunday, February 13. The surprising and wonderful news was received with excitement and tears of gratitude.[11]

Transforming the Tabernacle into a Temple

Just one week before the First Presidency's official announcement, the Temple Department turned to Roger Jackson of the firm of FFKR Architects to plan and supervise this momentous and unprecedented project. Immediately after he had received his master of architecture degree from the University of Utah in 1984, Jackson had gone to work with FFKR. Important projects included the remodeling of various school buildings and the expansion of the Utah State Capitol. He had become the lead architect for the remodel of the Hotel Utah into the Joseph Smith Memorial Building. This experience with older buildings would be valuable in Vernal.

Vernal Utah Temple. Courtesy of Intellectual Reserve, Inc.

When asked if it was a challenge to fit a temple into the tabernacle, Jackson responded with an emphatic "Yes!" The original thought was to have two stand-alone endowment rooms, but the flow would have been difficult within the tabernacle's walls. Instead, a new concept of "two-stage endowment room" was designed, allowing progression from one room to the other.[12] This plan was adopted for the Vernal Utah Temple and the St. Louis Missouri Temple, which was also under construction. Only the first room in the sequence would need projection equipment, and this plan could accommodate as many patrons as two independent fully equipped rooms. Ultimately, this two-stage endowment room would be commonly used in smaller temples throughout the Church.

In 1999 Roger Jackson would also become the lead architect in rebuilding the historic Nauvoo Temple. He received the same assignment for the 2005–7 renovation of the iconic Salt Lake Tabernacle. He remarked that these latter projects were "not once in a lifetime but once in ten thousand lifetimes experiences," marveling that he had two of them.

Preparations were also moving forward in Vernal. Local Church leaders organized a special open house so members of the community could visit the tabernacle one last time before its transformation began. During this five-day event, April 28 through May 2, 1994, more than 18,000 interested people walked through the building. There was never any opposition expressed from community leaders or residents regarding the new temple project. Where possible, equipment and furnishings were removed from the tabernacle. Fifty pews were set aside to be used in the future temple. Other items were donated to local historical societies and museums.

Gordon B. Hinckley with groundbreaking shovel at the Vernal Utah Temple. Courtesy of Kathleen Murphy Irving.

As groundbreaking approached, the weather had been showery. Saturday, May 13, 1995, however, dawned brisk but sunny. President Hinckley, who had become President of the Church just two months earlier, presided. He remarked that the approximately twelve thousand persons who had gathered for the groundbreaking were "a tremendous tribute to the faith of the Latter-day Saints in the work that goes on in the Houses of the Lord." He acknowledged that if the Church had thought of tearing down the tabernacle, "there would be a great shout go out across this entire valley." But the Church didn't want it "used for profane purposes of any kind. It was sacred. It had been dedicated." Therefore, "members will feel deeply grateful and profoundly touched by that which [will be] created out of this historic, dedicated, sacred structure. It will be beautiful."

It "will become a great spiritual center."[13] President Hinckley's second counselor, James E. Faust, affirmed that he "felt a special spirit and spiritual legacy of the devotion of the Saints who in their great poverty erected this magnificent building."[14] Elder W. Eugene Hansen of the Seventy, chair of the Temple Department, wondered "if any of those hardy souls who labored so diligently to construct this beautiful edifice ever had an inkling that one day it would be a temple."[15] President Hinckley offered the prayer dedicating the site. Then, at its southeast corner, the visitors from Church headquarters, local leaders, and others took their turn formally breaking ground for the Vernal Temple, which would "interlock pioneer craftsmanship with modern technology."[16]

Baptismal font, Vernal Utah Temple. Courtesy of Kathleen Murphy Irving.

First, the existing walls had to be stabilized by removing the inner wythe or layer of bricks and then spraying strong shotcrete onto the wall and around steel reinforcing rods, forming a layer several inches thick. Because all damaged bricks in the temple's exterior would be replaced, a source of period bricks was sought. Only at the pioneer-era Reader home were bricks with matching markings found, so they probably had come from the same clay pit and kiln and would match precisely. The owner, Nick J. Meagher, was a member of another faith. He had planned to tear down the old home but agreed to donate it to the Church. For the next two months, volunteers painstakingly dismantled the structure and cleaned sixteen thousand bricks, more than enough to restore the temple's walls. During this same time, the seminary addition to the east was removed, and the new annex was being constructed. The original plan was for it to be entirely underground, but when water was found at a depth of fourteen feet, the annex was raised to a depth of only nine feet. Thus, the upper ten feet of its block wall was above ground and was covered with a veneer of new bricks that closely matched the old.

With the original walls stabilized, the next step was to excavate inside for the baptistry. This required going down to twenty-two feet below ground level in an area

Dome placed on the Vernal Utah Temple. Courtesy of Kathleen Murphy Irving.

measuring forty by fifty feet. To keep ground water out, the floor and walls of this area were surrounded by a heavy-duty membrane, like a giant bathtub. The plan had been for the excavating equipment to be brought in through an opening created in the east wall, but this would delay construction on the annex for several months until work in the baptistry was completed. However, when the arch in the north wall was uncovered, it was wide enough for the machinery to pass through, thus avoiding the delay. Steel columns and horizontal beams were next erected within the former tabernacle to support the three reinforced concrete floors.

In mid-July 1996, the steel font was placed in the baptistry. The supporting oxen and exterior shroud were added the following spring, being the first in the Church to be made of fiberglass. For nearly two decades they had been part of an exhibit in the South Visitors' Center on Temple Square in Salt Lake City and became available for use in Vernal after the exhibit was changed. LaVar Walgren had pioneered the process of producing sculptures with fiberglass. He studied living oxen to assure that his reproductions would be realistic. The oxen and font had a "cultured marble" finish created by coating their surface with epoxy and ground marble.[17]

During the summer of 1996, the old roof was removed, the five original timber trusses were reinforced with steel, and the building was covered with a new green slate roof. The original plan had been to simply renovate the single twenty-four-foot tower atop the tabernacle's western facade. When President Gordon B. Hinckley was in Vernal for the groundbreaking, however, he expressed the concern that the steeple of the neighboring stake center would appear taller than the temple, so asked the architects to propose a new design. The decision was to add a thirty-two-foot tower topped by the angel Moroni to the east end and to reproduce the west tower using new, lighter materials. In early September 1995, therefore, the old tower was removed, and Vernal City made it into a gazebo in Ashley Valley Community Park. Chad Munns of Garland, Utah, received the contract to produce the new towers. He had fabricated many steeples for Latter-day Saint chapels but never for a temple. He would make them of Reynobond, stiff plastic laminated with a thin layer of aluminum. He calculated that he needed thirty sheets of this material, but the manufacturer indicated they had only twenty-four on hand and that no more would be produced in time to meet his schedule. Munns asked them to double-check by physically counting the sheets; they corrected their count to thirty-two. He bought them all. When he had finished the project, he had only a half sheet left over. The domes were fashioned of copper, which would weather to a dark green color.[18]

Pews saved from the tabernacle were stripped down to bare wood. They then were refinished, upholstered, and used in the temple chapel.

LaVar Walgren fabricated the eight-foot fiberglass statue of Moroni. The towers, midroof ventilation cupola, and Moroni were set in place atop the temple on Thursday, September 26, 1996. There was no public announcement, but the news spread quickly by word of mouth. An estimated crowd of four thousand interested observers filled the surrounding streets, singing hymns as they watched.[19] For the first time, the angel was simply painted gold rather than being gold-leafed. This was an experiment to test the weathering durability of this more economical alternative at the time the Church would be building scores of temples worldwide. The results were not as good as hoped. Therefore, during two weeks in February 1997, the angel was taken back off the temple, returned to Salt Lake City, thoroughly stripped down to the fiberglass surface, and then covered with 1,250 three-inch squares of 23 carat gold leaf. After the statue was back in place, even observers from a distance could discern the difference in brilliance: "it just looked more heavenly."[20]

Windows were installed late in 1996, enclosing the building so work could go forward during the winter. Most had patterned glass that afforded seclusion but also admitted natural light. The celestial room had eighteen windows; patrons were struck by the amount of light in this room.

Another striking feature of the building is the grand staircase at the east end of the former tabernacle. After three of the four newel post caps in the building were gone, Lloyd Hess was impressed to save the remaining one. It was in excellent condition so was refurbished to grace the banister at the base of the new stairway. A beautiful stained glass window was placed in the opening above the stairs. It depicted Christ as the Good Shepherd and was created by an unknown artist for the Mount Olivet Methodist Episcopal Church of Hollywood. The Church of Jesus Christ of Latter-day Saints purchased that building in 1937, and for decades it served as the Hollywood Ward chapel. When the old structure was torn down to make way for a more adequate meetinghouse, the window was saved for possible temple use. In Vernal, it was positioned so it appears at the end of the upper hallway serving the sealing rooms.

Pews saved from the tabernacle were stripped down to bare wood. They then were refinished, upholstered, and used in the temple chapel. A marker on the temple's exterior bears two dates—1907 and 1997—the years when the building was dedicated as a tabernacle and then as a temple.

Vernal Utah Temple brochure. Courtesy of the Church History Library.

Open House and Dedication

The open house took place in October 1997. Immediate neighbors and then VIPs were invited to come first. An estimated 118,700 visited during the two-week public open house from the 18th through the 25th. Approximately 25,000 volunteers assisted. A display on temple service and on the history of the Vernal Temple was set up in the cultural hall of the neighboring Glines Stake Center; workers connected that building with the temple by walkways enclosed with tent-like covers to help visitors reach the temple with cleaner shoes. Almost constant music was provided near the temple's entrance by various groups including ward choirs, children's choruses, quartets, and even family choirs. For example, descendants of William B. Smart, the stake president when the tabernacle was dedicated in 1907, scheduled a family reunion on the last day of the open house; a Smart family choir was one of the groups performing that day.

Following the open house, volunteers thoroughly cleaned the temple. It was then dedicated in eleven sessions from Sunday, November 2, through Tuesday, November 4 1997. President Hinckley presided and offered the dedicatory prayer: "We are grateful for this beautiful new structure which utilizes the historic tabernacle built by

Provo Tabernacle around 1885. Courtesy of Richard O. Cowan.

Thy people nearly a century ago. The original tabernacle came of a great spirit of faith and sacrifice on the part of those Saints who settled in this area. It was built as an offering unto Thee, and was held in the affections of the people long after it was used as a house of worship. Now that old and much-loved building has become the center piece of a new and beautiful House of the Lord. It has a quiet luster all its own."[21] He conducted the cornerstone ceremony in connection with the first dedicatory session on Sunday morning at 8 a.m. A large crowd had gathered at the southeast corner of the temple even before sunrise on this brisk fall morning to be part of this event.

Even though Lloyd Hess, the project manager in Vernal, had insisted that building the new temple in the shell of the former tabernacle had been less expensive than starting over and building from scratch,[22] many predicted that the Church would not undertake such a task ever again. Still, a devastating fire in Provo, Utah, just over a decade later would lead to a similar project once again.

The Provo City Center Temple

Another Historic Tabernacle

Fort Utah was established on the banks of the Provo River in 1849. Soon the settlement expanded beyond the fort and came to be known as Provo. By the early 1880s, the growing community needed an adequate place to worship.

The Provo Tabernacle was designed by William Harrison Folsom, one of the finest Latter-day Saint architects of the nineteenth century. He was born in Portsmouth, New Hampshire, on March 25, 1815. He worked with his father in a construction contracting business until he became a Latter-day Saint and moved to Nauvoo. He was sustained as Church architect in 1861 and became an assistant to Truman O. Angell Sr.[23] Folsom was an architect and construction superintendent on important projects throughout the territory—including the Salt Lake Theater, Salt Lake Tabernacle, and Manti Temple. He was asked to pattern the new tabernacle in Provo "after the Salt Lake Assembly Hall." The Provo Tabernacle's architecture was Eastlake or late Victorian, noted for many colors and a variety of design details. The building's interior hardly had a plain surface, even having wallpaper on the ceiling. The tabernacle reflected Gothic Revival architecture, which was popular during the late nineteenth century; the upper windows and corner towers have been described as pioneer Gothic.

Construction began in 1883, and the first major meeting in the yet unfinished building convened two years later—a memorial service for the late Ulysses S. Grant, eighteenth president of the United States. The audience of two thousand people sat

The Provo Tabernacle in 1997. Courtesy of Intellectual Reserve, Inc.

Interior of the Provo Tabernacle after restoration, 1986. Courtesy of the *Deseret News/Church News.*

The ornate interior was beautified by heavy ingrain wallpaper, ceiling panels, grained oak woodwork, and three chandeliers, "each holding twenty-four incandescent bulbs."

in temporary seats, as the unfurnished tabernacle did not yet have permanent floors, pews, doors, or windows. It continued to be completed and used in various stages.[24]

Because of the antipolygamy raids of the 1880s, many Latter-day Saint men—including some Church leaders—went into hiding to avoid arrest. For this same reason, five general conferences convened at locations away from Salt Lake City: both the April and October conferences of 1885 met in Logan, and it was rumored that the April 1886 conference was going to be held at the new tabernacle at Provo.[25] While the building would still not be completed, construction accelerated to accommodate the large crowds sure to gather at the upcoming spring conference. After a race against time, the 56th Annual General Conference was held in the nearly completed tabernacle on April 4, 1886. Large crowds gathered to the point that the tabernacle overflowed and "hundreds of persons surrounded the building." The October conference that year convened in Coalville, Summit County, Utah. The April conference of 1887 met once again in the Provo Tabernacle.[26]

While these conferences in Provo were a success, the tabernacle suffered serious financial setbacks, causing the building to remain unfinished for several ensuing years. On March 6, 1895, Abraham O. Smoot—former president of the Utah Stake and perhaps the most vocal champion for the tabernacle—passed away. His son Reed, a future member of the Quorum of the Twelve Apostles and United States senator, became a member of the Utah Stake presidency and helped to complete the struggle to raise the hundred thousand dollars (about $2.8 million in today's money) needed to finish the tabernacle. It was finally dedicated on April 16, 1898, by

President George Q. Cannon, first counselor in the First Presidency. The ornate interior was beautified by heavy ingrain wallpaper, ceiling panels, grained oak woodwork, and three chandeliers, "each holding twenty-four incandescent bulbs."

Due to structural deficiencies and winters of heavy snow, eventually the central tower began to cause the roof to sag. As a result, the upper octagonal part of the tower was removed in 1907—a difficult project for the period. Because this did not completely solve the problem, the remaining square base of the tower with its promenade walk was removed and the central part of the roof rebuilt in 1917. In this latter year, stained glass replaced the semifrosted glass in the windows, perhaps to help compensate for the loss of the tower. These changes significantly altered the exterior design as well as the interior ambient lighting.

A variety of community events took place in the Provo Tabernacle, including graduation ceremonies for Brigham Young University.[27] It also provided the setting for various civic meetings and hosted a variety of cultural activities, including lyceums and concerts. Still, over the years, stake conferences were the most common meetings held in the tabernacle.

From time to time, the tabernacle had needed maintenance and upgrades. A major renovation beginning in 1982 restored the interior to its original appearance, including treating woodwork to bring out its natural grain. Following this latest upgrade, the tabernacle was rededicated on September 21, 1986, with a capacity crowd present. President Benson presided and spoke at the meeting. "Husbands and wives must love and cherish one another. Selfish attitudes must be overcome. Faults must be overlooked. Contention must cease. Husbands and wives must be true and loyal to each other and to the sacred covenant of marriage." President Benson asked President Monson, his second counselor, to offer the dedicatory prayer. In his prayer,

The Provo Tabernacle on fire, December 2010. Courtesy of Shawn Beardall and the Church History Library (left) and Trevor Christensen (right).

Provo Tabernacle fire. Courtesy of Shawn Beardall and the Church History Library.

President Monson acknowledged, "We feel the spiritual influence of those who have preceded us in standing at this pulpit. Their lives become a living witness and testimony of thy work and we want to dedicate our lives that we might be true to the pioneer tradition of this building."[28]

An event in December 2010 would change the tabernacle forever. On Thursday evening the 16th, a full orchestra, members of the Millennial Choir, and several outstanding soloists gathered for a dress rehearsal of *Gloria*, a musical production by noted Latter-day Saint composer Lex de Azevedo that features events surrounding the birth of the Savior. The usual "church configuration" of the stand was modified to accommodate the production. Large lightweight arches had the appearance of stone. The hall was decorated with flowers, wreaths, garlands, and evergreen trees with twinkling lights. Even the building's stained glass windows were backlit by BYU Television, which planned to broadcast the production through its worldwide facilities. "It had the feel of old Jerusalem, with the modern-day Christmas. Just gorgeous. It really felt celestial," Kim Egginton, the event's producer, reflected. "I can't imagine that the . . . Provo Tabernacle could ever have looked more beautiful. . . . Everything just shone."[29]

During the night a fire broke out in the attic. By 3:30 a.m. flames broke through the roof, and at about 6 a.m. the entire roof collapsed with a thundering roar. The fire continued to burn for over a day and a half, leaving only the exterior brick walls standing. Normally such walls are toppled promptly as a safety precaution, but on this occasion the firemen inexplicably were instructed to leave them standing.

On Saturday afternoon, LeGrand "Buddy" Richards, president of the Provo South Stake, within whose boundaries the tabernacle was located, was among those taken by fire officials to visit the still-smoldering building. As he looked through one of the front windows, he could see a reprint of Harry Anderson's painting *The Second Coming*. He recalled that he could "clearly see the image of the Savior among the charred rubble." Even the wall that had supported the picture was gone. Nearly all of the material goods within the structure, some of significant value, had been destroyed, but that image stood as a clear reminder. The painting didn't make it through the ordeal without damage; it had been charred all around the edges except for the image portraying the Savior with outstretched arms. To Richards it seemed to say, "You know whose house this is. . . . What's it to you if I want to remodel it?" Immediately, Richards's spirit was lifted, and he was reminded "why there remains great reason to hope, even in the midst of smoking rubble." He left the experience confident that the Lord would yet do something spectacular there. He reminded his stake members, "Our faith does not reside in the house, but in its owner, and if He decides it is time to remodel His house or our lives, we should find great reason to rejoice and be grateful."[30]

Rebuilding the Tabernacle

John Emery, a project manager employed by Jacobsen Construction of Salt Lake City for a dozen years, received an order to head to Provo Friday morning while the building was still engulfed in flames. His assignment was to cooperate with the firefighters and to give attention to possibly preserving any parts of the building. Once the fire was put out, an immediate goal was to stabilize the brick walls of the tabernacle, making it safe for investigators to go inside to look for clues. On Monday, December 20, Jacobsen Construction began installing steel bracing around the building to preserve the brick walls as completely as possible.[31]

Less than a month after the fire, workers comb through burned debris for anything salvageable. Courtesy of Intellectual Reserve, Inc.

Like so many others, architect Roger Jackson was shocked by news of the Provo Tabernacle fire. During that weekend, at the urging of an architectural historian friend, he contacted Church officials with whom he had been working on the Vernal Temple and other projects and urged them not to allow the building to be torn down. Although the flames had gutted the wooden interior, the brick walls had likely remained sound. He reminded them that "we had done the same thing to the Uintah Stake Tabernacle except that we

The exterior walls of the Provo Tabernacle are secured for the construction of the Provo City Center Temple. Courtesy of Intellectual Reserve, Inc. All rights reserved.

They concluded, "The masonry system is in very good condition. We feel very strongly that this building can be renovated to its original grandeur."

didn't use fire but tore everything out on our own." He was able to display a photo of the future Vernal Temple when there were only gutted brick walls and point out that enough remained in Provo to allow the structure to be rebuilt. Emery invited Jackson to examine the brick walls with him because he valued his "knowledge of old masonry."[32] "After preliminary analysis" only four days after the fire, they concluded, "The masonry system is in very good condition. We feel very strongly that this building can be renovated to its original grandeur."[33]

Church leaders were eager to proceed with this project and within a few days appointed Roger Jackson of FFKR to be the architect. He would work closely with the Special Projects Department of the Church.

Andy Kirby, a native of Provo who had earned a degree in civil engineering at BYU, became the Church's site project manager. He worked closely with Emily Utt, Historic Sites curator with the Church History Department. She had received a bachelor of arts in both history and religious studies with a minor in sociology at Case Western Reserve University in Cleveland, Ohio. Church officials needed to know what had survived the fire. Kirby and Utt spent endless hours sifting through the tabernacle's remains. "We wanted to look through every inch of debris," Utt recalled. Andy remembered seeing Emily covered with soot as she sifted through buckets of material. This work was done during the winter. "It was really cold," she reflected. Even four or five months after the fire, they uncovered items encased in ice formed from the water used to fight the flames. The found a wide variety of items, including newel posts, pieces of railing or wooden molding, hardware from doors, hundreds of nails, and much more. In some cases, the fire had uncovered features hidden for decades. It burned away layers of later paint or remodeling to reveal original colors of paint or designs of wallpaper. The goal was to re-create a basic floor plan as well as detailed plans for specific features. "My favorite discovery," Emily Utt concluded, was some original stenciling that had been hidden behind two temporary walls, some mechanical equipment, and four layers of wallpaper—all burned away by the fire. The investigators took photographs and had architects prepare careful drawings of these items that would provide keys to an understanding of the building's original architecture and character.

They spent an interesting six months meeting with the architect and others, exploring possible options for what could be done with the Provo Tabernacle. Initial discussions during the winter and spring of 2011 had focused on restoring the Provo structure as a tabernacle. Several civic organizations and many residents in the community looked forward to its possible return as a venue for cultural as well as religious events. During June of that year, however, these plans changed. President Monson and Presiding Bishop H. David Burton confidentially discussed the possibility of rebuilding the tabernacle as a temple.

As had become the custom in recent years, in his opening remarks at the October 2011 general conference President Monson announced plans for several new temples. "First, may I mention that no Church-built facility is more important than a temple," the prophet emphasized. "Temples are places where relationships are sealed together to last through the eternities. We are grateful for all the many temples across the world and for the blessing they are in the lives of our members." Then he continued, "Late last year the Provo Tabernacle in Utah County was seriously damaged by a terrible fire. This wonderful building, much beloved by generations of Latter-day Saints, was left with only the exterior walls standing. After careful study, we have decided to rebuild it with full preservation and restoration of the exterior, to become the second temple of the Church in the city of Provo. The existing Provo Temple is one of the busiest in the Church, and a second temple there will accommodate the increasing numbers of faithful Church members who are attending the temple from Provo and the surrounding communities."[34] This announcement brought an audible gasp in the Conference Center and an outburst of emotions some forty miles to the south.

This announcement brought an audible gasp in the Conference Center and an outburst of emotions some forty miles to the south.

A great deal of planning had preceded President Monson's momentous announcement. A Church press release indicated "church leaders have worked with architects, engineers and historical experts to determine the future of the building." The new structure will include "a complete restoration of the original exterior," including even the tall central spire that had been gone for nearly a century.[35] With careful planning, architect Roger Jackson was able to fit most ordinance facilities into the historic building. Because plans called for restoring the tabernacle's exterior to its familiar appearance (of course with the addition of the original tall central spire), there were to be no above-ground additions to the building. Therefore, some of the space needed for a temple would have to be below the surface. Dressing rooms would be on a lower level to the north, and underground parking was planned on the south. The baptistry would be on the lower level directly below the east end of the tabernacle. The temple's chapel and two endowment instruction rooms, with one hundred sixteen seats each, would be on the ground floor. Temple patrons would begin their endowment experience in one or the other of these rooms before ascending the spiral stairs in one of the temple's corner towers to the second floor. They would then complete the endowment in the single large instruction room at the east end of that floor. A new session could begin once every hour. The celestial room and five sealing rooms were also on this upper floor.

The First Presidency instructed that the temple's interior should reflect elements of the tabernacle's original architecture—Eastlake Victorian on the main floor and pioneer Gothic on the second. The architect therefore examined objects which had survived the tabernacle fire and studied the interior of the Manti Temple, another building designed by William H. Folsom. The goal was to imagine how Folsom might have designed the Provo Tabernacle as a temple in the 1880s and then design the new structure accordingly. The architect also incorporated many specific features of the former tabernacle into the new temple. Newel posts and railings from the tabernacle's rostrum and details of the balcony are seen in the temple's grand staircase. The tabernacle's original elliptical ceiling is reproduced in the upper endowment room. The intricate Victorian stenciling, discovered following the fire, are featured in the brides' room. Before the production of *Gloria*, the tabernacle's pulpit had been

Provo Tabernacle shell on stilts. Courtesy of Church Newsroom/Intellectual Reserve, Inc.

removed from the podium and placed in storage; it therefore escaped destruction during the fire and was used in the temple chapel.

Construction Begins

Ground was broken by Elder Jeffrey R. Holland of the Quorum of the Twelve on a beautiful Saturday morning, May 12, 2012. He believed that the faithful 5,600 who had crowded onto the site was the largest group that had ever or would ever gather at that place. Elder Cecil O. Samuelson, Emeritus General Authority and president of Brigham Young University, rejoiced in "the rebirth of the iconic Provo Tabernacle, literally rising from the ashes of a horrible fire to become a temple of the Lord."[36] He insisted that a "BYU education is really not complete nor has it reached its heaven-intended potential unless it is joined with a consistent pattern of temple worship and service." He therefore felt it was fitting that the campus "be bracketed on the north-east and southwest by houses of the Lord."[37]

Elder Holland acknowledged the Utah Valley Saints' faithfulness. Speaking of the tabernacle, he asserted that "no other structure in this county has been such an integral part of the religious and civic life here." Therefore, he was grateful that the Brethren made their "inspired decision truly, to build this temple out of the ashes of this beloved tabernacle." He then offered the prayer dedicating "already sacred ground for an even more sacred purpose."[38] Ground was then broken using gold shovels taken from a rack constructed with timbers salvaged from the tabernacle.

Jacobsen Construction received the contract to rebuild the tabernacle, and John Emery became their senior project manager. Plans called for some temple facilities

The baptismal font under construction, Provo City Center Temple, January 2014. Courtesy of Intellectual Reserve, Inc.

Placing the statue of the angel Moroni was not announced publicly, but about a thousand people gathered to witness the event.

to occupy two levels beneath the historic tabernacle. Excavating for this basement directly beneath the original brick walls while preserving them intact posed "a significant challenge." The original lime mortar was soft, so the walls would probably not have survived the digging. Furthermore, they would likely have crumbled easily in an earthquake. How could the walls be preserved? Andy Kirby believed the solution came through following spiritual promptings which resulted in "an engineering construction marvel."[39] This plan would unfold dramatically during the latter half of 2012 and first half of the following year. The first major step was to reinforce the walls by lining them on the inside with reinforced concrete several inches thick. Piles were then driven ninety feet into the ground, some inside the walls and others next to them just outside. Each pair of piles was connected by a short steel beam that would support the walls above, an estimated total of 6.8 million pounds, while dirt was excavated below them. By the early spring of 2013, the tabernacle's shell appeared to be supported on stilts in midair.

The construction phase then began with pouring concrete for basement floors and walls. This provided a permanent new foundation for the walls, permitting removal of most of the piles. Once they were out of the way, the new temple could be constructed within the tabernacle's shell. The first steel beam was put into place on August 20, and the steel framework was "topped out" when the steel skeleton of the tall center tower was lifted into place on December 5, 2013.

Stained-glass window, Provo City Center Temple. Courtesy of Intellectual Reserve, Inc.

Brides' room, Provo City Center Temple. Courtesy of Intellectual Reserve, Inc.

This is the only temple in which the familiar "Holiness to the Lord" is proclaimed in stained glass.

Above: Sealing room, Provo City Center Temple. Left: Stained glass window. Courtesy of Intellectual Reserve, Inc.

Detail of stained glass window of Christ holding a lamb. Courtesy of Church Newsroom/Intellectual Reserve, Inc.

Placing the statue of the angel Moroni typically represented a major milestone in temple construction. This occasion in Provo was not announced publicly, perhaps because the temple was located on a major thoroughfare. Still, about a thousand people had gathered on the afternoon of March 31, 2014, to witness the event. As a large overhead crane lifted the figure into place atop the center tower, the gathered throng sang "An Angel from on High" and "I Love to See the Temple." During the summer, the roof was completed—of fireproof and durable slate rather than the original wooden shingles. Thus, the temple began to take on its completed appearance.

Since 1917, beautiful stained glass windows had been a beloved feature of the Provo Tabernacle. These would be restored in the new temple. In 1995 and 1996 the windows had been thoroughly cleaned and repaired as needed. The same local company who had done this work now received the contract to create the new windows. Fortunately, they had made detailed drawings of each window. While most of the new windows were recreations of those which had existed before, some, including ceilings in the brides' room and celestial room, were new. Another outstanding addition was the transom above the main ground-floor entrance; this is the only temple in which the familiar "Holiness to the Lord" is proclaimed in stained glass.

The temple's interior was also progressing. Several recent temples presented the endowment in a series of two rooms. In many cases, murals on the walls of the first

Above: Provo City Center Temple. Left: Three-story staircase inside the temple. Courtesy of Church Newsroom/Intellectual Reserve, Inc.

Provo City Center Temple cornerstone ceremony with Kristen Oaks and Dallin H. Oaks. Courtesy of Church Newsroom/Intellectual Reserve, Inc.

The temple was dedicated in three sessions on a beautiful spring day.

room depicted landscapes typical of the area where the temple was located. Murals for the two main floor instruction rooms of the Provo City Center Temple, however, set a new pattern. Each depicted scenes from the creation, the Garden of Eden, and the present world. By late fall, the temple was furnished and ready for dedication.

Dedicatory Events

Elder Steven J. Lund, who was the executive chairman of NuSkin Enterprises as well as a former mission president, Area Seventy, and future Young Men general president, chaired the committee responsible for the open house, cultural celebration, and logistics related to the dedication. Because of the Provo Tabernacle's historical significance and because thousands of Brigham Young University students and local Saints had fond memories of the building, Church leaders anticipated a greater-than-usual interest in the tabernacle's being rebuilt as a temple and scheduled an unusually long two-month open house. They were not disappointed. More than 800,000 persons attended the open house early in 2016. There were special tours for young women and their mothers on Sunday mornings when they could visit the brides' room, which could not be part of the normal itinerary. As individuals visited the beautifully restored building, they experienced countless special experiences or "tender mercies" (1 Nephi 1:20). The cultural celebration was staged in the Marriott Center

Right: Celestial room, Provo City Center Temple. Courtesy of Intellectual Reserve, Inc.

on the BYU campus on the Saturday evening before the temple's dedication. Some five thousand youth participated. The hour-long program focused on the revered Tabernacle and its story. The Lord's promise "to give unto them beauty for ashes" (Isaiah 61:3) became the inspired theme.

The temple was dedicated in three sessions on a beautiful spring day, Sunday, March 20, 2016. Presiding was Elder Dallin H. Oaks, a senior member of the Quorum of the Twelve and native of Provo. Proceedings were carried to stake centers throughout Utah. In his dedicatory prayer, Elder Oaks expressed gratitude for "the members of Thy Church whose faithful tithes and offerings have made possible the extensive restoration of this honored stake tabernacle that we now present unto thee as Thy house." He then petitioned blessings for "all who come within these walls that they may come in worthiness and participate with joy and understanding of the great teachings and ordinances and blessings of This house." The prayer asked for blessings upon all parts of the temple "and that Thy Spirit will ever be present to enlighten those who are present here."[40]

When the original Provo Temple was dedicated in 1972, it had become the 15th operating temple in the Church. Interestingly and significantly, the Provo City Center Temple became the 150th functioning temple. Hence, during the four decades between the dedications of these two neighboring temples there had been precisely a tenfold increase in the number of temples worldwide.

Notes

1. Kathleen M. Irving and John D. Barton, *From Tabernacle to Temple* (Vernal, UT: S. T. Tabernacle Enterprises, 1998), 2–6.
2. Irving and Barton, *From Tabernacle to Temple*, 7–19.
3. *Vernal Express*, August 30, 1907, quoted in Irving and Barton, *From Tabernacle to Temple*, 21.
4. Irving and Barton, *From Tabernacle to Temple*, 24.
5. Emily Utt communication, November 15, 2022, in possession of authors.
6. Irving and Barton, *From Tabernacle to Temple*, 28–30.
7. Irving and Barton, *From Tabernacle to Temple*, 29–30.
8. Irving and Barton, *From Tabernacle to Temple*, 32.
9. Irving and Barton, *From Tabernacle to Temple*, 32.
10. Quoted in Irving and Barton, *From Tabernacle to Temple*, 31.
11. Gerry Avant, "Shell of Old Tabernacle to House a New Temple in Eastern Utah," *Church News*, February 19, 1994, 3, 11.
12. Irving and Barton, *From Tabernacle to Temple*, 35.
13. John L. Hart, "Transformation Begins for Temple," *Church News*, May 20, 1995, 3.
14. Hart, "Transformation Begins," 3–4.
15. Hart, "Transformation Begins," 4.
16. Hart, "Transformation Begins," 3–4.
17. Irving and Barton, *From Tabernacle to Temple*, 62–63.
18. Irving and Barton, *From Tabernacle to Temple*, 57–58.
19. Gerry Avant, "Angel Moroni Tops Vernal Utah Temple Tower," *Church News*, October 5, 1996, 5.
20. Irving and Barton, *From Tabernacle to Temple*, 61.

21. Gordon B. Hinckley, in "We Thank Thee for This Sacred Structure," *Church News*, November 8, 1997, 4; Julie A. Dockstader, "Symbol of Heritage, Testimony," *Church News*, November 8, 1997, 3, 8–9.
22. Lloyd Hess, remarks, in possession of Richard O. Cowan.
23. See Nina Folsom Moss, *A History of William Harrison Folsom: March 25, 1815 to March 19, 1901* (Salt Lake City: William Harrison Folsom Family Organization, 1973).
24. Christensen, *Provo's Two Tabernacles*, 120, 123.
25. Andrew Jensen, *Church Chronology: A Record of Important Events Pertaining to the History of the Church of Jesus Christ of Latter-day Saints* (Salt Lake City: Deseret News, 1899), 119, 124.
26. Jenson, *Church Chronology*, 131, 138, 146.
27. Christensen, *Provo's Two Tabernacles*, 147.
28. "Provo Tabernacle Rededicated," *Ensign*, December 1986, 70; "Members Admonished to 'Refurbish' Their Lives," *Church News*, September 28, 1986, 3, 7.
29. Kim Egginton, interview by Richard O. Cowan, December 17, 2011.
30. Richards, "Reflections on the Provo Tabernacle," 2 (typescript in Richard O. Cowan's possession).
31. Jim Dalrymple, "Crews Work to Remove Debris and Stabilize Sections of Building," *Daily Herald*, December 29, 2010, A1–A2.
32. John Emery, statement to Richard Cowan, May 12, 2015.
33. Statement to John Emery by David Brenchley, December 21, 2010 (copy in Richard O. Cowan's possession).
34. Thomas S. Monson, "And So We Meet Again," *Ensign*, November 2011, 4–5.
35. Joseph Walker, "Temple to Rise from Ashes of Tabernacle," *Deseret News*, October 2, 2011, B1, B4.
36. Weaver, "Out of Ashes," 4.
37. Groundbreaking video.
38. Groundbreaking video; see also Weaver, "Out of Ashes," 4.
39. Andy Kirby, remarks at the Provo City Library, June 13, 2014 (notes in Richard O. Cowan's possession).
40. "Sacred Thanks of Our Souls," *Church News*, March 27, 2016, 5.

12 Filling in the South Salt Lake Valley

The Draper Utah and Oquirrh Mountain Utah Temples

Oquirrh Mountain Utah Temple. *Grassy Morning*, by Alan Fullmer.

Utah's temples dedicated up to 2010. Courtesy of Lee R. Cowan.

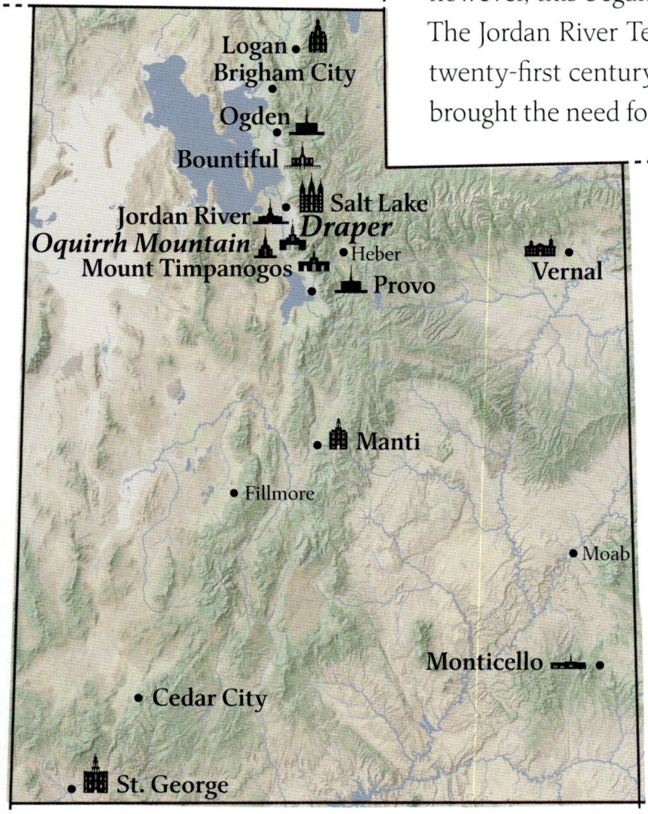

Soon after the pioneers arrived in the Great Basin, they established towns in the southern part of the Salt Lake Valley. For over a century, this area remained essentially agricultural, so population was small. During the later twentieth century, however, this began to change with an explosion of urban development in the area. The Jordan River Temple was dedicated in 1981 in response to this growth. As the twenty-first century dawned, accelerating growth in the southern end of the valley brought the need for yet more temples.

The Unfolding Announcement

As President Hinckley opened the October 2004 general conference, he pointed out that "the temples in the Salt Lake City area are extremely busy and at times are overloaded." He therefore announced, "We have determined to build a new temple in the Salt Lake Valley." He acknowledged that some may feel that "we are unduly favoring this area," but he insisted that the Church was simply attempting to accommodate the overwhelming temple activity in the valley. In fact, he then suggested that "if the present growth trends continue, we shall probably need yet another."[1]

When President Hinckley made this announcement, he did not specify an exact location. He indicated that it would be made known "shortly." Of course, this led to widespread speculation as to where precisely the new temple would be built. On Sunday, November 21, Church leaders read a First Presidency letter at meetings throughout the southern Salt Lake Valley indicating that the temple would be near Corner Canyon in Draper. This announcement was not totally unexpected. As early as 2002, Church real estate representatives told developers in the area that the Church was purchasing additional property next to a stake center site for the possible construction of a temple.

The 2004 announcement that a temple would be built in Draper represented the culmination of over a century and a half of efforts by faithful Saints in the area.

The Shoshone name for the southeast corner of the Salt Lake Valley was *Sivogah*, meaning "willows." As early as 1849 Ebenezer Brown, who had served in the Mormon Battalion, and his sons brought cattle into the area. The following year Ebenezer, his wife Phoebe, and their sons built cabins, settled their families there, and called the settlement South Willow Creek. In 1852 a branch was organized with Bishop William Draper, Phoebe's brother, as presiding elder, and the area came to be called "Draperville" (the name "Brownsville" was already taken).[2] As population in the southern part of the valley grew, Church units were divided and redivided. The first stake with headquarters in Draper, the Mount Jordan Stake, was formed in 1942; it was renamed the Draper Utah Stake in 1974. Thus, the 2004 announcement that a temple would be built in Draper represented the culmination of over a century and a half of efforts by faithful Saints in the area.

Just a year later at the October 2005 general conference, President Hinckley announced that the Salt Lake Valley's second new temple would be built in the Daybreak community located in South Jordan. He disclosed that the Church had two "excellent sites in the west and southwest areas of the valley through the kindness of the developers of these properties." The Daybreak site was one of these. Located on the brow of the bluffs at the foot of the west mountains, it had a spectacular view of the valley.[3]

President Brigham Young directed settlement in the south end of the valley west of the River Jordan as early as 1848. Isaac J. Wardle, Samuel Alexander Beckstead, and Archibald Gardner were the original settlers in the South Jordan area in 1859 when a canal brought water to the land. Two years later they erected the first permanent structure in the valley outside of Salt Lake City—the rock meetinghouse, now in West Jordan. Other people followed and South Jordan became a ward in the Salt Lake Stake in 1877. It covered fourteen square miles of farming and sheep-raising land. The fertile soil produced grain, hay, sugar beets, and vegetables. As urbanization spread into the area, the population grew; a separate South Jordan Stake was organized in 1969. The Kennecott Land Company opened the master-planned four-thousand-acre Daybreak community in 2004 in the west half of the city, accelerating population growth.

The two new temples would be similar in size and built concurrently—the first time two temples would be built simultaneously in the same valley. Hence, their stories would be somewhat intertwined.

Groundbreakings

On February 8, 2005, three months after the Draper site was announced, the city council approved a change in zoning regulations allowing houses of worship to reach a height of ninety feet (not including spires) in residential areas. This had been the only remaining obstacle to obtaining approval for the temple. On May 18 of the following year, the Draper planning commission approved plans for the fifty-seven-thousand-square-foot temple, a 492-space parking lot, and landscaping with a "large variety of trees."[4]

Groundbreaking on the windswept mountainside was on a warm summer Saturday morning, August 5, 2006. The entire First Presidency and several other General Authorities were in attendance. Cooled air was pumped to the stand, which was shaded by a canopy, while the audience sat in the sun on folding chairs assembled from the adjoining Draper Utah South Mountain Stake center. Proceedings were also carried by closed-circuit television to selected stake centers in the temple district. Elder Russell M. Nelson of the Quorum of the Twelve Apostles conducted the service.

The First Presidency (left to right: James E. Faust, Thomas S. Monson, and Gordon B. Hinckley) break ground for the Draper Utah Temple. Courtesy of *Deseret News* and Church History Library.

In contrast to the Draper groundbreaking, carried out in the hot summer sun, groundbreaking for the temple in South Jordan took place on a freezing day.

President Hinckley declared that "this is a remarkable time" and that "it is a great tribute to our people that they are so faithful in temple attendance." Since "temple service is a fundamental part of the gospel," President Hinckley insisted, "we must build temples where people can get to them" throughout the world. "They are costly to construct and costly to maintain, but we must have them, and fortunately because of the faith of the tithe-paying Saints we have the means to do so." President Thomas S. Monson, first counselor in the First Presidency, noted that Draper had been called "the egg basket of Utah." He challenged his listeners to "make a pledge this day to do a little temple building" in their own lives, "taking as their blueprint the passage in Doctrine and Covenants 88:119 pertaining to establishing a house of prayer, fasting, faith, learning, glory, order, a house of God." Looking out over the valley, President James E. Faust, second counselor in the First Presidency, appropriately cited Isaiah's prophecy that in the last days the Lord's house would be established "in the top of the mountains" and that "all nations shall flow unto it" (Isaiah 2:2–3). He then quoted the Lord's promise to Solomon as he built his temple that if the people would keep the

commandments, the Lord would dwell among them and not forsake them (1 Kings 6:12–13), and he prayed that this promise might be fulfilled for those building the temple in Draper.[5]

In the site dedicatory prayer, President Hinckley petitioned, "We pray that when [the temple] is completed it may be a place of refuge from the storms of life, a place holy and sanctified to all who will serve here, be they workers or patrons. We know the sacred work that will be done herein is a part of thine eternal plan for the happiness and well-being of thy children, both those in mortality and those beyond the veil of death."[6]

Groundbreaking for the temple in South Jordan took place four months later. By this time construction was progressing well on the Draper Utah Temple. Elder Paul E. Koelliker, a member of the Seventy with responsibility for temples, reported that the footings and foundations were completed. Even the cement shell for the baptismal font had been poured. "The first floor concrete walls are in place. It's above grade and it's moving along very well in the last four months."[7]

In contrast to the Draper groundbreaking, which was carried out in the hot summer sun, the December 16, 2006, groundbreaking for the temple in South Jordan took place on a freezing day. The invited audience gathered in a large, heated tent at the site; once again, proceedings were also broadcast in several area chapels. All three members of the First Presidency again attended and spoke. As he had done in Draper, Elder Russell M. Nelson of the Quorum of the Twelve conducted the services.

Peter McMahon, president of Kennecott Land, greeted the crowd. He reported that his firm had been negotiating with officials of The Church of Jesus Christ of Latter-day Saints and representatives of other faiths concerning possible chapel sites. Amid these discussions, "the Church approached Kennecott in 2005 to ask if the

"It seems appropriate to break ground for a new temple during a sacred holiday season. We couldn't have a better Christmas present than the house of the Lord."

company would be interested in having a temple built in the Daybreak development." This resulted in the site being donated. Mr. McMahon declared that the temple would be "a wonderful and iconic building on the edge of the valley, and so we're pretty excited about it."[8]

President Hinckley reflected, "It seems appropriate to break ground for a new temple during a sacred holiday season when members honor Christ's birth and the anniversary of Joseph Smith's birthday. We couldn't have a better Christmas present than the house of the Lord." Up to this point, the new edifice had generally been known as the South Jordan Temple, but to avoid confusing it with the Jordan River Temple just five miles away located in the city of South Jordan, President Hinckley announced that its official name would be the Oquirrh Mountain Utah Temple. This would be the first time two temples would be in the same city and ZIP code—84095. *Oquirrh* is a Goshute name meaning "wooded or shining mountain." "Patrons won't know how to spell Oquirrh, but they don't come to the temple to spell," President Hinckley quipped as the audience laughed. "They come to serve in the work of the Lord." While at the Draper Utah Temple groundbreaking, President Thomas S. Monson had recalled riding horses in that area as a youth. Now on this occasion, he spoke of riding bicycles and ice skating in South Jordan as a boy. He and President James E. Faust then gave counsel like that which they had shared four months earlier in Draper. President Faust also cited Brigham Young's prophecy of great growth west of the Jordan River and insisted that "we are seeing the realization of that in our time." In his prayer dedicating the site, President Hinckley petitioned that those building the temple might do so with "a spirit of worship."[9]

Both the Draper Utah and Oquirrh Mountain Utah Temples would be moderate-sized with a floor area of about 60,000 square feet and four 50-seat rooms for endowment presentation.

The service concluded with the traditional breaking of the ground with gold-colored shovels. After Church leaders had their turn, others were invited to participate. One of the first to respond was Peter McMahon of Kennecott Land. President Hinckley thanked him publicly for the donated site.[10]

Constructing the Temples

Both the Draper Utah and Oquirrh Mountain Utah Temples would be moderate-sized with a floor area of about sixty thousand square feet and four fifty-seat rooms for endowment presentation. Although these rooms would be arranged differently in the buildings, each temple had two sets of two rooms, meaning that groups would progress from one room to another during the endowment and that a new session could begin about every half hour. These temples would not include the cafeteria or clothing-rental facilities common in many earlier temples. The Draper Utah Temple was designed by Steven A. Goodwin of FFKR Architects, while the Oquirrh Mountain Utah Temple was designed by the firm of Naylor Wentworth Lund Architects of Salt Lake City. Both temples would be built by Okland Construction. The actual work of

Endowment room with mural, Draper Utah Temple. Courtesy of Church Newsroom/Intellectual Reserve, Inc.

building commenced shortly after groundbreaking, so the Draper Utah Temple was generally a few months ahead of the one in South Jordan.

The initial phase of construction took place in bitterly cold weather with record low temperatures. This phase consisted primarily of placing rebar and pouring concrete for foundations, floors, and walls. Because constructors needed to keep the cement at least thirty-five degrees so it could cure properly, they covered it with tarps or construction blankets and kept it warm by running hot water through tubes. The steel framework was erected during the spring and summer of 2007, the Draper Utah Temple topping out on July 20. In the fall the roof was completed, temporary windows were inserted, and the interior was heated so work could progress during the winter.

The Draper Utah Temple's interior features stone that had been quarried in France and then cut and polished in Italy. African Makore cherrywood was installed in such a way that no nails or screws were visible. Art glass in the windows by Tom

EXIT

Holdman reflects the temple's pioneer heritage by depicting the sego lily and a representation pattern typical of colorful block quilts. The sego motif was also carved into the woodwork and woven into carpets.

Left: Celestial room, Draper Utah Temple. Courtesy of Church Newsroom/ Intellectual Reserve, Inc.

Murals featuring mountain scenery typical of the West adorn the walls of the first in each set of two endowment rooms. The mural in one of these rooms, painted by Utah artist Linda Curley Christensen, depicts pine-covered mountains; the other, by Colorado artist Keith Bond, features a grove of aspens. The second room in each set has no murals but is more brightly illuminated to symbolize progress to a higher level. From the celestial room's fifty-foot ceiling hangs a chandelier that is thirteen feet tall and six feet in diameter; its two hundred lights are reflected by and through six thousand crystals from the Austrian Alps. The temple has five sealing rooms, one of which is the largest in any temple. Utah artist Dale Jolley added intricate stenciled paintings to the vaulted ceilings in the temple's most beautiful rooms. A painting of Moroni delivering the plates to Joseph Smith, which earlier had adorned the former Draper Tabernacle, now hangs in the temple's baptistry.

Placing the statue of the angel Moroni atop a temple's tower is a milestone event signaling the conclusion of exterior construction. Even though construction of the Draper and Oquirrh Mountain Temples was on different calendars, often months apart, setting the angelic figure took place on both temples within the same week. Still, the steps leading to this event at the two temples were quite different. A year before the figure was placed on the Draper Ttemple, the steel beams that would frame the tower were placed with great precision to assure that the angel would face due east. At Oquirrh Mountain, on the other hand, the spire was assembled on the ground and then set on the temple the same day as the angel; builders were careful to provide the spire a footing that not only could support the spire's weight but was secure enough to withstand the horizontal forces that strong winds would exert.

The eagerly anticipated but unannounced placement at Draper came on Tuesday, July 8, 2008. When two tall cranes were seen at the temple the afternoon before, rumors started flying. One crane raised the angel, suspending it long enough near the crowd so photographs could be taken. The other crane lifted two workmen in a basket so they could secure the statue in place. Just three days later, on Friday, July 11, the spire and angel were set on the Oquirrh Mountain Utah Temple. Motorists on the nearby Bangerter Highway saw what was happening, so a crowd quickly gathered.[11]

Statues for both temples were produced at 3-D Art, Inc. in nearby Kearns. Beginning in 1985, LaVar Wallgren had pioneered the process of producing fiberglass sculptures. The production of the figures for Draper and Oquirrh Mountain started eight months before they were placed. They were cast by Karl Quilter in three layers of fiberglass, each being allowed to cure before the next was applied. The finished statue was then painted with a sticky sizing that was allowed to dry overnight. This was the surface to which the 3.25-inch squares of gold leaf would adhere. Finally, the gold surface was buffed to a brilliant shine and then sprayed with a clear sealant to protect it from the weather. The figures were taken to the temple sites in a long

Sealing room, Draper Utah Temple. Courtesy of Church Newsroom/Intellectual Reserve, Inc.

open trailer pulled by a pickup truck. A large ring bolt in the figure's head facilitated it being lifted; once the statue was in place, the bolt was removed and replaced by a lightning rod as a top needle.

On August 25, 2008, just six weeks after the statue of Moroni had been placed, a wildfire erupted in the hills near the Draper Utah Temple. When Ray Buhler, one of the builders, was asked if he were concerned about possible smoke damage, he responded, "No! The Lord doesn't allow any smoking in the temple, so I don't think He would let that happen."[12]

Similarly, beautiful features were incorporated into the Oquirrh Mountain Utah Temple with its golden granite exterior quarried in the Quanzhou/Xiamen area in China. The interior features light limestone from Morocco and darker limestone from Egypt. Woods include oak from Indiana and Kentucky and sycamore from the Bavarian Alps. Art glass was by John Quist. Schonbek chandeliers with Swarovski crystals are shaped like five-pointed stars. The celestial room chandelier is fifteen feet tall and has 19,447 individual crystals.

As construction drew to a close, workmen reflected on what they had accomplished. Despite always wanting to do his best work on the temple, Ray Buhler realized that not everything could be perfect. "Our lives are like that. Because of the Atonement of Christ, we can be like the temple. As we stand before the Lord, even though we've made mistakes, He will make us perfect, and we will be with Him eternally someday."[13]

Project architect Steven Goodwin reflected on his work on the Draper Temple. "The temple is the most demanding project that I have worked on in my career as an architect." It represents "something other worldly, literally a house of the Lord. Designing and constructing a house that God's presence can dwell in is not a light effort. It requires many talented people and the vision of a prophet to guide our efforts." He considered how the temple "shapes and directs the thoughts and feelings" of patrons so that "light and revelation can be received and understood in the house of the Lord." The outside gardens are like "exterior rooms" that create a "sense of harmony and peace" as one arrives at the temple. "These feelings are enhanced as one then progresses through a series of spaces of varying sizes and finishing to the ordinance rooms," culminating in the celestial and sealing rooms with their high, vaulted ceilings that "immediately draw the eye heavenward."[14]

"The temple is the most demanding project that I have worked on in my career as an architect. Designing and constructing a house that God's presence can dwell in is not a light effort."

The Draper Utah Temple Open House and Dedication

The contractors officially turned the temple over to the Church on December 19, 2008, so final preparation for the open house and dedication went forward. During the first two weeks of 2009, special VIP visits were available for clergy of other faiths as well as for business, educational, civic, and other community leaders. After visiting the temple, guests participated in a reception with a buffet table in the cultural hall of the adjacent stake center. Displays provided information about the importance of temple ordinances, the worldwide construction of temples, and specifically about the Draper Temple. Between twelve and fourteen thousand persons took advantage of this opportunity to walk through the beautiful new Latter-day Saint temple.

General Authorities conducted many of these tours. Elder M. Russell Ballard of the Quorum of the Twelve Apostles, for example, sought to dispel the erroneous notion that members of other faiths were not welcome in any Latter-day Saint buildings. He felt sure that as a result of this tour members of the press would sense the sacredness of the special work done in the temples, but he noted that the Church's fifty-three thousand missionaries were "doing everything they know how" to encourage people to come and worship with us in one of our eighteen thousand meetinghouses worldwide.[15]

This was also the time when the General Authorities could bring their own families to see the temple. When eighty-four-year-old Elder Russell M. Nelson of the Twelve "was asked if he might like to conserve his energy by using the elevator

Draper Utah Temple. Courtesy of Church Newsroom/Intellectual Reserve, Inc.

instead of climbing the stairs," he respectfully declined, disclosing that he had spent the morning skiing. "The slopes offer a discount to those over eighty on Monday mornings," he added. He assured his attentive hosts that "the stairs posed no particular problem."[16]

The public open house commenced on Thursday, January 15. At this time of the year, winds and deep snow posed a significant challenge in the Corner Canyon area. Another challenge was the lack of sufficient parking adjacent to the temple. Open house tickets therefore specifically directed visitors to park at one of four chapels further down the mountain. Before boarding buses to the temple, they viewed a twelve-minute video introduction to temple service and to the Draper Temple. After walking silently through the building, they could enjoy cookies while viewing the exhibits in the stake center next door before being bused back to their cars. Tours were offered daily except Sunday. On any given day, up to six hundred volunteers performed such tasks as shoveling snow, operating audiovisual equipment, ushering visitors, playing reverent music in the reception area, or cleaning the temple each day after tours had ended. Thirty-five thousand volunteers served under the direction of Rodolfo C. Franco, president of the Draper Utah South Mountain Stake, who served as open house coordinator.

Visitors were invited to fill out comment cards at the end of their tour; their responses often reflected deep feelings. A visitor from another faith acknowledged, "When I was in the sealing room, I felt like I never wanted to leave." A faithful Latter-day Saint recalled "forty-two years ago kneeling with my husband and our four daughters and being sealed. Now he is gone, as are two of those girls, and how grateful I am for the sealing room." Another visitor conceded that he was not an active member of the Church, so "I felt so lucky to come and see the temple. Today I recommitted myself to come back to the Church." A young man who had recently lost his mother and who had faced other trials affirmed, "Today I decided I want to go on a mission." Yet another visitor who had been studying with the missionaries affirmed that "I was converted today."[17] A young family preparing to be sealed testified that "the Spirit was so strong, it" was hard to leave the sealing room. "The only thing more beautiful

Above: Temple dedication ticket. Below: President Monson at cornerstone with nine-year-old Justin Spainhower. Courtesy of *Deseret News* and Church History Library.

than the temple was the look of awe in my children's eyes."[18] Elder William R. Walker of the Seventy, who served as director of the Church's Temple Department, felt that it was significant that "there were numerous references to how people felt the Spirit. I think it is very significant that this was a temple that was not dedicated, and yet people still felt the Spirit and felt it very strongly."[19] By the time tours ended on Saturday, March 14, a total of 684,721 interested persons had visited the temple.

Upon the death of President Hinckley, Thomas S. Monson had become President of the Church early in 2008. He dedicated the temple in twelve sessions beginning on Friday, March 20, 2009, and continuing through Sunday, the 22nd. Speakers were members of the First Presidency, other General Authorities, Church auxiliary leaders, and members of the Draper Temple presidency and their wives. These proceedings were conducted in the temple's celestial room and viewed throughout the building by closed-circuit television. The tenth and twelfth sessions, both on Sunday, were also carried to stake centers in the temple district.

As was customary, after Church leaders had their turn, the president invited some young people from the audience to help place some mortar.

That was a beautiful spring weekend. Weather on Friday and Saturday was calm and sunny, while there were some showers on Sunday. According to President Dieter F. Uchtdorf, the beauty was not just outside: "It was as though there was sunshine inside, even within the enclosed walls. There is a beautiful feeling that another spot of heavenly light has come to the earth."[20]

The traditional cornerstone ceremony was part of the first session Friday morning. A youth choir of 189 teens from the temple district provided music. President Monson humorously announced that the mortar and trowels were ready, but that those who would use them were untrained and so might spill some of the mortar on the ground; he drew a chuckle from the crowd assembled outside of the temple when he assured them that the professionals would clean it up and make things right afterward. As was customary, after Church leaders had their turn, the president invited some young people from the audience to help place some mortar. First was Gracie Awerkamp, who gratefully reflected, "This was my first time to see the prophet" and to participate in a temple dedication. Then, as Justin Spainhower knelt to take his turn, President Monson commented that the young man was "already getting ready for a mission"; Justin later reported that when his mother confirmed that he was the one President Monson had called a future missionary, "she started hugging me like crazy." When the prophet invited thirteen-year-old Christoffer Hotvedt to come forward, he pointed to his younger sister Katrine, age seven, so both were invited to participate "as a pair." Obviously enjoying the occasion, President Monson handed a trowel to Becky Alexander, the conductor of the youth choir, and suggested she could use it instead of a baton.[21]

The cornerstone box contained the usual historical items plus some that were unique to this temple. Jim West, chair of the cornerstone committee, had crafted special writing pens from the roots of scrub oak trees cleared from the site as well as from pieces of the African Makore wood used in the temple's interior.[22]

"There is nothing like the dedication of a temple to bring out the best in people," insisted President Monson. It is as though there is a welcome sign inviting, "Come, here you shall find peace, here you shall find a formula for happy families." Boyd K. Packer, President of the Quorum of the Twelve Apostles, made an interesting observation: "If you drive a little way up the hill from the Draper Temple, you can see six temples"—the Draper, Oquirrh Mountain, and Jordan River—"in a line across the valley"; the Salt Lake to the north, and the Mount Timpanogos and Provo to the south. "With that many temples within our view, we have little reason to neglect our forebearers."[23]

President Monson offered the dedicatory prayer in all twelve sessions. It petitioned blessings for "those faithful members here and throughout the world who have contributed their tithes which have made possible this magnificent edifice." The prayer expressed gratitude for "the sacred sealing power" brought by Elijah the prophet "so that in this temple and all Thy holy houses Thy faithful Saints may be endowed with power from on high" and enter covenants that bring "all the blessings of Abraham, Isaac, and Jacob and all the holy prophets." The prayer affirmed that "the plan of salvation taught in the temple with simplicity, yet with power, will be as a never-failing beacon of divine light to guide our footsteps and keep them constantly on the pathway of eternal life." At a time of departure from safe moorings, the prayer asked that "youth of the noble birthright carry on in the traditions of their parents and grandparents." Similarly, at a time "when the family unit is under attack and things long held sacred are ridiculed by the world, we seek Thy help to make us equal to our tasks, that our homes may be havens of peace and happiness." As the temple was dedicated as "a house of baptism, a house of endowment, a house of sealing and a house of righteousness," the prayer acknowledged that "we [also] rededicate our very lives to Thee and to Thy work."[24]

Reflecting on the three days of dedication, President Henry B. Eyring, first counselor in the First Presidency, summarized, "It has been a wonderful experience. There has been a feeling of peace and joy in every session. . . . You could feel the faith of the people. Everything about it has been uplifting and marvelous."[25]

Cultural celebration. Courtesy of *Deseret News* and Church History Library.

A Joint Cultural Celebration

Beginning with the Ghana Temple in 2004, a "cultural celebration" had taken place the evening before temple dedications. Often held in outdoor stadiums where large audiences could be accommodated, these occasions allowed casts of several hundred or even thousands of youth to celebrate the history of their area culminating with the construction of the new temple. Because the Draper and Oquirrh Mountain Temples had been built together, the cultural celebrations in connection with their dedications would be held together. This event was scheduled for the last weekend in May 2009, several weeks after the March dedication of the Draper Utah Temple, and several weeks before the dedication of the Oquirrh Mountain Temple the following August. Youth from the twenty-five stakes in the Draper Temple district made their presentation on Friday evening, May 29, while those from the twenty-six Oquirrh Mountain district stakes had their turn on Saturday evening, May 30. A total of fourteen thousand participated. These events took place in the new twenty-one-thousand-seat Conference Center adjacent to Temple Square in downtown Salt Lake City.

The narration was the same both nights, but each group had its own costumes and choreography. Entitled *Come Up to the Mountain of the Lord*, the production honored the contributions of various groups beginning with Native Americans, early pioneers, and continuing to the multicultural population of recent years. As the drama reached its climax, "a glorious temple arose from the top of a great mountain," and concourses of teens carrying flags representing the groups that had been honored climbed the mountain as they gathered to the house of the Lord.

Ordinance room of Oquirrh Mountain Utah Temple. Courtesy of Intellectual Reserve, Inc.

On both nights, President Monson spoke to the youth before their dramatic presentation. "May I assure each of you that any effort you put forth will be rewarded many times over. You have had the opportunity to mingle with youth from other wards and stakes, you have made new acquaintances and forged new friendships." He insisted that "tonight will be a night you will never forget."[26]

Open House and Dedication of the Oquirrh Mountain Utah Temple

Two full months, Monday, June 1 through Saturday, August 1, were scheduled for the Oquirrh Mountain Utah Temple's open house. Ample parking near the temple was an advantage. The eight hundred volunteers who served on a typical day performed a variety of tasks including handing out cookies to visitors in the hospitality tent following their tours of the temple. Robert Homer, president of the South Jordan Utah Highland Stake, chaired this event. "Some volunteers were not active Church members. A few were not members at all," he recalled. "Still, they graciously filled shifts and did whatever they were asked to do to help the open house function smoothly."

Planners had anticipated that weather would be favorable during both months of the open house. June, however, was cool and stormy. In fact, during a thunderstorm on June 13, lightning struck the figure of Moroni atop the temple. Portions of the angel's face, arm, and trumpet were blackened. Church officials determined that it would be better to replace the statue rather than trying to repair it in place some 180 feet above the ground. This would be done on August 11, just over a week before the temple's dedication, the whole operation taking three hours. The new figure included lightning rods in the arm and trumpet as well as in the head.[27]

Seeing the temple affected individuals in different ways. An estimated 85 percent were Church members. Many visitors indicated that "they were eager to bring their young children to the temple and let them experience the beauty, wonder and spirit of the celestial room, baptistry, and mural-covered ordinance rooms." Some young people who may have been wavering in their faith were prompted to serve a mission or prepare to be married in the temple. Two BYU roommates with the same first name attended together and were moved by their experience. Whitney Benton reflected, "I love the temple's celestial room. I just imagined people dressed in white filling that room." Whitney Kluber added, "I had a feeling of togetherness and wanting to be there in the temple with my family." A single visit was not enough for Milvia Dique of West Jordan, even though she was a member of another faith. After touring the temple with friends, she returned with a relative vacationing in Utah from London. She returned yet a third

SUNDAY, AUGUST 23, 2009
9:00 A.M. OR 3:00 P.M.
MEETINGHOUSE

OQUIRRH MOUNTAIN
UTAH
TEMPLE
DEDICATION

NAME OF RECOMMEND HOLDER

SIGNATURE OF BISHOP OR BRANCH PRESIDENT

Temple dedication ticket. Courtesy of the Temple Department.

HOLINESS
TO THE
LORD
THE
HOUSE
OF THE
LORD

time with her husband and two of their children. For her, the open house was "a beautiful experience—I've enjoyed being inside the temple so much. The feelings I have felt there have been so strong." She acknowledged that she "gained an appreciation for temples. Any mystery that once surrounded the Church's most holy edifices has been replaced with understanding and respect. I know now why the temple is such a sacred place."[28]

Left: Oquirrh Mountain Utah Temple. Courtesy of Intellectual Reserve, Inc.

As visitors finished their tours, they were impressed not only with the Oquirrh Mountain Utah Temple but also with the scope of temple building. They could see the new Draper Utah Temple on the hillside southeast across the valley and the large Jordan River Utah Temple five miles to the northeast. By the time the two months were ended, nearly 590,000 had visited the temple.

President Monson dedicated the Oquirrh Mountain Utah Temple in nine sessions beginning Friday, August 21, 2009, through Sunday, August 23. Sunday meetings were cancelled throughout the state of Utah so Church members could view the dedicatory proceedings. Temple-worthy Church members gathered reverently in 657 stake centers, which were regarded as extensions of the temple. Still, an estimated total of 14,500 attended sessions in the temple during the three days of dedication.[29]

The customary cornerstone ceremony was part of the first session on Friday morning. A 187-voice choir sang spiritedly for the occasion. As President Dieter F. Uchtdorf, second counselor in the First Presidency, placed mortar on the cornerstone plaque, President Monson quipped, "For an airline pilot, that's perfect." The prophet then called for young volunteers to come forward to participate. When six-year-old Michael Branan in the back of the crowd raised his hand high, President Monson instructed, "Make way for the redhead." Michael was grateful for his red hair, believing this was why the prophet had singled him out. This was President Monson's

Thomas S. Monson celebrated his eighty-second birthday the same day as the Oquirrh Mountain Utah Temple cornerstone ceremony. Courtesy of Intellectual Reserve, Inc.

A choir sings at the Oquirrh Mountain Utah Temple dedication. Courtesy of Intellectual Reserve, Inc.

eighty-second birthday; as the cornerstone ceremony drew to a close, the assembled audience began singing "Happy Birthday." As they concluded, President Uchtdorf added, "And many more." President Monson good-naturedly commented, "I was waiting for that."[30]

In the dedicatory prayer, President Monson expressed gratitude: "We are grateful for the knowledge Thou hast given us that Thou art our Father, to whom we may turn for inspiration and guidance, for revelation and strength in times of trouble and distress." He also expressed gratitude for the Atonement of Jesus Christ and for guidance available through the Holy Ghost. The prayer continued, "We are grateful for this long-awaited day of dedication, when this, Thy holy house has been completed." The prayer petitioned that those who had contributed to the temple's construction might feel "the gratitude of those uncounted millions who have passed beyond this life, for whom the prison doors may now be opened and deliverance proclaimed through the devoted service of Thy people in this and other sacred temples."[31]

Temple president Alan S. Layton prayed that the families living in the new district might "do all they can to realize the blessings of the temple with parents, spouses, children, siblings and grandchildren. . . . It is here where the faithful can 'go up to the mountain' to learn His ways and walk in His paths." The Saints eagerly responded to this invitation. Even before daylight Tuesday morning, August 25, a large group of youth were at the temple, waiting for the door to open, wanting to be among the first who performed the sacred service of being baptized in behalf of their departed loved ones.[32]

Notes

1. Gordon B. Hinckley, "Condition of the Church," *Ensign*, November 2004, 4–5.
2. Andrew Jenson, *Encyclopedic History of the Church* (Salt Lake City: The Church of Jesus Christ of Latter-day Saints, 1941), 197–98; R. Scott Lloyd, "Dedication of Temple Is Sign of Renewal," *Church News*, March 28, 2009, 4.
3. "Opening Remarks," *Ensign*, November 2005, 4–5.
4. "Draper Utah Temple," https://churchofjesuschristtemples.org/draper-utah-temple/.
5. Lloyd, "Remarkable Time," *Church News*, August 12, 2006, 3.
6. Vicki Taylor and LaRayne Day, "The Draper Utah Temple" (unpublished manuscript), Church History Library, Salt Lake City, 43.
7. Sam Penrod, "President Hinckley Dedicates Building Site of New Temple," December 16, 2006, https://www.ksl.com/article/734498/president-hinckley-dedicates-building-site-of-new-temple.
8. Penrod, "President Hinckley Dedicates."
9. Jason Swensen, "AGreat and Wonderful Day," *Church News*, December 23, 2006, 3.
10. Penrod, "President Hinckley Dedicates."
11. "Draper Utah Temple," *Church News*, July 26, 2008, 13; "Oquirrh Mountain Temple," *Church News*, July 19, 2008, 14.
12. Taylor and Day, "Draper Temple," 108.
13. Taylor and Day, "Draper Temple," 109.
14. Taylor and Day, "Draper Temple," 128–29.
15. Scott Taylor, "Temple Tours," *Church News*, January 17, 2009, 6–7.
16. Taylor and Day, "Draper Utah Temple," 159.
17. "Speak Volumes," *Church News*, March 21, 2009, 5.
18. Taylor and Day, "Draper Utah Temple," 163.
19. "Speak Volumes," 5.
20. "A Feeling of Peace, Joy," *Church News*, March 28, 2009, 9.
21. Lloyd, "Dedication of Temple," 3–4; Taylor and Day, "Draper Utah Temple," 221.
22. Lloyd, "Cornerstone Box 'within Our Hearts,'" *Church News*, March 28, 2009, 10.
23. "A Feeling of Peace," 9.
24. "This, Thy Holy House," *Church News*, March 28, 2009, 6–7.
25. "A Feeling of Peace," 9.
26. Sarah Jane Weaver, "Temple Celebrations," *Church News*, June 6, 2009, 8–10.
27. "Statue Replaced," *Church News*, August 15, 2009, 7.
28. Jason Swensen, "Illuminating," *Church News*, June 13, 2009, 14; Swensen, "A Sacred Place," *Church News*, August 8, 2009, 3–4.
29. Jason Swensen, "Salt Lake Valley's Fourth Temple Opened," *Church News*, August 29, 2009, 3, 8, 9.
30. Jason Swensen, "Cornerstone Sealed amid Mild Sunshine," *Church News*, August 29, 2009, 3, 10.
31. "Oquirrh Mountain Utah Temple: Long-Awaited Dedication for 'Magnificent Edifice,'" *Church News*, August 29, 2009, 4–5.
32. Swensen, "Salt Lake Valley's Fourth Temple Opens," 3, 9.

13

A New Style of Temple

The Brigham City Utah, Cedar City Utah, Remodeled Ogden Utah, Payson Utah, and Remodeled Jordan River Utah Temples

Brigham City Utah Temple. *From on High*, by Alan Fullmer.

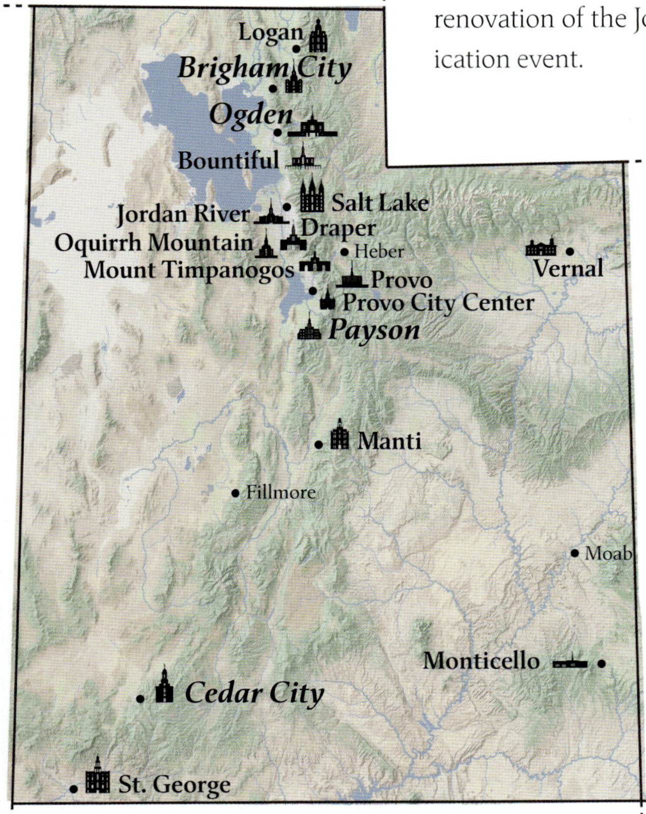

Utah temples with dedication dates from 1877 to 2017. Courtesy of Lee Cowan.

The second decade of the twenty-first century brought four significant temple construction projects to Utah. Two at opposite ends of the state—Brigham City and Cedar City—involved new temples that consciously reflected pioneer architecture. Another—in Ogden—was the unprecedented rebuilding of an existing temple. Then the large temple in Payson used a bold new design. The chapter ends with the renovation of the Jordan River Temple and the end of an era for one traditional dedication event.

The Brigham City Utah Temple

Fifty miles north of Salt Lake City in Box Elder County lies the town of Brigham City, Utah. Latter-day Saint settlement began in 1851 and then expanded in 1853 when Brigham Young directed apostle Lorenzo Snow to move to Box Elder and select fifty families to go with him.[1] As Brigham City developed, the Saints decided to build a tabernacle in the downtown area near Forest Street. Excavations began in 1865. However, on May 4, President Brigham Young visited the site and stated they were building in the wrong place, saying, "This is a commercial center, it is not the spot for your tabernacle."[2] Walking the workers two blocks south to Sagebrush Square, just outside the platted city, he pointed to the highest spot along Main Street and directed the tabernacle to be built there. Five days later, on May 9, 1865, Brigham Young helped lay the cornerstones for the tabernacle.[3] Work stopped and started over the years. Box Elder Tabernacle was finally dedicated on October 26, 1890, becoming the focal point of the religious community and a prominent building in Box Elder County.

A Century of Learning

Just west of the tabernacle on Second South and Main Street lay a three-acre parcel of land that served as the site for a house of learning until it later became the spot for a house of the Lord. In 1901 the three-story Central School was opened. One child attending elementary school there remembered walking up the dirt path in the 1930s to attend. His name was Boyd K. Packer, a resident of Brigham City and a future Latter-day Saint Apostle. The first school building burned to the ground on August 9, 1947, and then was rebuilt in 1950. The second elementary school served the Brigham City community for the rest of the century, then closed in May 2000.[4]

The building was razed. The land sat vacant. Jeff Packer, a real estate agent and nephew of Boyd K. Packer, tried to negotiate with various buyers, but to no avail. At one point he talked with the Church Real Estate Department about acquiring the land for extra parking for the Box Elder Tabernacle. During the discussions, Jeff mentioned the idea of building a temple there. The Church employee said, "Please don't use the T word," and expressed there would never be a temple in Brigham City. It was too close to Ogden and Logan. Yet in 2009, an unknown party became interested in the land. Jeff Packer later learned it was the Special Projects Division, and the Church bought the land.[5]

Announcement

In October 2009 President Thomas S. Monson announced five new temples, including one in Brigham City. Jeff Packer, who attended the general conference and was a member of the Box Elder Utah Stake presidency, went and visited his uncle between conference sessions. At that time Boyd K. Packer was President of the Quorum of the Twelve Apostles. Jeff told his uncle that stake members were texting and emailing him about possible sites for a temple. They were guessing the temple would be built across from the tabernacle. President Packer smiled and replied, "Well, let them speculate."[6]

Just weeks later, on Tuesday, October 27, President Monson called President Packer about visiting possible temple sites. The prophet said, "I'd like you to come with me. We're leaving in thirty minutes." They were joined by President Dieter F. Uchtdorf, second counselor in the First Presidency, and Elder William R. Walker of the Seventy, executive director of the Temple Department. When the foursome arrived at the block west of the Box Elder Tabernacle, President Monson asked Elder Walker where the Brigham City Temple could be situated. He said it would look east, directly facing the tabernacle. Then President Monson asked President Packer's thoughts about this site. He replied, "I think this is the perfect place for the temple." President Monson then responded, "That's good enough for me," and raised his arm to the square.[7]

This moment captured an unusual beginning to how the Brigham City Temple would develop. The First Presidency personally oversees the Temple Executive Committee and temple projects. However, President Monson asked President Packer to direct the design and many aspects of the Brigham City Temple even though he was not a member of the committee. Elder Walker was asked why he believed President Monson gave such an honor and responsibility to President Packer. Elder Walker suggested it was because of the love between these two leaders and President Packer's home ties to Brigham City. He also added that with President Packer serving as President of the Quorum of the Twelve, it was also good training—in case President Packer outlived President Monson.

The stake members were guessing that the temple would be built across from the tabernacle. President Packer smiled and replied, "Well, let them speculate."

Brigham City Utah Temple design. Courtesy of David Hall.

Latter-day Saints believe the east and west towers in Latter-day Saint architecture symbolize the Melchizedek and Aaronic Priesthoods.

A Historic and New Temple Design

With President Monson's assignment, preparations were made for the first group meeting between President Packer, Bishop Keith B. McMullin of the Presiding Bishopric, and David Hall, director of Temple Design Services. Brother Hall was requested to bring photographs of historic temples, including St. George, Manti, Logan, Salt Lake, and Vernal. Additionally, Hall received a prompting to include a rendering of the new Kansas City Missouri Temple with his packet of materials and placed the photo at the bottom of the pile.

David Hall and Bishop McMullin joined Elder Walker for the meeting in President Packer's office on November 10, 2009. At one point in the discussion, Brother Hall asked permission to show President Packer a drawing of the Kansas City Temple even though it was not a nineteenth-century temple. Seeing the Kansas City rendering changed the course of the conversation. David Hall had asked himself some hypothetical questions about the Kansas City Temple. How would a Missouri temple have looked if the early Saints had been able to stay in the state instead of fleeing west? If the Saints had returned to reclaim Missouri at the end of the nineteenth century as they had hoped, how might a Missouri temple look as a sister to Logan or Manti?[8]

Kansas City reimagined the pioneer temples of Logan and Manti into a neoclassical, two-tower temple for the twenty-first century. Brother Hall later added that architecturally, our Church is the only religious tradition that includes two separated towers, with one on the east and one on the west. Comparatively, Catholic cathedrals have two towers that are usually together on one side of the building. Because of Brigham Young's inspiration for the Salt Lake Temple, Latter-day Saints believe the east and west towers in Latter-day Saint architecture symbolize the Melchizedek and Aaronic Priesthoods. This unique two-tower design was adopted for Brigham City. Similarly in the 2010s, it was employed for two historically significant temples amid strong architectural traditions. The two-tower style was used in Rome, the heart of early Christianity in Europe, and in Philadelphia, the birthplace of the United States Declaration of Independence.

Other pioneer temples and designs also influenced Brigham City. Hall recalled that "the historic precedence of patterns such as Salt Lake's windows and Manti's curved towers brought Brigham City closer to its nineteenth century predecessors than even Kansas City." At the conclusion of the design process, President Packer commented on the stylistic similarity between Brigham City and Salt Lake: "It is like a child to his father."[9]

President Packer suggested interior design connections to the Box Elder Tabernacle, a peach blossom motif in round windows, an instruction room with murals that have animals and birds in the landscape, a mural of "the Presidency," mountain peaks above Willard, and an interior of white-painted wood like the Manti and Salt Lake Temples. President Packer also contributed some of his own artwork of birds.

Details in the Brigham City Utah Temple. Above: Instruction room with landscape murals featuring animals and birds. Left: Peach blossom motif in round windows. Courtesy of Intellectual Reserve, Inc.

Linda Curley Christensen and Michael Malm painting *Work to Do, Ere the Sun Goes Down* on screen during the temple cultural celebration. Courtesy of Clinton D. Christensen.

"I can see in my mind's eye a temple sitting here in about two years' time. It will be gorgeous. It will be a beacon from all over the valley."

Building the Temple

Groundbreaking for the temple was held on July 31, 2010. The temple rendering was unveiled for the community displaying a three-story, thirty-six-thousand-square-foot temple. The basement would house the baptistry, mechanical rooms, administration offices, and marriage guest waiting room on the main floor, the dressing rooms and a chapel on the second floor, and two progressive endowment rooms leading to a celestial room and three sealing rooms on the third floor.

President Packer presided at the groundbreaking and was joined by Elder Russell M. Nelson of the Twelve, who had ties to nearby Perry, Utah, where his first wife, Dantzel, was raised. President Packer began his remarks, "I am home. I can see in my mind's eye a temple sitting here in about two years' time. It will be gorgeous; it will be white. You will see in the design of it reflections of previous temples that have been built, particularly the Salt Lake Temple. It will be a beacon from all over the valley."[10]

Construction proceeded very quickly in a two-year time frame. The interior colors were a desert sage green and blue, tile was from China and Turkey, and a custom-made baptismal font included twelve unique bronze oxen. When President Packer was asked if the oxen should be the same or different, he referenced the twelve sons of Israel and replied, "Asher and Dan were not twins."[11]

Far left: The Christensen family participates in the cornerstone ceremony. Courtesy of Clinton D. Christensen. Left: Ticket to the Brigham City Utah Temple dedication. Courtesy of the Temple Department.

Below: After completing the cornerstone ceremony, President Boyd K. Packer waves toward children (not shown). Courtesy of Clinton D. Christensen.

The baptistry also contained a confirmation painting created by Linda Curley Christensen and Michael Malm entitled *Work to Do, Ere the Sun Goes Down.*[12] The painting shows a Shoshone man being confirmed by missionary George Washington Hill and is based on an event on May 5, 1873, when 101 members of the Shoshone band were baptized in the Bear River north of Brigham City and confirmed until sundown. The painting also includes a half circle of witnesses of the confirmation. All are dressed in different tribal clothing. They symbolize the nearly twelve hundred men, women, and children from nine different tribes that joined the Church throughout Utah, Wyoming, and Idaho between 1873 and 1877.[13] The painting pays tribute to the great contributions of the indigenous peoples of the Americas who were living throughout the West when the Latter-day Saints arrived in the valley. This confirmation painting has been used elsewhere and can be found in the Cedar City Utah Temple, Provo Utah Temple, and Star Valley Wyoming Temple.

Left: The baptismal font in the Brigham City Utah Temple includes twelve unique bronze oxen. Courtesy of Intellectual Reserve, Inc.

A Trio of Apostles at the Dedication

As the temple reached completion, President Monson deferred from having the First Presidency attend the dedication so that President Packer could return to his hometown and preside. At the time, it was a rare exception for a member of the Quorum of the Twelve to be assigned to dedicate a temple. Early in Church history, Elder Orson Hyde of the

Above: Grand hallway, Brigham City Utah Temple. The temple interior features white-painted wood like the Manti and Salt Lake Temples. Courtesy of Intellectual Reserve, Inc.

Left: The brides' room in the Brigham City Utah Temple displays the temple's interior colors: desert sage green and blue. Courtesy of Intellectual Reserve, Inc.

Brigham City Utah Temple. *Spring*, by Alan Fullmer.

Twelve had dedicated the Nauvoo Temple. In 1999 two Canadian temples were dedicated on the same day, November 14. President Packer, as Acting President of the Twelve, was assigned to go to Regina at the same time President Hinckley was in Halifax. President Packer dedicated the Brigham City Utah Temple on September 23, 2012, and was joined by fellow Apostles L. Tom Perry and Russell M. Nelson. In the future this new style of sharing the responsibility with members of the Quorum of the Twelve to dedicate temples would become standard when President Nelson became Church President.

President Packer was eighty-eight when he dedicated the temple and would live almost three more years. He was a living link to early settlers of the Brigham City area. As if to bind together the Saints of today with the pioneers of the past, President Packer exclaimed in the dedicatory prayer, "We honor the memory of those who came to this valley as pioneers and have raised their families to honor the order of the principles and ordinances of the gospel.... We sense the presence today of Presidents Brigham Young and Lorenzo Snow and Elder Rudger Clawson, each of whom would be very interested in the dedication of this temple."[14]

The Cedar City Utah Temple

Right: Cedar City Utah Temple. Courtesy of Intellectual Reserve, Inc.

The Cedar City area was first settled by Latter-day Saint pioneers in 1851. In addition to being an agricultural outpost and way station for travelers along the Mormon Trail to Southern California, this Iron Mission sought to develop the mineral resources of the area. The Parowan Stake was organized the following year with Cedar City as one

HOLINESS TO THE LORD
THE HOUSE OF THE LORD

of its wards. In 1923 a rail branch opened to Cedar City, which became a major travel destination as the jumping-off point for tours to southern Utah's national parks and the North Rim of the Grand Canyon in Arizona. Since 1962 the annual Shakespeare Festival has also made Cedar City a cultural center. In recent decades, the area's economy has broadened to include manufacturing. This brought growth, and Cedar City became a separate stake which has been divided and redivided. Population grew from fewer than ten thousand in 1970 to more than 30,000 in the second decade of the twenty-first century. Faithful Latter-day Saints in the area understandably looked forward to the time when they might have a temple of their own.

The planning for new temples "often starts with the stirrings of the Spirit among the local leaders."

Cedar City is also an educational center. The Branch Normal School, established in 1897, grew over the years, becoming a state college and finally Southern Utah University in 1991. A student stake was organized in 1966, and during the 1990s two more were formed. On December 28, 2009, Elder Daniel M. Jones, the Area Seventy assigned to the Cedar City region (and future temple president), told the leaders of the student stakes that he believed the explosion in the number of SUU students was the factor "that tipped the scales" because it "added a very compelling component" to their petition for a temple to serve thousands of students in the area. Elder Yoshihiko Kikuchi of the Seventy, who was serving with the Temple Department, affirmed that the planning for new temples "often starts with the stirrings of the Spirit among the local leaders." The other stake presidents in the area were excited when they heard of this conversation, so they drafted a formal request for a temple.[15]

Securing the Site

Several steps were necessary before the eventual site for the temple would be ready. For years, the city had planned for Cove Drive to be a major thoroughfare for its western suburbs, connecting Second North with the south interchange accessing the I-15 freeway. However, property for the last key half-mile segment down the hill at the north end was not for sale. A grant from Iron County in 2010 and a swap of state for federal money made funding for the needed canyon route available the following year. The owner could see how the new road would enhance the value of his property and was finally willing to sell the right-of-way. Maureen Einfeldt, who lived in the area, later recalled: "We began to have backhoes come into our neighborhood, which was a dead end at the time. In no time, there was a new, beautiful road leading to the top of the hill. I had the thought that perhaps it was clearing the way for a new temple," but time passed and nothing was said.[16]

Right: Stained glass portrayal of the Savior in the Cedar City Utah Temple. This is one of two stained glass windows in the temple that came from the Astoria Presbyterian Church in Queens, New York, which had been razed a few years earlier. Courtesy of Intellectual Reserve, Inc.

Just three months after the road was completed, three people appeared at the city offices identifying themselves as "developers looking to do their due diligence on several properties they hoped to develop." About five months later, near the end of August 2012, one of them returned, stated that he was an architect with The Church of Jesus Christ of Latter-day Saints, and asked for a closed-door meeting with city officials. He disclosed that the Church "had chosen a potential site for a possible temple in Cedar City" which had the three needed qualities of being in "a nice area,"

and having good visibility and easy access. The Church bought the temple site in November. Plans for a temple in Cedar City were announced at the Church's general conference in April 2013.[17]

Planning the new temple occupied the next year and a half. As had been the case at Brigham City, this 39,802-square-foot building was intended to be "a tribute to the region's rich pioneer heritage." Designed by Architectural Nexus, it incorporated features of the St. George and Manti Temples as well as of other historic buildings in St. George, Beaver, and Fillmore.[18]

Construction

The temple district included about forty-five thousand members in seventeen stakes, from Ely, Nevada, on the northwest to Boulder and Escalante in south-central Utah on the east. Each stake had a particular assignment. For example, the Cedar City Stake set up 1,625 folding chairs at the site for the groundbreaking ceremony on Saturday, August 8, 2015. A blowing rain Thursday evening and Friday morning resulted in the

Mural in the endowment room of the Cedar City Utah Temple. Courtesy of the Cedar City Utah Temple historical subcommitee.

Baptistry in the Cedar City Utah Temple. Courtesy of Intellectual Reserve, Inc.

chairs being caked with mud. Early Saturday morning, however, dozens of volunteers had them clean and dry for the event.

Two General Authorities participated. Elder L. Whitney Clayton of the Presidency of the Seventy presided over the hour-and-a-half ceremony; Elder Kent F. Richards, executive director of the temple department, conducted. Elder Dane Leavitt, the local Area Seventy, planned the event. Elder Clayton recalled the Apostle Paul's teachings to the Corinthian Saints that "ye are the temple of God" (1 Corinthians 3:16) and then added, "God intends not to just build this [tangible] temple, but [also] to make us temples." He challenged the Saints to invigorate their family history work so that the new temple can be kept busy performing ordinances for people identified entirely by those who live in this temple district. Elder Richards referred to Ezekiel's imagery of water flowing from the temple and giving life to everything it touched (Ezekiel 47:1–12). He then taught, "Just as finding a renewable, sustainable source of water was essential to settlers of this arid region, finding a well of living water is essential to spiritual nourishment." In his prayer dedicating the site, Elder Clayton affirmed that "by revelation this choice spot of hilltop land has been selected." Then, in addition to the seventeen stake presidents and other leaders using the traditional gold-colored shovels to break ground, Elders Clayton and Richards used a large track hoe to symbolically begin excavating for the temple.[19]

Despite icy weather, concrete for the temple's three levels was poured beginning in January 2016. As precast concrete panels formed the temple's walls beginning in March, the building quickly took on a completed appearance. The figure of Moroni was hoisted to the top of the cupola on September 15. Work on the temple's interior went forward during the winter of 2016–17. Three motifs unified decorations throughout—juniper branches and berries, columbine flowers, and clusters of feathers to honor the area's indigenous peoples. The color scheme featured deep rusts and blues. Many paintings beautified the temple's rooms; while most illustrated scenes from the Savior's ministry, others depicted the red-rock scenery of southern Utah. Two particularly striking features were stained glass windows which came from the Astoria Presbyterian Church in Queens, New York, which had been razed a few years earlier. One showing the Lord in a red robe and with outstretched arms is positioned behind the recommend desk, while the other, depicting him praying in Gethsemane, adorns the temple's west entrance.

Above: Cedar City Utah Temple sealing room. Left: Celestial room. Courtesy of Intellectual Reserve, Inc. The red and blue flower in the stained glass window is the columbine flower motif, used both throughout the temple and in the stained glass.

Open House and Dedication

By the fall of 2017, the temple was ready for its open house. VIP tours for special groups began Saturday, October 21. Elder Larry Y. Wilson of the Seventy and executive director of the Temple Department personally led the tour for the press. He declared that the temple had forever changed Cedar City. "It becomes a symbol that there is a House of God—a place more holy than any other—in this community. Every time you drive by it you can't help but be inspired by its beauty and to have your thoughts drawn toward God and His purposes for this earth and for your life." He explained that the transition from dark brown woodwork on the lower floors to the white on the floors above "is meant to represent a very literal rising above the earth [to be] closer to heaven." When the group entered a sealing room at the end of their tour, Elder Wilson told them how as a seven-year-old boy he was sealed to his parents in the Idaho Falls Temple: "It gave me a sense of eternal belonging."[20]

Ticket for the Cedar City Utah Temple dedication. Courtesy of the Temple Department.

Other VIP tours were conducted by members of stake presidencies in the temple district. In preparation for this experience, Elder Wilson spent four hours with these leaders and their wives, numbering over one hundred. As they walked through the temple, he taught with an openness most of the group thought was rare and instructed them how to approach the sacred workings within the temple in an appropriate way. Especially striking was their experience in the beautiful celestial room which most in the group were seeing for the first time. "They were filled with pure joy coupled with reverence and awe for what that room represents. The silence of such a large group . . . was powerful."[21]

Several visitors had rather special experiences at the open house. One had grown up in Queens, New York, where she attended the Astoria Presbyterian Church as a little girl. When she heard about the open house, she made a trip to Cedar City so she could see "her stained glass windows" once again. When she saw them, "she became very emotional and began to weep" and stated, "We were very grateful that the glass had been preserved and was not lost" in the demolition of her old church building.[22]

A couple from the Phoenix area happened to be traveling through Utah on their vacation. At dusk as they approached Cedar City on the freeway, they saw directions to "event parking" and wondered what event this might be. They decided to check it out. After parking, they boarded a bus, noting that "everyone was so happy." As they approached the illuminated building, the woman from Arizona asked the lady behind them, "What is this place?" She replied, "This is the temple; it is the house of the Lord." As they entered the temple, she felt something she had felt at the Mesa Arizona Temple while attending the Easter pageant there. "What is this feeling?" she wondered. In the baptistry she learned about baptisms in behalf of those who had died without this ordinance and thought of her grandmother who had died recently. She had been afraid she might go to hell because she had never been baptized. "Could this be done for my grandma?" the traveler from Arizona pondered. When the tour reached the celestial room, she found a place where she could be alone. "As I looked around the beautiful room, thoughts I previously had in the baptistry came back to me. Then I heard a voice say to me, 'Now you know what you need to do for me.'" She recognized her grandmother's voice. Finally, in a sealing room, she learned that couples could be united for eternity. "As I pondered this idea, I heard the same voice say to me, 'Do this for your grandpa and me.'" In their motel that evening, she reflected: "I could not stop thinking about what had just happened to me. I felt such peace." The next morning, she told her husband that she wanted to go back to the temple. During the next three days she repeated the tour seven times. "Each time I heard the voice and felt the same way," she affirmed.[23] The public open house extended from October 27 through November 18. In all, some 187,614 persons were able to visit the temple.

The youth celebration took place Saturday evening, December 9, in the events center on the Southern Utah University campus. President Henry B. Eyring, first counselor in the First Presidency, greeted the four thousand youth and encouraged them to record in their journals how they felt while they participated in this event. "That record will help you when you tell your children and your grandchildren what it meant to you to be a part of the celebration of the completion of a temple of God in Cedar City." The production, entitled "A Light on a Hill, Iron in the Will," depicted scenes from the history of the area. It featured two well-known hymns that were written in Cedar Valley: Joel H. Johnson wrote "High on the Mountain Top" two years after the first pioneers had arrived, and John M. Macfarlane later authored "Far, Far Away on Judea's Plains." As a result of participating in this event, the youth affirmed that they felt more connected with each other and with their Heavenly Father.[24]

President Eyring dedicated the temple in three sessions on Sunday, December 10, 2017. In his dedicatory prayer, he testified that "the presence of this house is an answer to the prayers of Thy people. We thank Thee for it and ask for Thy Spirit to dwell continuously within its walls. We pray that this beautiful temple will be a haven for all who enter." He prayed that students in the area might be blessed. He also prayed that the example of faithful Saints may "lead others to seek Thine everlasting truth." The prayer affirmed that the temple is "our gift to Thee, dear Father, given in acknowledgment of Thy great gifts to us, most notably the gift of Thy beloved Son."

Rebuilding the Ogden Utah Temple

The Ogden Utah Temple is located downtown, and the Church's *Ensign* magazine commented, "Centrally located in downtown Ogden amid the businesses and institutions of man, the Ogden Temple effectively symbolizes the power of the gospel to reach down and out to the daily life of each of us, to bless, guide, and protect us as we walk and work and live in the real workaday world."[25] This very location, however, also had its downside. Ogden's downtown was old, and the temple's immediate surroundings had become dilapidated. The Church took steps to remedy this, notwithstanding some in the community who were reticent of the Church heavily investing

Rendering of the remodeled Ogden Utah Temple. Courtesy of Intellectual Reserve, Inc.

in revitalizing downtown Ogden. In 1999 it bought the block to the west, demolished old and often boarded-up houses, and constructed attractive apartments. As President Hinckley dedicated these new housing units, he declared that downtown Ogden would prosper again and become beautiful. The Church later bought portions of the blocks to the north and east to similarly upgrade the temple's environment.

Ogden city officials were also sponsoring efforts to beautify downtown. Other investors and developers followed the Church's example, purchasing hundreds of acres for redevelopment projects valued at hundreds of millions of dollars. The old mall in the block to the south of the temple was demolished and replaced with new office and retail space and entertainment facilities. In the decade after President

Hinckley's prophetic statement, eight thousand new jobs were created and the value of taxable property in the area increased by one-third. This improvement was called "the Ogden miracle." As early as 2001, Ogden officials discussed possible improvements to the temple itself with the First Presidency and Presiding Bishopric. In October 2009, Mayor Matthew R. Godfrey met with President Thomas S. Monson and his counselors to discuss this matter. An announcement came the following February.[26] The Ogden Temple would be the first temple totally reconstructed in the history of the Church by choice, compared to the Nauvoo and Apia Samoa Temples that were rebuilt due to damage by fire.

The momentous announcement came at a news conference held in the Ogden Tabernacle on Wednesday, February 17, 2010. Elder William R. Walker of the Seventy and Bishop Keith B. McMullin, second counselor in the Presiding Bishopric, disclosed that "a major remodel of the Ogden Temple" would "dramatically change its appearance." The reshaped exterior would feature new white stone, art glass, and a more timeless design. Some compared the new building to the Bountiful and Draper Temples. The temple's main entrance would be shifted from the west to the east side where it would face Washington Boulevard, Ogden's principal business street. Inside, some rooms would be rearranged, "but the core building design" would "remain the same." "Modern energy-saving equipment" would replace old mechanical, electrical, and plumbing systems. Underground parking would be added, and the entire "Ogden Temple Square" would be completely relandscaped. "This is like Christmas for a mayor to have an announcement like this," Mayor Godfrey enthusiastically responded. He believed that nothing else attracted so many visitors and that "a more beautiful temple" would boost Ogden's economy.[27]

Reconstruction

The temple closed Saturday, April 2, 2011. As this date approached, it became increasingly crowded as Church members in the area were eager to serve in their historic and beloved temple just one more time. The final session Saturday evening was an emotional occasion for the capacity group. Everyone in the company who had come with a partner participated in the prayer circle, which "completely encircled the entire room."[28]

Demolition by Big-D Construction followed quickly. Workmen removed and preserved the temple's original cornerstone box. Soon only a skeleton of concrete floors and support columns remained. By early 2012 the process of rebuilding had begun, including a new white granite exterior. On Monday, May 6, 2013, a large crane lifted the gleaming white spire into its place. The next day workers placed a fourteen-foot version of the fiberglass statue of the angel Moroni, weighing eight hundred pounds, atop the spire, its gold leafing sparkling in the sun. This brought the total height of the temple to 188 feet 8 inches. On Thursday, May 23, the copper box from the original cornerstone was placed in the southeast corner of the new building. The temple's exterior now appeared nearly completed.

Above: The brides' room in the Ogden Utah Temple features a unique rug with desert rose and prairie grass motifs. Right: Temple entry waiting area. Courtesy of Intellectual Reserve, Inc.

Far right: The celestial room, Ogden Utah Temple. Courtesy of Intellectual Reserve, Inc.

As has always been the case, the finest materials available were used in the temple's reconstruction. Mahogany came from Africa. Marble was quarried in Egypt and fabricated in China. Prevailing motifs are the desert rose and prairie grass. These were especially well displayed in a one-of-a-kind rug that adorned the beautiful brides' room. Both these plants grow wild in the area, and the rose may recall the prophecy that the desert would "blossom as the rose" (Isaiah 35:1). Some artwork from the

The remodeled Ogden Utah Temple, 2022. Courtesy of Intellectual Reserve, Inc.

original Ogden Temple was returned to the new structure. Robert Shepherd's mural, originally behind the recommend desk in 1976, now occupies a central location on the ground floor; it depicts the Mount of Transfiguration where priesthood keys were conferred, including the power to bind on earth and in heaven. Other pieces were new. One particularly striking print, a copy of an Elspeth Young painting in the Johannesburg South Africa Temple showing an African woman kneeling in fervent prayer, is located at the entrance to the sisters' dressing room. Another print, copied from a painting in the El Salvador Temple, portrays the Savior with Native American children, recalling his visit to ancient America. Rather than having a single large chandelier, the celestial room features a lighted etched dome surrounded by four smaller chandeliers.[29] The temple's floor area was reduced slightly from 115,000 to 112,232 square feet, but architects believed it was used more efficiently. At the same time, the Ogden Tabernacle, located on the north side of the same block, also underwent a renovation. Its steeple was removed because the designers did not want the two buildings to compete.[30]

"This beautiful temple has been a haven of peace. It has served well. Showing the effects of such service, it has been necessary to renovate and improve it."

Rededication Events

The public open house extended five weeks from Friday, August 1 through Saturday, September 6. An estimated total of 550,000 visitors attended. An usher asked a

A sealing room in the Ogden Utah Temple. Courtesy of Intellectual Reserve, Inc.

Youth participate in Ogden Utah Temple cultural celebration before the temple's rededication. Courtesy of Intellectual Reserve, Inc.

member of another faith how he had enjoyed the tour. He replied, "Your temple is just beautiful, but the real effect is right here in my heart."[31] More than sixteen thousand youth participated in the cultural celebration held in the Dee Events Center on the Weber State University campus the day before the temple's rededication. Because of the large numbers, half of the youth performed on Saturday afternoon and the other half in the evening. Based on the theme "Shine the Light," the pageant reviewed the area's history as a lantern was carried from one scene to another. In addition to the costumed performers, a massive chorus of several thousand singers performed. One of their original numbers was "I Am Prepared." When four youth from Syracuse High School were tragically killed in separate accidents during the weeks just before this event, music director and the song's composer Brita Miles wrote a fourth verse for this number which inspired the youth as they sang with emotion: "One day in white, I'll return to His side, Father is waiting for me; Home in His care, with loved ones there, crowned with celestial glory, I am ready!" Near the end of the performance, hundreds of youth seated on the floor held large cards side by side that formed a huge picture of the original Ogden Temple. Then, upon a signal during the climaxing song, all turned their cards over, revealing a picture of the newly rebuilt temple as house lights were turned on bright.[32]

President Monson dedicated the rebuilt temple in three sessions on Sunday, September 21, 2014. The proceedings were carried by satellite throughout the state of Utah and into southwestern Wyoming, which was part of the temple district. The customary cornerstone ceremony was not needed because the original unopened cornerstone box was already in place.[33] In his dedicatory prayer President Monson acknowledged, "This beautiful temple has been a haven of peace. It has served well. Showing the effects of such service, it has been necessary to renovate and improve it. We are grateful for this long-awaited day of rededication when the renovations have been completed."[34]

A Large Temple in Payson

Payson had its beginning late in 1850 when Brigham Young sent settlers to the south end of Utah Valley. Fertile soil enabled this area to become noted for farming, stock raising, and especially fruit growing. It was part of the valley-wide Utah Stake until 1901 when the Nebo Stake was formed with headquarters at Payson.

A Special Site

The first temple in Utah Valley was dedicated in Provo in 1972. The Mount Timpanogos Utah Temple in the north entered service in 1996. Then, as the population in the southern part of the valley exploded during the early twenty-first century, the possibility and necessity of a temple there became more evident. As early as 2009, real estate representatives of the Church's Special Projects Department began searching for appropriate sites from Springville to Santaquin. Soon they "felt strongly" they should concentrate their efforts in the Payson area. They wanted a site that was visible, accessible, and ideally next to a meetinghouse whose parking lot might be shared. Before long, a piece of land in the southwest corner of the community became their favorite, but it was not for sale.

Mark and Denise Y. (Dee) DeHart had owned their farm since the early 1990s and operated it as part of a sod-producing business. In 2004 they began actively planning to build their dream home on a ten-acre plot that sloped up to a hill at the southeast corner of the farm. They had "stood many times on it and marveled how far we can see from this tiny little rise." They began working with an architect, but despite repeated attempts, nothing seemed to work out. "Neither the good architect nor we could figure out the problem, so we decided to table the project for a little while. That is when the economy faltered," so they concluded to begin raising another crop on this piece of land. Wheat seemed to be the best choice because of the rocky

For three years, the family "experienced great joy tending the wheat and anonymously giving it away through the bishops of [the] stake."

Payson Utah Temple site. Courtesy of Church Newsroom, Inc.

and sloping nature of the plot. As the first harvest approached, the family "decided to dedicate the ten acres to the Lord, and grow, harvest, clean, and bag the wheat and give it away" to people in the ward who could not afford to buy it. The next year, the harvest was even more abundant, so the scope was expanded to the whole stake; at this time the farm came to be called "the giving field."[35] For three years, the family "experienced great joy tending the wheat and anonymously giving it away through the bishops of [the] stake."

In the fall of 2009, Dean M. Davies, managing director of the Special Projects Department (and future member of the Presiding Bishopric), and Lynn Bailey, real estate manager, contacted the DeHarts and the owners of a few other sites to ascertain whether or not the properties could be purchased. When the intended use of their property was disclosed to the DeHarts, Dee was touched. "Then uncharacteristically for me," she reflected, "I began to cry as I described the joy involved with the last three years." The Church employees, also in tears, explained that "the prophet himself would likely come and look at all of the areas being considered and would make the decision." Dee assured them that "we knew the Lord would put the temple where it should be" but were pretty sure it would be in Spring Lake or Elk Ridge. The

DeHarts discussed this possibility with their children Audrey, Emmy, Maddie, their son Ben and his wife Haley, "as it would require them to eventually sacrifice a portion of their inheritance and our retirement. It was a quick and unanimous decision in favor of donating the property to be used for a temple site. We had never been asked to donate the property," Dee affirmed, and "not one family member has had a problem since then with that decision."[36]

About two weeks later, in December 2009, Dean Davies brought the First Presidency to personally inspect four sites. They stopped first at the DeHart property. "President Monson just rolled down the window and looked out and didn't get out of the car." After they had been to the other sites, he asked the group to return to the first. This time "he walked out onto the ground and said, 'Brethren, this is where the Lord wants His temple built.'" Presidents Eyring and Uchtdorf concurred. Dee DeHart later reflected, "We had the amazing opportunity to be the stewards of this hallowed piece of ground for eighteen years before returning it to the Lord for a much greater purpose that will benefit many thousands more."[37] The property was located near the intersection of 930 West and 1550 South, about a mile from the 800 South exit from Interstate 15.

"We had the amazing opportunity to be the stewards of this hallowed piece of ground for eighteen years before returning it to the Lord for a much greater purpose that will benefit many thousands more."

The First Presidency did not wait for general conference to announce plans for the Payson Temple. On Monday afternoon, January 25, 2010, they announced, "A new temple of The Church of Jesus Christ of Latter-day Saints is to be built in Payson, Utah." The "new temple will help meet the needs of a growing Church membership in the area and will ease the heavy use of the Provo Temple, which is one of the busiest in the Church." President Monson stated that "temples answer those soul-searching questions of the purpose of life, and why we are here and where we are going. They are sanctuaries from the storms of life and bless the lives of members of the Church who worship within their sacred walls."[38]

Groundbreaking and Construction

Saturday, October 8, 2011, the day for the temple's groundbreaking, brought an early taste of winter for the six thousand who braved the elements. Four General Authorities had places on the covered platform, including Elders Dallin H. Oaks of the Quorum of the Twelve, Steven E. Snow of the Presidency of the Seventy, William R. Walker of the Temple Department, and Jay E. Jensen of the Seventy, who was born in nearby Mapleton. Elder Walker conducted the services. He referred to the rich pioneer heritage of the communities in the Payson Temple district, and noted that its twenty-six stakes from Mapleton to Nephi included approximately eighty-nine thousand members and that twenty-nine thousand of them held temple recommends. Two hymns authored by individuals who had lived in Payson were sung during the proceedings—"High on the Mountain Top," by Joel H. Johnson, and "Sweet Is the Work," by John J. McClellan.

Elder Dallin H. Oaks conducts the Payson Utah Temple groundbreaking. Courtesy of *Deseret News* and Church History Library.

Elder Steven E. Snow, who was responsible for the Church's Utah areas, pointed out that the Payson Utah Temple would become the sixteenth in the state of Utah. He recalled that when he and his wife, Phyllis, were married, only thirteen operating temples were in all the Church and that they had set a goal of visiting all of them. "Well, President Hinckley and President Monson have ruined all that; we're not going to make it," he good-naturedly conceded, noting that there were then 135 temples in service worldwide with many more announced or under construction.

In his remarks, Elder Oaks, a native of Provo, declared that he also regarded Payson as one of the places where he grew up. When he was seven years old, his father died, and Oaks came to live for two years with his Harris grandparents, who had a farm just a half mile south of the present temple site, and he was baptized there. As a teenager, he returned to Payson during the summers to help on the farm; he played the oboe with the high school band and gave his first church talk in Payson. While attending the Brigham Young High School in Provo, he became interested in radio and announced some local basketball games. He gratefully recalled that while broadcasting a game at the high school in Payson, he met his first wife, June Dixon from Spanish Fork; they were married fifteen months later.

As part of his groundbreaking remarks, Elder Oaks also quoted what President Monson had taught about temples: "No Church-built facility is more important than a temple," and "true joy is found in holy temples of our Heavenly Father. I can think of no greater incentive to inspire compliance with God's commandments and entry into His holy house than the beckoning love of those who have gone ahead and plead for us to follow." Elder Oaks testified that temples are houses of the Lord, so "this temple will be His house. Here will be exercised the ordinances of His holy priesthood." Hence, "the ultimate purpose of this temple is the exaltation of the children of God."[39]

Right: Completed Payson Utah Temple. Courtesy of Intellectual Reserve, Inc.

Grand staircase in Payson Utah Temple. Courtesy of Intellectual Reserve, Inc.

Endowment room, Payson Utah Temple. Courtesy of Intellectual Reserve, Inc.

Elder Oaks offered the prayer dedicating the temple site. He expressed gratitude "for the preservation of this land for that purpose, and for the generosity of those who have made it available for Thy work." He prayed "for angels to watch over and guard this site" from harm. He petitioned that "the workmanship of the House of the Lord will be beautiful and worthy of a house to be dedicated to Thy name and to the work of Thy Son." He also asked blessings on the people that they might be prepared for the sacred service to be carried out in the temple.[40]

Meanwhile, Architectural Nexus was preparing plans for the new temple, which would follow the floor plan of the temple then being built in Gilbert, Arizona, but with a distinctive bold exterior. The basic arrangement of facilities had symbolic significance: the font, which symbolizes the grave (Doctrine and Covenants 128:13) and where the entry gospel ordinance is received, is the lowest part of the temple. Initiatory ordinances, in preparation for the endowment, are received on the ground floor. Three endowment rooms, each seating about ninety patrons, are on the second floor; each of these rooms offers the complete endowment presentation, so patrons do not progress from room to room before entering the celestial room. Hence, three groups can receive the endowment at the same time, allowing a new session to begin approximately every forty minutes. Seven sealing rooms, in which the climaxing ordinances of the temple are received, are located on the uppermost floor; three of these rooms are large enough to accommodate seventy guests. The floor area of 96,630 square feet makes it one of the larger modern temples.

Construction commenced in May 2012, Wadman being the general contractor. Before concrete could be poured for footings in the deep excavation, 107 geopiers were driven deep into the ground to provide more solid support. Just one year later, concrete for the main roof was poured. A prominent feature of the building is the outward-curving windows on each of its four facades, especially the east, where the celestial room is located. Columns for these radius windows were installed during June. Construction of the tower culminated in the fall, with the completion of the dome and twenty-foot spire at the tower's top. Then a major event was placing the angel Moroni atop the tower, bringing it to its full height of 208 feet. Thursday morning, October 10, 2013, was cool and misty. When Susan Leavitt caught a glimpse of something gold being taken toward the temple, she "raced to the site to see if it was, in fact, Moroni." Later, when a construction worker unexpectedly allowed her to stand next to the statue, "she cried uncontrollably." When Deidre Henderson, a state senator, learned what was happening, "she dropped everything," loaded her children in the car, and drove to the site. "I thought it was really important for my kids to witness that event." Even though there was no formal announcement, thousands of people packed

Celestial room, Payson Utah Temple. Courtesy of Intellectual Reserve, Inc. A prominent feature of this temple is the outward-curving windows on each of its four facades, especially the east, where the celestial room is located.

Sealing room, Payson Utah Temple. Courtesy of Intellectual Reserve, Inc.

the area, cars lined the streets, and even on the freeway people slowed to have a look. Elaine Williams set up a ladder and helped people to climb it for a better view over the construction fence. "It's absolutely exciting," exclaimed Margaret Allred, who lived near the temple. "It's a blessing of the Lord for us. I think it will touch people's hearts."[41]

Interior

The rooms were adorned with beautiful woodwork of Sapele mahogany from Africa and Emperador marble from Spain. The pallet of cream, light green, and light burgundy of the temple's interior reflects "the land and its people." Two decorative motifs were employed throughout the temple—wheat, in keeping with the recent previous use of the temple site, and the apple blossom, reflecting the numerous fruit orchards in the area. Here again there is an element of progression. On the lowest floor, the blossoms are shown only as buds on the branches. As one ascends through the temple, the blossoms are represented as increasingly open. In the sealing rooms on the upper floor, they are presented as fully open flowers. The beautiful red and green hues in carpeting complemented the apple motif. At least nineteen original paintings would adorn the temple, including works by Ken Stockton and Elspeth Young. Striking art glass features were created by Tom Holdman in his Lehi studio at the other end of Utah Valley.

By March 2015 construction was completed. The temple was then officially turned over from the Special Projects Department, which had built it, to the Temple Department, which would operate it.[42]

Open House, Youth Celebration, and Dedication

Larry Duffin headed the committee in charge of events surrounding the temple's open house and dedication. The sixteen members of this group headed subcommittees responsible for such matters as history, traffic, security, hospitality, equipment, and the youth celebration; members of these groups totaled about three hundred. In all, some twenty thousand volunteers would then assure the success of these events. As Brother Duffin thought of the temple he was about to present to the public, he asserted confidently, "The inside will take your breath away." Still, he reflected, it isn't the building's beauty or the hectic preparations to exhibit it that matter most. "Our greatest hopes are that individuals will feel closer to their God, which leads them to living better lives. We've heard quite a bit from stake presidents, since the temple was announced, that people have felt the need to change their lives. Thousands have been motivated by the presence of the temple."[43] The temple impacted all those that came during the month-long open house, where a total of 475,542 visitors toured the temple.

The youth cultural celebration filled LaVell Edwards Stadium on the Brigham Young University campus Saturday evening, June 6. More than thirteen thousand youth came together to present their production before the huge audience as an offering of gratitude to God. The youth were dismayed when a "typhoon-like rainstorm" struck just before starting time, pelting the area with hail and destructive

Youth participate in cultural celebration for the Payson Utah Temple. Courtesy of Intellectual Reserve, Inc.

winds while thunder and lightning threatened overhead. Participants and spectators were directed to clear the stadium and seek refuge under the stands as the fury raged for over an hour. Finally, the clouds parted, the sun shone, and the program began.[44]

As the program drew to a close, the youth in section after section in the stadium removed their white shirts, revealing T-shirts in coordinated bright colors that created a rainbow that spread across the full length of the stand. Just as the Lord had placed a "bow in the cloud" as a token of His covenant (Genesis 9:13) after a terrible flood in Noah's time, the youth had endured their own torrential downpour that very day. What had been designed as an event for the youth to unfold the rainbow in the stadium as a sign of their commitment to seek temple blessings took on added meaning after the storm. As the final note of music faded, a light rain began to fall, mingling with tears of reverent gratitude on thousands of upturned faces.[45]

President Eyring conducted the cornerstone ceremony and presided over the three dedicatory sessions the following day, Sunday, June 7, 2015. In addition to those gathered in the temple, thousands of faithful Saints viewed the proceedings in stake centers throughout the temple district.[46] President Eyring's dedicatory prayer expressed gratitude "for this beautiful edifice which has been erected in our midst. It stands magnificent where it may be seen by all in this community and those who pass by. May it be a constant reminder to those who see it of the obligation of Thy covenant people to walk in righteousness before Thee. . . . May this house be ever sacred to those who enter it and to all who look upon it. May it truly be the House of the Lord, a place of holiness." The prayer also petitioned blessings for those who would serve in the temple: "May Thy faithful Saints be edified and strengthened through the endowment they will here receive. May Thy servants who go from this Thy House to represent Thee be endowed with power to bear witness before the world of Thy great cause and kingdom restored to the earth for the blessing of Thy sons and daughters, both those living and those beyond the veil of death. May all who kneel at these sacred altars feel the power of Thy binding covenant for them and their posterity through all eternity."[47]

The temple went into service immediately after its dedication. W. Blake Sonne and his wife, Elizabeth, became the temple's first president and matron. Youth groups lined up outside of the temple early on Monday morning to be the first to perform baptisms in behalf of the dead. The beautiful sealing rooms were already booked solid for several weeks.

When nine-year-old Kaylee Tervort's parents asked her and her siblings where they wanted to be married, Kaylee confidently replied, "In the Payson Temple." This was about six years before anyone knew there would be a Payson Temple. On the day the announcement was made, her parents picked her up from school, told her about the announcement, and drove her to the site of where the Payson Temple would be. Kaylee was in fact married there in 2017.[48] She was just one of the many Saints in the area who were truly anxious to enjoy the blessings available in the new Payson Temple.

A new locally designed fountain graces the front entrance of the renovated Jordan River Utah Temple. Courtesy of Intellectual Reserve, Inc.

Jordan River Utah Temple Renovated

The Jordan River Utah Temple had closed in February 2016 for extensive renovation. The building was strengthened seismically. All heating, air-conditioning, electrical, and plumbing systems were replaced or upgraded so that future operating and maintenance costs would be reduced. The interior was completely refreshed, including new carpeting, mahogany fluted millwork, Turkish marble floors, interior art glass, and a "new art deco motif" in the celestial room ceiling. Wall finishes were redone and were adorned with "new murals and other art features." As had been done in the Ogden and Provo Temples years before, escalators were removed from the grand stairway and replaced by fixed stairs supplemented by high-speed elevators. Outside, a new locally designed fountain graced the front entrance. A new exit on the west side enabled newly married couples to greet family and friends without blocking the main entrance. Over two years were needed to complete all these improvements.[49]

Top: The celestial room ceiling in the renovated Jordan River Utah Temple features an art deco motif. Bottom: The brides' room. Courtesy of Intellectual Reserve, Inc.

Leaders wanted to involve all 17,000 of the temple district's youth in activities leading up to the temple's dedication.

Open house and dedication events came in the spring of 2018. On Saturday, March 10, persons with disabilities were given all day to go through the temple at their own speed; this, for example, enabled blind visitors to examine features by touch. More than 452,000 visitors came during the public open house which extended from March 17 to April 28. Those hosting special groups could go off path to spend some time in one of the temple's seventeen sealing rooms where they discussed temple ordinances, covenants, and worship; individuals having this experience left changed. Many Church members were heard to express the need to become actively involved

again. A less-active couple with children said, "I think it's time we return." An excommunicated man remarked to his wife, "We've got to come back and be sealed here as soon as this repentance process is completed."[50]

Leaders were anxious to involve all the temple district's seventeen thousand youth in activities leading up to the temple's dedication so they organized a variety of events. There was a special day for the youth during the open house. Then, on a rainy Saturday morning, May 12, the youth discovered how close the temple was as they gathered at their meetinghouses and walked as groups to the temple. They filled the temple's lawn as they sang hymns and recited scriptures. They felt a spirit of unity as they saw friends from school who they had not realized were fellow Latter-day Saints.[51] The climax was the cultural celebration Saturday evening, May 19, at the Conference Center next to Temple Square downtown. This production, entitled *Ready*, traced the history of temple building beginning with the Old Testament tabernacle and culminating with the Jordan River Utah Temple. Youth from the temple district nearly filled the huge auditorium. This celebration was different, because those in the orchestra, choir, and dance groups were presenting their program to fellow youth rather than to their parents.[52] This would be the Church's last youth cultural celebration. At this time Church leaders were stressing that activities and programs should be "home-centered and Church-supported."[53] The pattern

Cultural celebration in the Conference Center. Following the cultural celebration for the Jordan River Utah Temple rededication in 2018, President Russell M. Nelson began the practice of youth devotionals prior to temple dedications. Courtesy of Intellectual Reserve, Inc.

of holding "youth devotionals" instead of cultural celebrations began with the dedication of the Concepción Chile Temple in October of that same year.

President Eyring, second counselor in the First Presidency, rededicated the Jordan River Utah Temple on Sunday, May 20, 2018. He felt that the temple's 1981 dedicatory prayer by President Spencer W. Kimball was "terrifically appropriate to our time," so he quoted from it extensively in his prayer of rededication.[54] Worthy members eight years of age and above were able to attend. Regular church meetings throughout the Jordan River Temple district and the adjoining Oquirrh Mountain and Draper Temple districts were cancelled, and the rededicatory proceedings were carried to stake centers so many thousands more could participate. The nine-year-old Baker twins from Sandy were excited that they could personally attend in the temple. "I felt safe and happy," Daxton remarked. "I'm just glad I attended." His sister Elsie concurred: "I felt like I was being baptized again. And when President Eyring said the prayer, it felt like the Holy Ghost was there—I thought the room was getting brighter."

The reconstruction of the Ogden Utah Temple and renewal of the Jordan River Utah Temple foreshadowed a thorough renovation of Utah's early pioneer temples. This would be a major focus during the 2020s.

Notes

1. Clinton D. Christensen and Michele Peck, *Harvest of Faith: The Brigham City Utah Temple*, (n.p.: Temple Department, 2013), 48.
2. Frederick M. Huchel, *A History of Box Elder County* (Salt Lake City: Utah State Historical Society, 1999), 148.
3. Huchel, *History*, 148.
4. Christensen and Peck, *Harvest of Faith*, 17–18.
5. Christensen and Peck, *Harvest of Faith*, 21–22.
6. Christensen and Peck, *Harvest of Faith*, 23.
7. Christensen and Peck, *Harvest of Faith*, 12.
8. Christensen and Peck, *Harvest of Faith*, 40.
9. Christensen and Peck, *Harvest of Faith*, 39.
10. Church Newsroom "President Packer Presides at Groundbreaking of Brigham City Utah Temple", July 31, 2010, https://newsroom.churchofjesuschrist.org/article/president-packer-presides-at-groundbreaking-of-brigham-city-utah-temple.
11. Christensen and Peck, *Harvest of Faith*, 135.
12. Christensen and Peck, *Harvest of Faith*, 152.
13. Christensen and Peck, *Harvest of Faith*, 143.
14. "Dedicatory Prayer: Brigham City Utah Temple, 23 September 2013," https://www.churchofjesuschrist.org/temples/details/brigham-city-utah-temple/prayer/2012-09-23.
15. Beverly Burgess and historical committee, *Come Ye, Let Us Go Up to the Mountain of the Lord: Cedar City Utah Temple History* (Salt Lake City: Church of Jesus Christ of Latter-day Saints, 2019), 7.
16. Burgess and historical committee, *Come Ye*, 2, 4.
17. Burgess and historical committee, *Come Ye*, 4–5.
18. Jason Swensen, "The Dream Has Now Been Realized," *Church News*, October 29, 2017, 5.
19. Rachel Steizer and Valerie Johnson, "Site Dedicated for New Sacred Edifice," *Church News*, August 16, 2015, 3; Burgess and historical committee, *Come Ye*, 19–25.

20. Swensen, "The Dream Has Now Been Realized," 5.
21. Burgess and historical committee, *Come Ye*, 56.
22. Burgess and historical committee, *Come Ye*, 75.
23. Burgess and historical committee, *Come Ye*, 76.
24. Rachel Sterver, "More Than 3,000 Youth Celebrate," *Church News*, December 17, 2017, 6–7.
25. "The Ogden Temple," *Ensign*, February 1978, 80.
26. "Rededication: The History of the Ogden Utah Temple" (prepared by the Ogden Temple Rededication Committee, 2014), 31–32.
27. *Ogden Standard-Examiner*, February 18, 2010; Scott Schwebke, "Renovated Ogden Temple Will Look Similar to Bountiful," *Standard-Examiner* (Ogden, UT), September 10, 2010, 2A.
28. *Rededication*, 32.
29. Bryon Saxton, "Ogden Temple Renovation Elicits 'Oohs' and 'Ahhs,'" *Standard-Examiner*, October 21, 2012; *Standard-Examiner*, July 30, 2014; R. Scott Lloyd, "Media Tour Newly Renovated Edifice," *Church News*, August 3, 2014, 3.
30. "Rededication," 43.
31. Julie Dockstader Heaps, "Ogden Utah Temple," *Church News*, September 14, 2014, 11.
32. Marianne Holman Prescott, "Shine the Light," *Church News* September 28, 2014, 6–7; Heaps, "New Verse for Song Memorializes Teens," *Church News*, September 28, 2014, 7.
33. Sarah Jane Weaver, "President Monson Rededicates 14th Temple," *Church News*, September 28, 2014, 3–4.
34. "A Haven of Peace," *Church News*, September 28, 2014, 5.
35. Janene Baadsgaard, "The Payson Utah Temple, 2010–2015" (unpublished manuscript), 7–9.
36. Baadsgaard, "Payson Utah Temple," 9.
37. Baadsgaard, "Payson Utah Temple," 9.
38. "Temple in Payson," *Church News*, January 30, 2010, 2.
39. Lloyd, "Construction Begins," 3.
40. Baadsgaard, "Payson Utah Temple," 32–33.
41. Genelle Pugmire and James Roh, "A Golden Gleam," *Daily Herald*, October 11, 2013, 1.
42. Baadsgaard, "Payson Utah Temple," 51–90.
43. Genelle Pugmire, "Payson Temple a Symbol of Faithfulness," in *Payson LDS Temple*, 26, 28, in author's possession.
44. Baadsgaard, "Payson Utah Temple," 251.
45. Marianne Holman Prescott, "Fill the Earth with Love," *Church News*, June 14, 2015, 8–9; Pugmire, "Payson Temple," 35–36; Baaddsgarard, "Payson Utah Temple," 250–53.
46. Gerry Avant, "Faith and History Resonate," *Church News*, June 14, 2015, 5.
47. "Accept it as Thy Holy House," *Church News*, June 14, 2015, 7.
48. Yvonne Cheney to Richard O. Cowan, August 14, 2020.
49. Jason Swensen, "Welcome Back to the Jordan River Utah Temple," *Church News*, March 18, 2018, 8–10.
50. Scott Taylor, "A Call for Unity and Righteousness," *Church News*, May 27, 2018, 3–4.
51. Marianne Holman Prescott, "Youth Walk Outside Their Comfort Zones," *Church News*, May 20, 2018, 4–5.
52. Prescott, "17,000 Youth are 'Ready' for Temple," *Church News*, May 27, 2018, 6–7.
53. "Home-Centered, Church-Supported," *Church News*, September 2, 2018, 14.
54. Rededicatory prayer, in "Temple Is an Offering," *Church News*, May 27, 2018, 5.

14

Refreshing, Renovating, and Restoring Pioneer Temples

The St. George, Salt Lake, and Manti Utah Temples

Manti Sunset from on High, by Alan Fullmer.

While new temples were under construction during the twenty-first century from one end of Utah to another, Church leaders disclosed a major effort to preserve the Beehive State's four nineteenth-century houses of the Lord. At the October 2018 general conference, President Russell M. Nelson affirmed, "The proper care and maintenance of these temples is very important to us. With the passage of time, temples are inevitably in need of refreshing and renewal. To that end, plans are now being made to renovate and update the Salt Lake Temple and other pioneer generation temples."[1]

He elaborated on this theme at the conference six months later: "The earliest [temples] stand as monuments to the faith and vision of our beloved pioneers. Each temple constructed by them resulted from their great personal sacrifice and effort. Each one stands as a stunning jewel in the crown of pioneer achievement. Ours is the sacred responsibility to care for them. Therefore, these pioneer temples will soon undergo a period of renewal and refreshing, and for some a major restoration. Efforts will be made to preserve the unique historicity in each temple wherever possible, preserving the inspiring beauty and unique craftsmanship of generations long since past."[2] Elder David A. Bednar of the Twelve said that the Brethren had known for a long time that these temples had to be brought up to modern building codes, "but the time was not right" because the needed "technology, equipment, and the right team were not yet available" until now.[3]

The temples in St. George and Salt Lake closed in 2019 for renovation. The Manti Temple followed in 2021. With the announcement in April 2021 of a second temple to be built in Cache Valley and located in Smithfield, Utah, the impact of the closing of the Logan Temple will be lessened when its renovation time is announced.

The St. George Utah Temple

For months, experts from the Church's Special Projects Department thoroughly examined the condition of the St. George Utah Temple inside and out. They could see that the structure needed to be updated and strengthened. Historic Sites curator Emily Utt and architectural historian Elwin Robinson and others had the assignment to carefully document the building's architectural style and furnishings. They discovered that original construction workers had left their signatures and even bits of poetry in some hidden places within the walls. "It's been really fun to go back and see those things as we've gotten into this project," Utt admitted.[4]

Representatives of various Church departments traveled to St. George on Wednesday, May 22, 2019, to conduct a news conference announcing details for the upcoming renovation of the temple there. Brent W. Roberts, managing director of the Special Projects Department, started by emphasizing that after the temple closed in November, it would "undergo extensive structural, mechanical, plumbing, and finish work," and should reopen in about three years. Emily Utt reminded the group

Rendering of St. George Utah Temple exterior. Courtesy of Intellectual Reserve, Inc.

that the temple had been built through the "great personal sacrifice of St. George residents" and with "the unified effort of Latter-day Saint communities hundreds of miles apart." She explained that it had been renovated on several previous occasions and expressed the expectation that the present renovation would honor and build on the "contribution" and "diligence of those who had come before."

Andy Kirby, director of Historic Temple Renovations, then laid out the scope of the work to be done. The temple would be strengthened from foundation to tower. Original wooden floors, trusses, and joists would be reinforced with steel. The annex on the north and the stairway addition on the west, both built during the 1970s, would be replaced with updated structures whose exteriors "sympathetically" match the architecture of the original temple. Ordinance spaces would be moved into the temple itself, while mechanical facilities would be shifted to the annex. The street on the north would even be raised a few feet, making it more level with the temple's entrance and thus eliminating the need for steep ramps. Interior furnishings and

Rendering of St. George Utah Temple interior recommend desk. Courtesy of Intellectual Reserve, Inc.

accessories would be "consistent with the dignity and beauty of the historic temple" and reflect the mid-nineteenth century when it was built. New murals in instruction rooms would be inspired by those that had been in the temple earlier. The large assembly room on the fourth floor would be restored. Enhanced landscaping would include more trees and feature a plaza where bridal parties exiting the temple could greet families and friends. Hence, the project would include "preservation, restoration, renovation, and new construction." Andy Kirby affirmed that it was "an honor to be entrusted with this important task."

In the foreground, steel fabricated stairs stand ready for installation in the St. George Utah Temple as workers prepare the exterior temple for painting. Once completed, the historic temple and the new north and west additions will be seamless in appearance. Courtesy of Intellectual Reserve, Inc.

Michael Suhaka, who would become managing director of the Temple Department on July 1, explained that the temple presidency and workers would all be released when the temple closed, that Saints in the St. George district were encouraged to attend other temples during the closure, and that the Cedar City and Las Vegas Temples were gearing up for increased activity.

After the St. George Temple closed on November 4, 2019, the temple's historic east doors were removed for preservation, and plywood filled the openings. Protective plywood coverings were also placed over the long stairways leading up to these doors. The annex on the north and the stairway addition on the west needed to be removed so new construction could begin. Strengthening the temple's hand-laid stone foundation was an early priority. Trenches along the temple's walls provided access. At each corner, steel pipes were driven thirty-five to forty feet into the ground, and the load of the temple's weight would be shored up by these micropiles. The fourteen interior stone support columns were strengthened by having their bases wrapped in resin-infused fiberglass. Timber beams were clad in steel. The temple has stood for nearly a century and a half, noted Eric Jamison, field project manager for the Special Projects Department. "After beefing this up, we're going to be able to ensure that the foundations last far beyond that."[5]

In February excavation for the new annex was underway, and soon concrete was being poured for the foundation and basement floor. During the next six months, structural steel girders and beams were put in place for the three-story facility. As the precast concrete

Arched doorways of maple and poplar in the north addition of the St. George Utah Temple replicate original millwork in the historic temple, January 2022. Guests will experience a seamless transition from the north addition to the historic part of the temple. Courtesy of Intellectual Reserve, Inc.

> The notion that "St. George will blossom like a rose is a very important part of this community. When people come here for the open house, it will be green and lush and beautiful."

Above: Aerial view, St. George Utah Temple. Below: Palm trees outside the temple. Courtesy of Intellectual Reserve, Inc.

exterior cladding was added in September, one could see how the round windows, columns, and battlements in the annex matched those of the temple. While interior walls were being constructed in the annex, four efficient state-of-the-art plumbing, electrical, heating, and air-conditioning systems replaced decades-old equipment throughout the temple itself.

Typically, landscaping begins only after most exterior construction is completed. As early as May 2020, however, many new trees and shrubs were being planted to provide additional shade and serenity. The notion that "St. George will blossom like a rose is a very important part of this community," observed Emily Utt. "This town is very proud of its landscape, of its trees, of its plantings." The goal was to have the landscaping well established and flourishing by the time the temple was ready for its rededication, Eric Jamison explained. "When people come here for the open house, it will be green and lush and beautiful," Utt added.[6] Later, two rows of palms were added to frame the iconic view of the historic temple's east front. The octagonal tower's dome was also removed and replaced by one of darker metal which was closer to the original.

Groundwater concerns, a problem the pioneer builders also had to overcome, delayed work on the west elevators and stairways extension for over a year. Spring water under the temple needed to be channeled away.[7] By mid 2021, foundations were being poured for this structure, and during the fall its walls began to rise. Completion of this facility was the final major construction in the temple's renovation. Finishing interior cabinetry, painting, and furnishing as well as final touches on exterior landscaping would complete the project in 2023 and be ready for rededication. "It's quite beautiful," Andy Kirby affirmed. "I'm so excited to have people see that beautiful historic temple refreshed and renewed. They'll recognize their temple when they go back," he continued. "It will be more functional; it will be easier to get around with the new elevators and stairs."[8]

The Salt Lake Temple

At a news conference conducted in the South Visitors' Center on Friday, April 19, 2019, President Nelson asserted that the building of temples worldwide is evidence that the Savior's Church has been restored. "Temples are precious to us," he continued, "because in them Church members and their families participate in sacred ceremonies and ordinances that are the crowning facet of the gospel of Jesus Christ. The highest blessings that God offers to His faithful children are available only in a temple." He affirmed that for more than a century and a quarter, the Salt Lake Temple had been "a beacon of light." Because the pioneer-era temples are outstanding examples of "architectural design, engineering, and the use of materials then available" and because they are among the most heavily utilized temples in the Church, "we have a sincere desire, we have a sacred responsibility to care for them." Church leaders then announced specific plans to renovate the Salt Lake Temple and its surroundings so they might continue to bless the Saints "for generations to come." The temple would close at the end of the year and reopen about four years later. At the heart of the project was an extensive seismic upgrade to protect temple patrons as well as the temple itself in the case of a major earthquake. In the process, temple facilities would be enhanced to better accommodate their sacred purposes. At the same time, Bishop Dean M. Davies, first counselor in the Presiding Bishopric, explained that the hope was that visitors would "feel more welcomed and invited to enjoy historic Temple Square."[9]

The desire was to restore the temple's interior to its original character. Planners worked closely with Emily Utt, studying the original design, tracing modifications over the years, and analyzing paint samples to return the temple more faithfully to the earlier Victorian palette of colors. Even outside, the grounds were to be returned more to their appearance at the time the temple was built. The plaza over to State Street on the east was to be refurbished with more seating and other changes to enhance the visitor experience; artwork would specifically focus more on Jesus Christ. President Nelson assured the group, "We promise that you will love the results." Jacobsen Construction, who had built a number of other temples, was appointed to be the general contractor.

Preparation for Renovation

Following the last endowment session on Saturday evening, December 28, 2019, the Salt Lake Temple closed for renovation. Greg and Jill Tingey, who had been temple workers for twenty years, were among those serving on this last day. "There were a lot of tears," Greg acknowledged. "There were a lot of people who just didn't want to leave, and neither did we." Jill concurred: "It felt like home. It was hard to see that come to a close. It was very tender." Adding to their emotion, that day was their wedding anniversary. Before leaving the temple, they were able to spend a few quiet moments in the very room where they had been sealed thirty-five years earlier.[10]

Following the last endowment session on December 28, 2019, the Salt Lake Temple closed for renovation. "There were a lot of people who just didn't want to leave, and neither did we."

On a wintry Thursday morning, January 2, 2020, protective fences began going up around the projected construction area. Eventually the plywood fence would be fitted with plexiglass windows so visitors could view the progress of this momentous renovation project.

During this same week, a lesser known but important process was unfolding inside. Known as "decommissioning" the temple, it started with workers removing records, clothing, and other sacred items used in temple ordinances from the building. It technically was transitioning from being a working temple into a construction site. The laundry, offices, and custodial closets were cleaned out. Furniture was removed and placed in storage. Historic stained glass and light fixtures were removed and preserved. Historic surfaces inside the temple were also covered. Emily Utt reflected on how the temple had been carefully protected for over a century and affirmed, "It is a sacred experience to be involved in preparing it for this next important step." "Even as this temple becomes a construction site," Andy Kirby assured, "we never lose sight of its sacred purpose and history."[11]

Outside, monuments, sidewalks, planter boxes, shrubs, and trees needed to be cleared so the project could begin. A prized cedar of Lebanon tree, however, was preserved, its root system carefully protected. On January 15 the South Visitors' Center was demolished. A portion of the historic wall around Temple Square was also removed so eventually there could be a less obstructed and more inviting view of the temple from busy South Temple Street. As had been done in St. George, the historic doors were also removed from the east and west ends of the temple for preservation, their openings being filled with plywood. Inside, HVAC units were placed throughout the building to regulate temperature and humidity and to protect fine surfaces and historic woodwork.

The first devotional for construction workers took place Wednesday morning, March 4, 2020. Emily Utt spoke on "a sense of the sacred" in her devotional address. "High on the east tower of the Salt Lake Temple are carved the words 'Holiness to the Lord,'" she noted. "That phrase is a reminder to everyone who walks past that it is a holy building. A sacred building. The temple isn't a common public building. It was built for a higher purpose." She insisted that "Holiness to the Lord" also was an affirmation by the temple's builders that they were giving "their very best to Him.

Rendering of the south side of the Salt Lake Temple and future Temple Square. Courtesy of Intellectual Reserve, Inc.

The temple was the place where they would make sacred promises, called covenants, with God. It was the place they would create relationships that would last forever. Even if they didn't live to see it completed, the temple would be a place of holiness for their children and the generations after." She then told her audience that this same attitude could elevate their own work on the temple. "Keeping a sense of the sacred is giving our very best to the project. It is taking the time to do the job right even if no one sees it. It is asking for God's help as we work. If we approach our problems with a sense of the sacred, we will be guided to the right solutions. Even though this is a messy and noisy construction site," she concluded, "we can keep this a holy place. Your daily efforts to keep a sense of the sacred will keep this temple holy until it is rededicated."[12]

During March 2020 the COVID-19 pandemic swept across the land. Renovation work continued with proper precautions. If that weren't enough, the Salt Lake Valley had a 5.7 magnitude earthquake early Wednesday morning, March 18. Several Church buildings sustained structural damage, especially in the West Valley and Magna areas, where the quake centered. Damage to the Salt Lake Temple was minor. A few pinnacle stones on the towers were dislodged. Witnesses saw the statue of the angel Moroni swaying back and forth, the suspension system inside the tower doing

Above: Emily Utt shows paper items to the First Presidency (left to right: Dallin H. Oaks, Russell M. Nelson, and Henry B. Eyring). Courtesy of Intellectual Reserve, Inc.

Right: Coins from the Salt Lake Temple capstone. Courtesy of Intellectual Reserve, Inc.

its job. In the process, the angel's horn was shaken loose. Within a day or so, workmen had retrieved the crumpled horn from battlements lower on the tower where it had fallen. Church spokesman Daniel Woodruff noted that this event emphasized why the project of renovation "is so necessary to preserve this historic building and create a safer environment for all our patrons and visitors."[13]

Exactly two months later, on Monday, May 18, the statue and three-foot ball it stood on, together weighing five thousand pounds, were removed from the temple and carefully set on the ground with a huge crane. The plan was for the angel to be stored, refurbished, and eventually returned to its place on the temple's east center tower. Pinnacles were also removed from the towers and carefully inventoried so they could eventually be returned to their exact same places; inserting steel pins would prevent them from ever sliding out of place again. Conservator Emiline Twitchell and curator Emily Utt were anxious to examine the capstone's historic contents. They found that the books, photographs, and other paper items were badly deteriorated despite being wrapped in silk oilcloth. Only the approximately four hundred coins were in relatively good condition.[14]

Angel Moroni and capstone being removed from the Salt Lake Temple. Courtesy of Intellectual Reserve, Inc.

A major goal of the renovation was to strengthen the temple's foundations. Jacobsen Construction turned to Forell/Elsesser Structural Engineers, a renowned engineering firm in San Francisco, for help with the seismic design. This "next stage is probably the hardest," acknowledged Andy Kirby. "We seek the inspiration of Father in Heaven," he testified, "and we know He will give us His guidance in building His house." He firmly believed that "the engineers have been guided in working through all the details."[15]

The foundations first needed to be uncovered so they could be fortified. The underground tunnel along the temple on the south had been demolished in February 2020, and the sealing room addition on the north was dismantled in July. Great care was taken to protect the historic wall of the temple itself. During that same month, the temple annex on the north, including offices, a chapel, dressing rooms and other support facilities, was also removed. Rubble was carefully sifted so metal, concrete, and other usable materials could be recycled. Once the temple's foundation was uncovered inside and outside, steps were taken to solidify the sandstone footings. Many three-inch shafts were drilled through the stones at various angles from inside

Salt Lake Temple construction site. Courtesy of Intellectual Reserve, Inc.

Because the Salt Lake Temple's historic murals had been painted directly on the lath and plaster walls, they could not be preserved as part of the project.

as well as outside and then filled with special high-strength grout which also pushed out to fill voids and joints. Threaded steel rods or "rock anchors" were also drilled through the footings and then fitted with nuts which were tightened to hold the stones together. "Secant walls" of interlocking columns of steel and concrete forty feet deep were constructed against the outside edge of the foundation to keep the soil on which the temple rested in place while adjoining ground was excavated.

An Adjustment in Plans

Because the Salt Lake Temple's historic murals had been painted directly on the lath and plaster walls, they could not be preserved as part of the project. This was a great disappointment to those who had looked forward to the murals remaining in place. Hence, the murals were "carefully photographed and documented," and some original portions were "preserved in the Church's archives."[16]

Another need grew out of the temple's location at Church headquarters. Saints from all over the world flocked to "the top of the mountains" (Isaiah 2:2) to attend the historic Salt Lake Temple. Hence, the capacity of the temple needed to be greater, and Church leaders wanted visitors to have the same kind of experience as in any other temple, and to enjoy it in their own language, which would be difficult in sessions presented by live actors.

The First Presidency testified, "We have felt the Lord's hand guiding us in modifying several aspects of the renovation." On March 12, 2021, the Presidency announced the following changes:

- There would be two baptistries, both located on the lower floor of the new annex.
- Two new endowment instruction rooms in the space formerly occupied by the baptistry would be added, bringing the total to five. Four would be on the first floor, and one on the second. Each would seat 150 patrons. New sessions could begin every twenty or thirty minutes rather than just one each hour.
- Rather than being progressive, moving from room to room, and presented by live actors, all endowment sessions would be conducted in a single room by film (in more than eighty languages). That would greatly reduce the amount of memorization required of temple workers. "There is a desire to ensure that the learning and experience are similar for all who come to the temple from anywhere in the world," the First Presidency affirmed in their statement. "The same

Rendering of the second baptistry in the Salt Lake Temple. Courtesy of Intellectual Reserve, Inc.

ordinances, covenants, and authority are available in every temple and will now be presented in the same way, and now in more than eighty languages."

- Ten new sealing rooms would be added, bringing the total to twenty-three. They would be of varying sizes, the largest accommodating seventy-five guests.
- The cafeteria would be discontinued, the space being needed for functions more directly connected with the ordinances.
- Changes would make the temple more readily accessible to patrons with mobility challenges, complying with all government accessibility requirements.

The Work Continues

Because the pioneers had relied primarily on gravity and mortar to hold the temple together, its high masonry walls and towers would be particularly vulnerable in a strong earthquake. The whole building therefore needed to be reinforced to keep it together in a quake. The pioneer foundations had already been bonded and strengthened. Work on the temple's roof commenced in 2021. A tower crane installed the previous October south of the temple made this possible. It was 250 feet tall—40 feet higher than the temple's tallest tower. The old copper roof was removed and replaced by a temporary covering, like a heavy tarp. The thousands of stones forming the battlements and buttress caps along the edge of the roof were carefully removed to make way for a structural concrete bonding beam running the length of each wall

Russell M. Nelson and Wendy Watson Nelson at the Salt Lake Temple site. Courtesy of Intellectual Reserve, Inc.

and completely around the perimeter of the roof, to which new steel trusses would be secured. These new trusses, eighty-eight feet long and weighing thirty-five thousand pounds, were installed next to the original steel trusses. They were added two at a time, filled with crossbeams to provide horizontal stability, and bolted rather than welded to avoid the possibility of fire. Thus, only one section of roof had to be opened at a time, limiting exposure of the interior to weather before the permanent copper roof was put into place. This reinforced roof was a key part of the overall seismic strengthening of the temple. Steel frameworks nicknamed "Christmas trees" were constructed to strengthen the six towers, which were then anchored to the bonding beam surrounding the roof. Next, four-inch-diameter channels were precisely drilled down through the walls, so steel cables could tie or clamp the roof structure to the reinforced foundation eighty feet below.

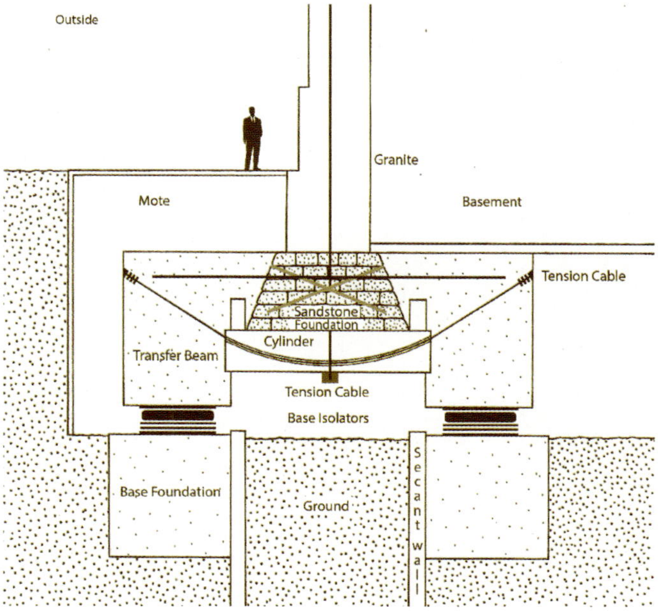

Salt Lake Temple foundation cross section showing seismic upgrades. Courtesy of Lee R. Cowan.

President Nelson toured the construction site Saturday, May 22, 2021. While there, he recorded part of his message for October general conference: "As I examine the craftsmanship of this entire building, I marvel at what the pioneers accomplished." Nevertheless, he observed, "These many decades later, however, if we examine the foundation closely, we can see the effects of erosion, gaps in the original stonework, and varying stages of stability in the masonry. Now as I witness what modern engineers, architects, and construction experts can do to reinforce that original foundation, I am absolutely amazed. Their work is astonishing!"[17]

Jack and bore used to insert a row of cylindrical steel casings crosswise under footings around the Salt Lake Temple. Courtesy of Intellectual Reserve, Inc.

An exposed portion of the original sandstone foundation of the Salt Lake Temple. Holes (shown above) have been drilled preparatory to inserting rod fasteners that will tie the foundation together and give additional support. Courtesy of Church Newsroom.

With the temple's historic footings thoroughly consolidated, the next step, beginning in late August 2021, was to use a carefully planned "jack and bore" process to insert a row of cylindrical steel casings crosswise under these footings all around the temple. These giant cylinders were four feet in diameter, one inch thick, and long enough to extend out a few feet both inside and outside from under the sandstone footings. A web of heavy No. 18 steel rebar called a "cage," including conduits for steel tension cables, was inserted. When all were in place, the temple rested on them. An array of laser sensors warned of even the slightest movement in the temple.

The next step was to deepen the excavations next to the foundations and cylinders, both inside under the temple and outside, by an additional sixteen feet. In these huge trenches, new parallel footings of reinforced concrete were then constructed. Ninety-eight base isolators were next placed atop these new footings in pairs, one on the inside and the other on the outside of the temple walls. Each base isolator, all stainless steel, consisted of two disks, one on top of the other, about seven feet in diameter. Their inner surfaces were concave, with something like a giant ball bearing that could roll between them and allow the upper plate to shift from side to side, the whole assembly being about two and one-half feet high.

Huge transfer beams of reinforced concrete, about fifteen feet high and up to fifteen feet wide, were next constructed on top of the base isolators against the inside and outside of the temple's historic stone foundations. The steel in the cylinders was welded at each end to the steel inside these transfer beams. The maze of steel cables passing through the conduits inside the cylinders was attached to the inside beam and the outside beam; tension was increased, pulling the transfer beams tight against the sandstone and granite blocks and making the whole into a single and larger foundation. The soil was then cut out from underneath the cylindrical casings, thereby transferring the massive weight of the temple atop the support cylinders through the base isolators to the new footings. In effect, the temple was floating above the ground. Thus, the building could remain relatively still if the earth shook beneath it.

The isolator allowed movement up to five feet in any direction, so there needed to be a gap or "moat" up to five feet wide on all sides of the temple. The Salt Lake Temple has six underground entrances bridging this gap. Each was fitted with an accordion-like section that allowed it to flex. Ducts and other utilities that cross the moat were likewise fitted. On the surface, the gap was covered with large metal plates that could slide back and forth during a quake; they in turn were covered with pavers or other landscaping materials.

Meanwhile, excavation for the new facilities north of the temple also continued during 2021. Steel columns sunk deep into the ground around the perimeter of the excavation and connected by heavy planks kept the outside soil from caving in. As the digging went deeper, more of a heavy secant wall constructed north of the

The area where the North Visitors' Center once stood is refilled with soil to build up a level surface and prepare for the construction of additional restrooms for guests of the Tabernacle and Assembly Hall, Salt Lake City, March 2022. Courtesy of Intellectual Reserve, Inc.

Top to bottom: Interior renderings of the veil room, an endowment room, and a sealing room in the Salt Lake Temple. Courtesy of Intellectual Reserve, Inc.

temple was exposed; it needed to be strengthened so it could withstand forces created by the temple's weight of about 185 million pounds.[18]

When the excavation reached a sufficient depth, a 180-foot-long pedestrian tunnel was constructed under North Temple Street. As the rocks and dirt were removed, steel support arches were inserted every four feet. It would connect the underground parking garage at the Conference Center more safely and conveniently with the grand hall on the middle level of the new entrance to the temple.

In December 2021 the excavation on the north reached its maximum depth of eighty-five feet, and preparations began for construction. A second tower crane had been set up on the north side of the temple to assist. A steel mat was laid down to support the forty-two-inch-thick reinforced concrete mat foundation of the new annex. Three pumper trucks for eight to ten hours delivered eighteen hundred cubic yards—the largest single cement-laying operation of the entire project.[19] This new facility would embrace two entry pavilions on the surface and three stories underground. It would house a waiting room for guests attending temple weddings, a larger chapel, the two new baptistries, dressing rooms, sealing rooms, offices, and other facilities.

Meanwhile, work on the Church Office Building Plaza had begun. After the area between Main and State Streets was closed in February 2021, the fountain, which had leaked into the parking garage below, was removed. Landscaping was then taken out and soil scraped away so the garage's cement roof could be thoroughly waterproofed before landscaping was reconstructed. The new design called for a crescent-shaped array of bases for the flags of the world, emphasizing the scope of the Church's mission to share the gospel of Jesus Christ.

In June 2021 the First Presidency announced that the former North Visitors' Center would be demolished. This area would be replaced "with gardens and contemplative space" offering "a more direct and clear view of the Salt Lake Temple." This would be consistent with President Nelson's goal to "enhance, refresh, and beautify

Renderings of the creation room (left) and garden room (right) in the Salt Lake Temple. Courtesy of Intellectual Reserve, Inc.

the temple and its surrounding grounds." Additional public restrooms would also be provided in the northwest corner of Temple Square.[20]

In May 2022 excavation began for the two new visitors' pavilions on Temple Square south of the temple. These two buildings, connected by a common underground level, were designed to afford an unobstructed view of the temple from South Temple Street where many visitors passed by. A unique feature of the lower floor would be replicas of rooms in the temple. Thus, visitors could see what the baptismal font, a sealing room, and even what an endowment instruction room were like. Exhibits would focus on eternal families and other doctrinal principles undergirding the work done in temples.

While all this was being accomplished, another huge project needed to be completed in the historic temple's interior. This would include not only the renovating and refreshing of the General Authorities' council rooms and the large priesthood

The "seismic strengthening of the Salt Lake Temple and the extensive remodel of the temple and surrounding areas are sacred and significant undertakings."

Rendering of the world room, Salt Lake Temple. Courtesy of Intellectual Reserve, Inc.

Rendering of Salt Lake Temple celestial room. Courtesy of Intellectual Reserve, Inc.

assembly room on the upper floors but also the creation of the five new endowment presentation rooms below. Four would be on the lowest floor in the space formerly occupied by the creation and garden rooms and the baptistry. The fifth would be on the next floor where the world room had been located. The area of the terrestrial room would become the veil room where patrons would complete their endowment instructions. The celestial room would be thoroughly refurbished.

Thus, after the renovation of the Salt Lake Temple had passed its two-year mark, much had been accomplished, but a great deal remained to be completed. The First Presidency insisted that the "seismic strengthening of the Salt Lake Temple and the extensive remodel of the temple and surrounding areas are sacred and significant undertakings." As the work unfolded, the First Presidency acknowledged that Church leaders had "learned a great deal about the temple and its surroundings." As a result,

A view of the Salt Lake Temple from the tunnel underneath North Temple Street that will eventually connect the Conference Center parking lot to the temple, June 2021. Courtesy of Intellectual Reserve, Inc.

"inspired modifications and additions to the project and scope have been made so the temple and Temple Square may serve many generations yet to come." Therefore, the estimated completion date was pushed back. The Presidency reiterated, "We look forward to welcoming the world at that time to visit, tour, and learn about this sacred temple and The Church of Jesus Christ of Latter-day Saints."[21] Following this open house, the temple would then be rededicated and resume its service as a consecrated house of the Lord.

The Manti Utah Temple

When the First Presidency announced in March 2021 modifications in plans for the renovation of the Salt Lake Temple, they disclosed the first details concerning similar work to be done at Manti: "Beginning later this year, the Manti Temple will begin a multiyear renovation that will include mechanical updates and other changes to prepare the temple to serve for generations." Plans anticipated that the progressive room-to-room presentation by live actors would transition to single-room presentations by film. Therefore, "some elements of the temple's structure" would need to be remodeled and "updated to accommodate these changes and improve accessibility for patrons." The statement assured that "the historic staircases in the Manti Temple are being preserved during the renovation." These changes, however, meant that the murals painted on the walls of some of the larger rooms could not be saved. The announcement assured that they would be thoroughly photographed and documented before being removed. At least portions of the murals would be preserved and exhibited "in a public setting." Still, newspapers and the Internet were full of

The pioneer temple needed "upgrades and other changes to keep it useful and safe."

letters or statements decrying their impending removal from the temple. Even a group of marchers in Provo demonstrated their opposition to the plan.

Members of stake presidencies throughout the Manti Utah Temple district, civic leaders from Manti and neighboring Ephraim, and their wives were invited to a special meeting in the Manti Tabernacle on Saturday morning, May 1, 2021. In a prerecorded statement, President Nelson unfolded a new vision for the Manti Utah Temple. He reiterated that the pioneer temple needed "upgrades and other changes to keep it useful and safe. It also needs to be revised to offer the revealed ordinances and covenants to members who speak languages other than English. That will be made possible by filmed presentations." However, the endowment presentation in Manti would still be "progressive," moving from room to room as in a few other recent temples.

Manti Utah Temple with scaffolding. Courtesy of Lee R. Cowan.

President Nelson explained, "We have continued to seek the direction of the Lord on this matter," and, he added, "we have been impressed to modify our earlier plans for the Manti Utah Temple so that the pioneer craftsmanship, artwork, and character will be preserved, including the painted murals loved by so many." He emphatically announced, "We will leave those murals where they are located now, inside the Manti Utah Temple." The circumstance of the murals in the Manti Utah Temple was different than Salt Lake. While the murals in the garden and world rooms of the Salt Lake Temple were painted directly on the plaster walls in the 1890s, those in Manti were painted on canvas during the 1940s. Thus, their preservation would be easier to accomplish. C. C. A. Christensen's mural in the Manti Temple's creation room, however, would need to be redone. The plan was to photograph it carefully and then have artists reproduce it precisely.[22] President Nelson also announced that a new temple would be built in nearby Ephraim (see the following chapter); he explained that this would enable the Church to solve the problems of accessibility and capacity while at the same time "preserve the unique classical character and useful life of the historic Manti Utah Temple."[23]

Elder Ronald A. Rasband of the Quorum of the Twelve, who had been assigned to preside at the news conference in Manti, insisted that the change was not the result of protests, but rather he testified that it was an example of the Lord revealing "his secret unto his servants the prophets" (Amos 3:7). While the faithful were praying that they might accept the Lord's will, the prophet was pondering and praying about several options that had been presented to him. He then received one of his during-the-night promptings directing him what to do. He shared his revelation with a small group of Church leaders, and during the next ten days to two weeks, plans came together with what Elder Rasband described as "moving with all due haste or warp speed." President Nelson wanted the Saints in Manti to be the first to hear, so the matter was kept strictly confidential.[24]

This was the first time since Payson, over a decade and a hundred temples earlier, that such an announcement had not come as part of a general conference. Brent W. Roberts, managing director of the Special Projects Department, was grateful that they could get to work right away rather than needing to wait for the next conference. He indicated that much of the planning had already been done. They had researched the history of the original design, soil composition, and limestone strength, as well as waterproofing methodologies. The original plan would have required over three years, but without needing to make such major changes as moving walls, Roberts estimated the work could be done in eighteen months to two years. Waterproofing the foundation and the east wall would be a major task. The interior would be refreshed, protecting historic surfaces including the murals. Thus, as Roberts put it, the project would be a "mix of preservation, restoration, and installation of new equipment."[25]

W. Christopher Waddell, first counselor in the Presiding Bishopric, called Manti a "jewel of a temple." He insisted that its renovation will "not only honor the Lord, but will honor our pioneer forebears whose sacrifice and talents will continue to be

The temple renovation will "not only honor the Lord, but will honor our pioneer forebears whose sacrifice and talents will continue to be on display for generations to come."

Manti Utah Temple. Courtesy of Intellectual Reserve, Inc.

When you see the beauty of what the early pioneers have done, it "is just a remarkable thing."

on display for generations to come as members of the Church worship in this sacred House of the Lord." Bishop Waddell asserted that "President Nelson truly is a prophet to the world, and his concern is for all of God's children." When you think of people speaking over eighty languages, many first-generation pioneers in their own lands, being able to enter these iconic temples and see the beauty of what the early pioneers have done, it "is just a remarkable thing."[26]

The Manti Utah Temple closed October 2, 2021, so the work could begin. One of the first projects was to stop water from leaking into the temple through its east wall where the building was cut into the mountainside up to the level of the third floor. A deep excavation exposed this wall so improved waterproofing could be inserted. "It has been a very persistent leak for many, many years with several attempts to try to fix it," Andy Kirby acknowledged. "We hope we will be the final attempt to fix it." Work can then focus on cleaning and preserving the interior.[27]

While renovation was moving forward in the Manti and Salt Lake Temples, Latter-day Saints in the Cache Valley area awaited further word concerning plans for the Logan Temple. During this same time, there also was a series of announcements of about a dozen new temples for the Beehive State.

Notes

1. Russell M. Nelson, "Becoming Exemplary Latter-day Saints," *Ensign*, November 2018, 114.
2. Nelson, "Closing Remarks," *Ensign*, May 2019, 111.
3. Rachel Sterzer Gibson, "Five Lessons Learned from Renovation of the Temple," *Church News*, October 25, 2020, 10.
4. Emily Utt, news conference in St. George, May 22, 2019, recording in Richard O. Cowan's possession.

5. "St. George Utah Temple Renovation Hits One-Year Milestone," November 2020, Church Newsroom (https://newsroom.churchofjesuschrist.org/article/one-year-milestone-for-st-george-temple-renovation-project).
6. "St. George Utah Temple Hits One-Year Milestone."
7. Rick Satterfield, email message to Richard Cowan, June 7, 2021.
8. Trent Toone, "St. George, Manti Renovations Continue," *Church News*, April 2, 2022, 12.
9. The *Church News* of April 27, 2019, published a special issue on the Salt Lake Temple renovation.
10. KSL-TV, *The Salt Lake Temple*, aired April 3, 2021, recording in authors' possession.
11. Sydney Walker, "What It Means to Decommission a Temple," *Church News*, January 12, 2020, 3.
12. "Construction Update," March 6, 2020, Church Newsroom (https://newsroom.churchofjesuschrist.org/article/temple-square-renovation-project-updates-january-march-2020).
13. Walker, "Salt Lake Temple Sustains Minor Damage in Quake," *Church News*, March 22, 2020, 2; Walker, "Church Buildings Damaged in 5.7 Quake," *Church News*, March 29, 2020, 21.
14. Sarah Jane Weaver, "Angel Moroni Statue, Capstone Removed for Preservation, Restoration," *Church News*, May 24, 2020, 11; Walker, "What's Inside the Salt Lake Time Capsule?," *Church News*, August 2, 2020, 9–11.
15. "Salt Lake Temple Renovation," September 25, 2020, Church Newsroom video (https://newsroom.churchofjesuschrist.org/article/salt-lake-temple-renovation-update-september-2020); Scott Taylor, "Salt Lake Temple Foundation Stones Link Past to Present," *Church News*, October 4, 2020, 6–7.
16. Taylor, "First Presidency Announces Salt Lake Temple Changes," *Church News*, March 20, 2021, 12–14.
17. Russell M. Nelson, "The Temple and Your Spiritual Foundation," *Liahona*, November 2021, 93.
18. Trent Toone, "A Look 1 Year into the Salt Lake Temple Renovation," *Church News*, January 16, 2021, 14–15.
19. Christine Rappleye, "Vertical Drilling Above, Pipes Below," *Church News*, December 18, 2021, 16.
20. Scott Taylor, "North Visitors' Center to be Demolished," *Church News*, June 19, 2021, 15.
21. Sarah Jane Weaver, "Work on Temple Renovation Project 'Truly Remarkable,'" *Church News*, December 18, 2021, 15.
22. Emily Utt and Laura Price Howe, email messages to R. Devan Jensen, November 7, 2022.
23. Nelson, prerecorded remarks, May 1, 2021.
24. Quoted in official announcement, May 1, 2021, Church Newsroom (https://newsroom.churchofjesuschrist.org/article/ephraim-utah-temple-manti-temple-renovation); Ronald A. Rasband, remarks at Manti, Utah, recording in Richard O. Cowan's possession.
25. Quoted in official announcement, May 1, 2021.
26. Quoted in Tad Walch, "How President Nelson Received the Revelation about Two Temples," *Church News*, May 6, 2021.
27. "Update on the Manti Temple," *Church News*, April 2, 2022, 12–13.

15

A New Wave of Temples during the Twenty-First Century

The Saratoga Springs, Layton, Red Cliffs, Deseret Peak, Orem, Taylorsville, Ephraim, Syracuse, Lindon, Smithfield, Heber Valley, and Reconstructed Provo Utah Temples

Saratoga Springs Utah Temple.

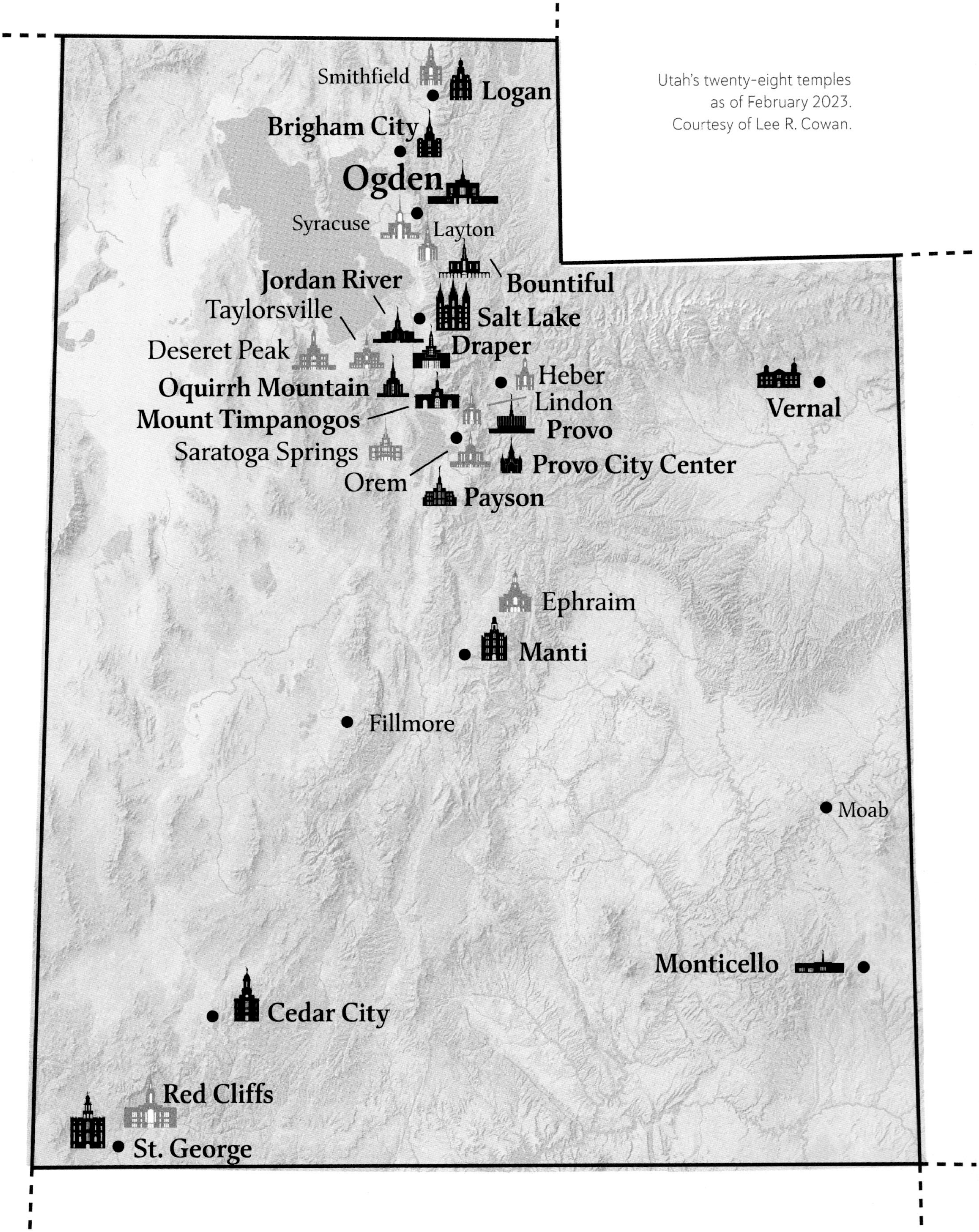

Utah's twenty-eight temples as of February 2023. Courtesy of Lee R. Cowan.

During his brief, nine-month administration (1994–95), President Howard W. Hunter powerfully directed the Latter-day Saints' attention toward the temple. He challenged them to "establish the temple of the Lord as the great symbol of their membership" and then added, "It would be the deepest desire of my heart to have every member of the Church temple worthy. I would hope that every adult member would be worthy of—and carry—a current temple recommend, even if proximity to a temple does not allow immediate or frequent use of it."[1] President Gordon B. Hinckley (1995–2008) then became noted for dedicating or rededicating far more temples than all of his predecessors combined. President Thomas S. Monson (2008–18) announced plans for the construction of forty-four new temples.

When Russell M. Nelson became President of the Church in 2018 at age ninety-three, some wondered if he would be able to keep up the pace. He increased it significantly, announcing plans for a hundred more temples during just his first four years as prophet, including temples in India, mainland China, Russia, and eleven in Utah, the latter being the subject of this chapter. He also spoke regularly about the importance of temple worship. At the October 2018 general conference, he announced plans to thoroughly renovate Utah's four pioneer temples and plans to build twelve new ones in Africa, Asia, South America, Mexico, and in Washington County, Utah. He then commented, "Building and maintaining temples may not change your life, but spending your time in the temple surely will. . . . I invite you to worship in the temple and pray to feel deeply the Savior's love for you, that each of you may gain your own testimony that He directs this sacred and ageless work."[2]

"Building and maintaining temples may not change your life, but spending your time in the temple surely will. . . . I invite you to worship in the temple and pray to feel deeply the Savior's love for you, that each of you may gain your own testimony that He directs this sacred and ageless work."

During the early months of 2020, a novel coronavirus swept across the world and was declared to be a pandemic. To slow the spread of COVID-19, governments banned most group meetings and required individuals to wear masks. The Church responded by shifting normal Sunday meetings to an online format and closing all temples. After a few months, the Church began a phased reopening of temples, a few at a time according to local conditions, first for only the sealing of living couples and then later for the endowment and other ordinances for living members. A year later, four temples in the Pacific Area began the process of reopening temples for limited proxy ordinances. Not until June 2022 did temples in Utah return to a more normal schedule. Even though during these years Latter-day Saints were not allowed normal access to the temples, the Church nevertheless continued to announce plans for constructing more of these sacred structures. This evidenced the importance Church leaders attached to temple worship and service.

The new wave of temples in the Beehive State would fill in the map, making them closer to Church members. All would be moderate in size, those in more populated areas ranging from seventy to ninety-six thousand square feet of floor area. They would not be as large as the Jordan River, Ogden, and Provo Temples, but they would be larger than the Draper and Oquirrh Mountain Temples. Only the Ephraim Utah Temple, located in the more rural Sanpete Valley, would be about the size of the Brigham City Utah Temple, about half as large as the others.

The Saratoga Springs and Layton Temples

Planning for the temples in Saratoga Springs and Layton was underway before President Nelson became President of the Church. Plans for the former had already been disclosed, while the latter was announced just a few weeks after he became the Church's leader.

The Saratoga Springs Utah Temple

Thermal springs near the northwest corner of Utah Lake were named for the well-known Saratoga Springs resort in New York, and the area had been a popular fishing place for Native Americans for centuries. Early European explorers to the area included Father Escalante, who visited the shores of Utah Lake in 1776, and Parley P. Pratt, the first Latter-day Saint explorer, in 1847.[3] The city of Saratoga Springs was incorporated in 1997, and it became one of the most rapidly growing areas in the United States during the early twenty-first century. President Thomas S. Monson announced plans to erect a temple there at general conference on April 2, 2017. This would be the fifth temple in Utah Valley.

Saratoga Springs Utah Temple. Courtesy of James Turner.

The Special Projects Department worked closely with Mayor Jim Miller of Saratoga Springs, and he was "very pleased" with how the new structure would "blend in with the community."[4] The 22.5-acre temple site would be in the Beacon Pointe subdivision, just west of Redwood Road. Situated on a sloping hillside, it afforded a good view of the north end of Utah Lake with Mount Timpanogos beyond. The temple would have approximately eighty-seven thousand square feet of floor area, have a basically square footprint, be three stories high, and be surmounted by a central tower. It would be on a new road to be known as Ensign Drive. A twenty-one-thousand-square-foot meetinghouse would also share the site.[5]

About a thousand invited guests were present for the temple's groundbreaking on a breezy overcast Saturday morning, October 19, 2019. Elder Craig C. Christensen of the Seventy, president of the Utah Area, presided. He recalled how a month earlier he had spent about an hour walking over the site and how he could envision construction of the future temple. "I started to think what will take place within the walls of the temple once it is completed and dedicated. I realized in a more profound way how this particular temple will bless many individuals and families." Chad Wilkins, a long-term local resident and chairman of the groundbreaking committee, recalled how years earlier Elder Neal A. Maxwell of the Twelve had affirmed that "the Lord

Audience at Saratoga Springs Utah Temple groundbreaking. Courtesy of Intellectual Reserve, Inc.

would bring people to this area."[6] He certainly had done so. "As we prepare to break ground for this new temple," Wilkins urged, "may we silently commit today to prepare the soil of our hearts to do our part to qualify for the powerful promises offered us by the Lord and His holy prophets." David Durfey, member of one of the stake presidencies, emphasized that this was a very young area with an abundance of children and youth, and that the temple was being built "because of their faith and what they need in order to grow up unto the Lord." He predicted an abundance of marriages here, saying, "It will be amazing." In his site dedicatory prayer, Elder Christensen petitioned that the youth would be drawn here and that they would "recognize through Thy spirit that this is truly a special, even holy, gathering place."[7]

Construction progressed rapidly. By the end of 2020 the temple's exterior had taken shape, with only the spire needing to be finished. This was completed the following year, and on August 20, the figure of the angel Moroni was placed atop the temple. This was over a year after the spring 2020 decision to no longer include the angel (see the discussion of the temple in Tooele Valley later in this chapter), but architectural plans for the Saratoga Springs Temple had been released in 2019 several months before that decision was made. Because of supply chain problems and delays related to the COVID pandemic, an additional year and a half would pass before the temple was ready for dedication. The First Presidency announced that the public open house would run from April 15 through July 8, 2023—an unusually long time. The temple would then be dedicated by President Henry B. Eyring on August 13 of that year.[8]

The Layton Utah Temple

North Davis County was already densely populated, so a temple located there would relieve pressure on the busy Ogden and Bountiful Temples. Plans for a temple in Layton were announced at the April 2018 general conference, and the specific site was disclosed a year later, on July 15, 2019. It would be built on a beautiful 11.89-acre site at the corner of Oak Hills Drive and Rosewood Lane in southeast Layton.[9]

The community was named for Christopher Layton, an early pioneer in Davis County. In the bench areas next to the foothills, early settlers developed dry farming, the raising of wheat and corn without irrigation. Fruit and vegetables grew in the fertile land lower in the valley.[10] While Layton originally was an agricultural area, it grew steadily in population, especially with the coming of Hill Field (now Hill Air Force Base) near the beginning of World War II. Layton is now the largest community in Davis County.

> The design for the Layton Utah Temple was released early in 2020. Like other Utah temples announced at about the same time, it would be a three-story structure and would have a floor area of about eighty-seven-thousand square feet. Its appearance, however, would be unique. Echoing the design of the historic Logan Utah Temple and the more recent Brigham City Utah Temple, it would have two attached towers, one at the east end and the other at the west.[11]

Layton Utah Temple. Courtesy of Marshall Thompson.

At the time the architectural rendering was released, the First Presidency announced that the groundbreaking would take place on Saturday, May 30. President Thomas K. Checketts, of the Layton Utah Holmes Creek Stake, headed the committee making arrangements for this event. Well over a thousand interested Saints were expected to attend, so careful planning began. Just a few weeks following this announcement, however, the COVID-19 pandemic hit, and gatherings of large groups were prohibited. Plans for the groundbreaking had to change completely. Only twenty people were invited to be present, all wearing masks and maintaining social distance. A video recording would be made available to members in the temple district.

Groundbreaking was quietly moved to May 23, 2020, so the recording could be released on the original appointed day one week later. The video combined music by The Tabernacle Choir and air views of the temple site with a recording of the brief program. Elder Christensen conducted. He likened the small gathering "to the Church's first meeting in 1830 with just a few people present" and added, "That's how this feels to me." The site dedicatory prayer was given by Randy D. Funk, a General Authority Seventy and first counselor in the

Attendance was limited at the Layton Utah Temple groundbreaking because of the COVID-19 pandemic. Courtesy of Intellectual Reserve, Inc.

Utah Area presidency. He emphasized that his prayer dedicated the land, initiated the process of construction, and petitioned blessings for the workers as well as for the people in the district. "It is an opportunity for really all to have the blessing of the Lord as we go forth and construct this beautiful temple in this site."[12]

As construction moved forward, the temple's basic form rapidly took shape by the end of 2021. The angel Moroni was added to the west tower on March 10, 2022, with the temple expected to be completed by the middle of 2023 and ready for dedication.

Temples in Washington County and Tooele Valley

The next two Utah temples, announced in October 2018 and April 2019, were close to historic centers of Latter-day Saint population. Interestingly, both would be named after broad geographical areas and would subsequently be renamed after specific geographical features.

A Temple in Washington County

The St. George Temple, Utah's first, had been built in Washington County in the extreme southwest corner of the territory and later state. At first this temple had served a broad area, including even southern California. Construction of other temples made the temple district smaller geographically, but more recent population growth in the St. George area has kept this historic temple busy. A second temple in

Progress of Red Cliffs Utah Temple in September 2022. Courtesy of Doug Tice.

Washington County would ease the pressure. Plans for this temple were announced at the October 2018 general conference. President Daniel K. Frei of the nearby Santa Clara Utah Stake "was grateful that there would be a second temple in the area: We do have a temple, but only so much work can be done.... We are already at capacity." He noted that the new temple would allow more members to serve. "It is also an indication of the Lord's confidence in the people who live in the area."[13]

The specific site was announced about a year later. While the original St. George Temple was located close to the center of town west of I-15, the new temple would be built east of the freeway in an area where fields of hay and grain were rapidly being replaced by spreading residential neighborhoods. The fourteen-acre site would be

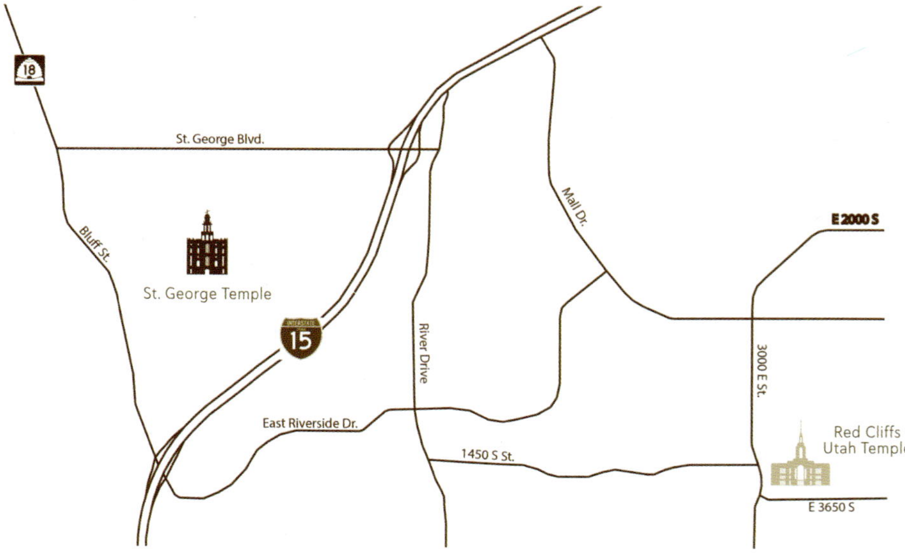

City map showing both temples in Washington County, Utah. Courtesy of Lee R. Cowan.

northeast of the intersection of 3000 East and 1580 South.[14] A rendering of the temple's design was released in April 2020. It would be a three-story structure, having about eighty-eight to ninety thousand square feet, and a central spire.[15]

At first, this temple was simply identified as being in Washington County, Utah. This wouldn't be the first time the official name of a temple was determined sometime after its initial announcement. For example, the name Provo City Center Temple was adopted several months after plans were announced to rebuild the burned-out Provo Tabernacle. The *Church News* describes the interesting way the new temple in southern Utah received its name: Elder Jeffrey R. Holland of the Quorum of the Twelve and his wife, Patricia, both of whom had grown up in southern Utah, "were driving in the proposed area of the new temple, knowing the need for a name since St. George has had its namesake temple for nearly a century and a half. He recalled his wife looking north toward Pine Valley and mention[ing] Red Cliffs as a possibility because of the dominating geological feature in the expansive view." They later suggested this name as an option to the First Presidency, commenting that "the name represents not only the immediate area, but also honors much of the entire temple district that encompasses the Virgin River region."[16] The Presidency adopted their suggestion.

Groundbreaking for the Red Cliffs Utah Temple took place on Saturday, November 7, 2020. For several days the weather had been typical of St. George, pleasant and warm. On the appointed day, however, it turned cold and blustery. The First Presidency assigned Elder Holland to return to his hometown to preside. Elder

Jeffrey R. Holland and Patricia Holland at the Red Cliffs Utah Temple groundbreaking. Courtesy of Intellectual Reserve, Inc.

Red Cliffs Utah Temple. Courtesy of Gary Davis.

Christensen conducted. Several dozen church and civic leaders and their wives were invited to be present. All wore masks and observed other precautions related to the COVID-19 virus.

"As we talk about home, safety, peace and people who love you," Elder Holland remarked, "that is a description of the temple—it is the safest, the most welcoming and reassuring place in the world." In his site dedicatory prayer, Elder Holland affirmed that the original St. George Temple had stood for a century and a half as a symbol of "the area's faith and commitment." He called the land he was dedicating "a sister site." While present-day Saints do not face the same challenges as the pioneers, Elder Holland insisted that "they have their own modern-day challenges" and that "temple attendance and worship" help us meet them.[17]

A Temple in Tooele Valley

Tooele Valley is located over the Oquirrh Mountains just west of the Salt Lake Valley. The origin of the name Tooele is uncertain. It may be the name of an early Goshute chief Tuilla, or it may be derived from the tules or bulrushes growing in a marshy or swampy section of the area.[18] As population along the Wasatch Front continued to expand, it increasingly overflowed into this valley to the west. Saints in this area were assigned to the Salt Lake Temple, some thirty miles away. Then plans for a temple in this area were announced at the general conference in April 2019. Stake president Todd C. Thompson of the Tooele Stake remarked, "This is something we've been hoping for but knowing it might not happen in our lifetimes. We were trying to just be patient and humble, and we're grateful that the Lord is answering those prayers."[19]

The design for the Deseret Peak Utah Temple (at that time called the Tooele Valley Utah Temple) was released on April 7, 2020. Its three stories would have approximately seventy thousand square feet of floor space. The exterior would be cast stone with a roof of copper shingles. Flowers native to the Tooele Valley—the cliffrose and the silvery lupin—would be featured. Architects drew details from the historic tabernacle in the area.[20] The temple's central spire reflected a change in policy regarding statues of the angel Moroni.

Since the early 1980s, virtually all new temples included figures of the herald angel atop their chief tower.[21] Some temples were dedicated without the angel because of legal restrictions but added the figure as soon as this became possible; these included Sydney (1984) and Boston (2000). Other temples had omitted the statue because of local sensibilities. Examples include the Freiberg Germany Temple, dedicated in 1985 behind the Iron Curtain in the communist-controlled German Democratic Republic, and the Paris France Temple (2017), located near Versailles,

Rendering of Deseret Peak Utah Temple. Courtesy of Intellectual Reserve, Inc.

where a golden angel might have been regarded as an attempt to outdo the world-famed palace. A few others omitted the figure for security concerns, especially small temples in less affluent areas where a statue apparently made of gold might be a temptation for vandalism or threaten the safety of patrons who might be viewed as wealthy targets for personal attack. Kinshasa, in the Democratic Republic of the Congo, and the temple in Port-au-Prince, Haiti, (renderings released in 2016 and 2017 respectively) are recent examples. All these instances, however, were regarded as exceptions to the norm of having Moroni on temples.

New Church logo. Courtesy of Intellectual Reserve, Inc.

The Deseret Peak temple's design was different because it was the first of a long series of temples planned without the statue of Moroni. This change came at a time of greater emphasis on the Savior.

The announcement of the Deseret Peak Utah Temple's design in April 2020 was different, however, as it was the first of a long series of temples planned without the statue of Moroni. This change came at a time of greater emphasis on the Savior. At the October general conference in 2017, President Nelson had emphasized the importance of the Church being known by its revealed name, The Church of Jesus Christ of Latter-day Saints (Doctrine and Covenants 115:4). Then, at the conference in April 2020, he unveiled the Church's new official logo featuring a depiction of the Savior. Previously, the angel Moroni was used as a symbol on many Church materials. The design for the temple was released just three days later. The last temple design with the familiar angel Moroni (for Durban, South Africa) had been released two months earlier in February 2020.

The original site for the Deseret Peak Utah Temple in Erda had been announced September 25, 2019.[22] In May of the following year, the county approved the Church's request to zone 167 adjoining acres for a planned community having more than four hundred residences. There were to be thirty-two acres of open space, walking trails, and parks. Still, "some local residents voiced concern about the high-density impact on the small, rural community of Erda," leading to a divisive controversy. Finally, on August 8, the First Presidency emphasized that there was "a sincere desire on the part of the Church to avoid discord in the community," so they withdrew their residential zoning request. The Presidency expressed gratitude for the faith and prayers Church members had exhibited during this process and encouraged "all people to treat one another with kindness and Christlike love."[23]

Eventually a new location was selected for the temple. In November 2020 President Nelson confidentially made the trip out to Tooele so he could personally inspect several sites the Presiding Bishopric had selected for his consideration. After having been taken to each of them, he asked to return to one. He wanted to be sure. Standing on the spot, he declared, "This is where we build the temple." Richard Droubay, who would head the local temple committee, later commented, "To have his stamp on this piece of property is amazing!"[24] This 17.98-acre site would be west of the intersection of 2400 North and 400 West in Tooele, about 2.6 miles southwest of the earlier site. It was donated by Perry Homes Utah and was amid a major new suburban housing area being developed by this corporation. Its selection was announced on January 19, 2021. At the same time the Church disclosed a new name,

Elder Brook P. Hales conducts the Deseret Peak Utah Temple groundbreaking service. Courtesy of Intellectual Reserve, Inc.

the Deseret Peak Utah Temple.[25] Deseret Peak in the Stansbury Range is probably the most conspicuous landmark in the area.

Ground was broken on a warm and breezy Saturday, May 15, 2021. Richard Droubay believed he had witnessed a series of miracles leading up to the event. Landscaping trees and shrubs, worth thousands of dollars, had been borrowed to beautify the site. On the day before the groundbreaking, a powerful wind-driven storm passed through the area. It seemed to split in two and pass by on either side of the site, thus avoiding potential significant damage. Because the pandemic was easing, 238 church and civic leaders were invited to attend. They were seated where the future temple's celestial room would be located. Elder Brook P. Hales of the Seventy, secretary to the First Presidency and a longtime resident of Tooele, presided. Previous groundbreakings during the pandemic had been recorded and then made available for viewing within a few days. The groundbreaking in Tooele was the first to be streamed live, so anyone interested could view it in real time. Speakers included Saints from the area. Kim A. Halladay, who had presided over two stakes and was now a sealer in the Salt Lake Temple, described how he had to get up at 3 a.m. in order to be on the road at 4:00 and reach that temple in time for his early shift; he affirmed that this was a privilege rather than a sacrifice. Elder Hales spoke of the factors attracting people to a temple, including its "peaceful, comforting connection

The groundbreaking in Tooele was the first to be streamed live, so anyone interested could view it in real time.

Progress of the Deseret Peak Utah Temple, September 2022. Courtesy of Carolyn Richards Baker.

between heaven and earth; and the blessing to receive covenants that bind one to God." In his site dedicatory prayer, he expressed gratitude to the Perry family who had generously donated the ground and then petitioned that the Saints "may feel the godly power" of the future "sacred edifice."[26] As the program ended, Kim Halladay was observed rushing away even before having the long-anticipated opportunity to take part in turning soil with the gold-colored shovels. "I've got to run," he called out, "I've got to fill an assignment in the [Salt Lake] temple."[27]

Temples Adjacent to College Campuses

During the women's session of general conference in October 2019, President Nelson emphasized that women as well as men may access God's power through temple ordinances and covenants. As part of this message, he announced plans for eight new temples, including two in Utah—in Orem and Taylorsville.[28] Their sites have two things in common besides the unusual session in which they were announced: both are next to a freeway, and both are located within walking distance of college campuses. The Orem Utah Temple is only a few blocks from Utah Valley University, and the Taylorsville Temple is even closer to a major campus of Salt Lake Community

College. Then in 2021, a third temple adjacent to a college was announced, the Ephraim Utah Temple, which will be close to Snow College.

The Orem Utah Temple

The Orem Temple is the sixth in Utah Valley and the third in the Provo-Orem metropolitan area. Orem's mayor, Richard Brunst, felt "surprise and excitement" when he heard the announcement. "Wow," he exclaimed, "what a great thing to happen for the residents of Orem and members of the Church throughout Utah County."[29] Concerning the planning of this and other temples, Brent Roberts, managing director of the Special Projects Department, later explained that this is not done in the same way as most buildings are planned. "We pray and attend the temple. . . . It's more of a spiritual opportunity" because planners need to know they have "a mandate" from the Lord.[30]

Both the Orem and Taylorsville Temples are next to a freeway and located within walking distance of college campuses.

Along with the excitement, there was the inevitable speculation about exactly where the new temple would be located. Church representatives had visited with officials of Vineyard, the community just west of Orem on the shores of Utah Lake, so some regarded this as the chosen site. But on December 11, 2019, just seventy days after the initial announcement, the First Presidency disclosed that the Orem Utah Temple would be built on Geneva Road just south of University Parkway. The promptness of the announcement was unexpected; at this time, site announcements typically took from six months to two years. The sixteen-acre parcel was already

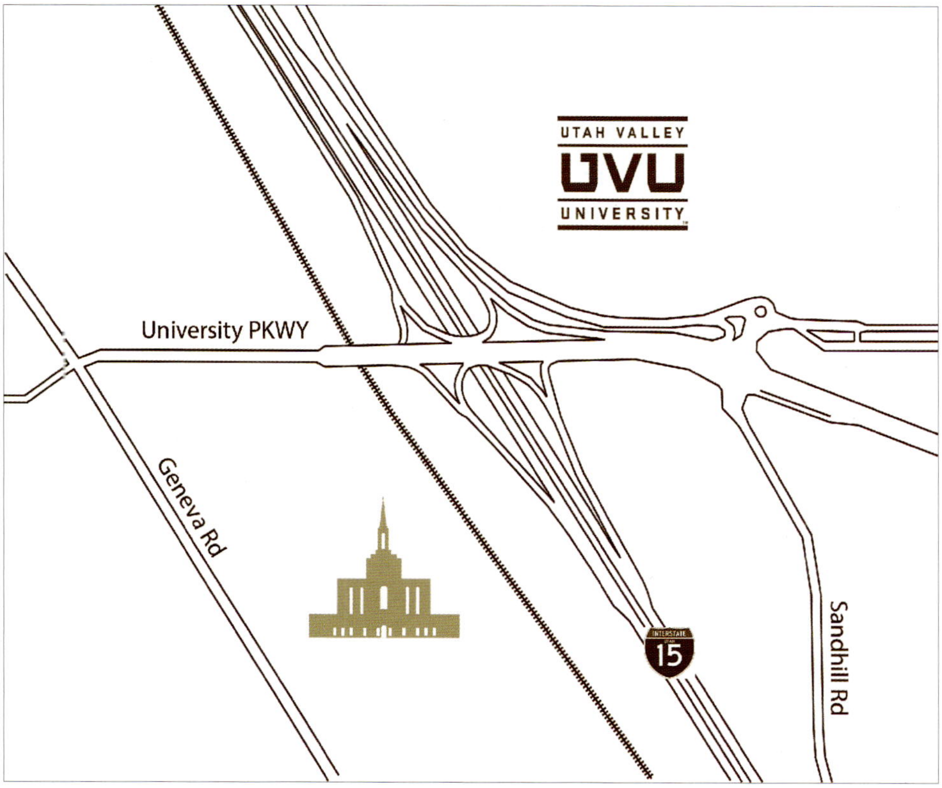

Orem Utah Temple neighborhood. Courtesy of Lee R. Cowan.

Rendering of Orem Utah Temple. Courtesy of Intellectual Reserve, Inc.

owned by the Church, having been purchased several years earlier by Brent Roberts for another purpose when he was president of the Orem Utah Lakeview Stake. The First Presidency's announcement indicated that a stake center would also be erected on the property.[31]

A series of meetings resulted in approval of plans to build the temple. In all these gatherings there was no opposition, just curiosity about what the temple would look like and how quickly it would be built. First was a meeting with neighbors on March 5, 2020. Then on April 1 the planning commission addressed some concerns: They adopted the new PD-50 zone, which had been "designed specifically for the temple." A seven-foot masonry wall would separate the site from the Frontrunner commuter rail right-of-way. Zoning regulations called for a minimum of 280 parking places, but plans provided for 520. Improvements to be made by the Church and the Utah Department of Transportation would handle anticipated traffic without widening Geneva Road, which had been a source of concern to some residents. The planning commission unanimously approved these plans. Finally, on April 14, the city council also gave its unanimous approval.[32]

On June 24, the First Presidency announced that groundbreaking would be on September 5. "The city looks forward to the groundbreaking," affirmed city manager Jamie Davidson. He noted that "the Church has served as a wonderful partner in addressing concerns and issues associated with the development of the temple site. As a community of faith that prides itself on being family-centered, the temple and associated buildings will be a welcome addition to Orem." Mayor Brunst added, "The edifice will be a blessing to the community," and, "We are blessed and lucky to have it." Referring to the rendering which the First Presidency had released with their announcement, he observed, "it is a beautiful design, even though there is no angel Moroni on top." He had hoped to see the iconic symbol atop the temple, but he acknowledged that recent designs for other temples had omitted it. Still, he believed the Church had "taken time to understand the history of the area" and that this would be reflected in other features of the design.[33]

Floral design on the temple spire, Orem Utah Temple. Courtesy of Lee R. Cowan.

Because of the COVID pandemic, only a few people, including church and civic leaders, were invited to be present for the groundbreaking on Saturday, September 5, 2020. Many of the guests had local connections. Utah's governor, Gary Herbert, for example, was from Orem. Brent Roberts, managing director of the Special Projects Department, had presided over an Orem stake; the Orem Utah Temple would be just one of the fifty-five temple building or renovation projects moving forward under his direction. Proceedings were recorded so they could be viewed later by members in the temple district. Elder Christensen once again presided. Elder Walter F. Gonzáles of the Seventy, who conducted the ceremonies, greeted the audience in English and Spanish, reflecting the diverse composition of Church members in the area. Elder Christensen declared that the temple "will become an added refuge of strength in an increasingly uncertain world—a holy place where we learn and live more fully the great plan of happiness made possible by our Savior, Jesus Christ." He pointed out that in addition to dedicating the temple's site, they would also be dedicating "the process of getting it built"; hence, this was a time of gladness and thanksgiving. Elder Evan Schmutz, also of the Seventy, declared that the temple would "act as a beacon, drawing the gaze of millions as they pass by this hallowed ground, and inviting the devoted service of hundreds of thousands of faithful Latter-day Saints as the ordinances of salvation are offered to the living and the dead."[34]

As the groundbreaking activities were concluding, Sister Zulma Gonzáles called attention to a small group of people in Sunday dress across the site standing behind the fence in a corn field. They turned out to be three great-grandchildren of Niels Williamson and their spouses. Niels had been the original owner of the temple property, having bought it in 1870. This group felt they should be present to respect

Orem Utah Temple, fall 2022.
Courtesy of Lee R. Cowan.

Williamson family attendees at the Orem Utah Temple groundbreaking. Courtesy of Intellectual Reserve, Inc. Niels Williamson was the original owner of the temple property site.

the significant event taking place on what had once been their family's land. Elder Gonzáles remarked, "I like to think that also on the other side of the veil there were witnesses cheering what was taking place."[35]

After the site was graded, excavation began for the foundation and basement. By February 2021, cement walls could be seen at ground level. On March 1, the first steel beams were delivered to the site, and within days the steel framework was rising, easily seen from the nearby thoroughfares. On December 10, the prefabricated steeple was hoisted to the top of the temple and the finial was installed. A prominent and unique feature on the steeple is a representation of a wild phlox flower prominent in the area. Within a few days the tower was being illuminated and the temple's exterior appeared to be complete. The significance of this moment was much like the placing of Moroni atop earlier temples.

The Taylorsville Utah Temple

Taylorsville, near the center of the Salt Lake Valley, had some of the best land for farming and sheep raising in pioneer days. It remained mostly agricultural until the 1940s when suburbs of Salt Lake City began spreading, particularly following World War II. Originally part of the Salt Lake Stake, Church units in Taylorsville multiplied with the growth in population. This growth led to the announcement of a temple in the area. Taylorsville mayor Kristie Steadman Overson was convinced that the future temple would "forever change the city."[36]

Rendering of the Taylorsville Utah Temple. Courtesy of Intellectual Reserve, Inc.

This would become the fifth temple in the Salt Lake Valley. The sites for the Taylorsville and Orem Temples were disclosed at the same time, a scant two months after their initial announcement. The 7.5-acre site in Taylorsville was just west of the I-215 belt route, on the south side of 4700 South, a major east–west artery in the area, only two blocks from a major campus of Salt Lake Community College. A meetinghouse on the property would be removed and not replaced.[37] This took place the following June, after which the site was cleared, graded, and made ready for construction. The future temple would be three stories high with a floor area of about seventy thousand square feet and a central spire. Although this description matched that of the Orem Utah Temple, the two buildings would look quite different.

Groundbreaking took place on October 31, 2020. Presiding was Elder Gerrit W. Gong of the Quorum of the Twelve Apostles, whose wife, Susan Lindsay Gong, grew up in Taylorsville. Elder Gong noted that Latter-day Saints in the community included fifth- or sixth-generation members whose ancestors helped settle the area, as well as "relative newcomers" who were enriching the community. He also recognized "the

Left: Susan Gong and Gerrit W. Gong turning soil at the Taylorsville Temple groundbreaking. Below: Current progress on the temple. Both images courtesy of Intellectual Reserve, Inc.

Watching the Taylorsville Utah Temple being built will be "a foundational piece for the faith of the Saints that live in this area."

rich blend of heritages, languages, and cultures that define Taylorsville." He affirmed that the new temple was "already connecting people 'in deep ways' across generations and cultures." Elder Christensen also spoke during the service. He insisted that "the multiple temples being built in the Utah Area reflect the faithfulness of the Saints." He believed that watching the Taylorsville Utah Temple being built would be "a foundational piece for the faith of the Saints that live in this area."[38]

The Ephraim Utah Temple

In his prerecorded message at the special meeting in the Manti Tabernacle on May 1, 2021, President Nelson not only disclosed updated plans for renovating the historic Manti Temple (see the preceding chapter) but also indicated that Church leaders had given "prayerful foresight to the growing number of faithful members of the Church who now live or will yet live in this central sector of Utah." He specifically referred to "the thousands of students who come to Snow College in pursuit of their education" and affirmed, "We care about their well-being and their future." He then continued,

Rendering of the Ephraim Utah Temple. Courtesy of Intellectual Reserve, Inc.

President and Sister Nelson arrive at the Ephraim Utah Temple groundbreaking. Courtesy of Intellectual Reserve, Inc.

"After much study and prayer, with our deep gratitude for the Lord responding to our pleadings, I am pleased to announce that we have been impressed to build a new temple in Ephraim."[39] Other General Authorities in attendance at the press conference then provided more information. Elder Kevin R. Duncan of the Seventy, executive director of the Temple Department, indicated that the temple would have four endowment rooms, each seating thirty persons, so a new session could begin about every half hour. There would also be three sealing rooms and a baptismal font. He also affirmed that Church leaders were "especially thrilled" that students at Snow College could now have the blessing of serving as patrons or workers in an accessible nearby temple. One student, Jacob Semadeni, acknowledged that a new temple close to campus would be "a special opportunity" for all the Latter-day Saint students. Abby King, another student, concurred: "That's because many students at the college are living away from home for the first time and must [consciously] choose to connect with the Church."[40]

W. Christopher Waddell, first counselor in the Presiding Bishopric, explained that as soon as the site could be secured and necessary approvals obtained, about two years would be needed to build the temple.

Elder Ronald A. Rasband of the Quorum of the Twelve Apostles presided at the meeting. He indicated that half of his ancestors, who were from Denmark, came to

Ephraim through great sacrifice. With emotion he affirmed, "I am absolutely positive there is joy on the other side of the veil with this announcement."[41]

Five months later, Church authorities announced that a three-story temple having an area of thirty-nine thousand square feet would be built in Ephraim on a 9.16-acre site on 400 East at 200 North, just a block northeast of the Snow College campus.[42]

Because a member of the Seventy usually presides on these occasions, the group gathered in Ephraim was amazed when President Nelson arrived to participate.

Groundbreaking was on Saturday, August 27, 2022. Because a member of the Seventy usually presides on these occasions, the group gathered in Ephraim was amazed when President Nelson arrived to participate. They greeted him with "reverent, sacred silence and many tears." The prophet's roots run deep in Sanpete Valley. He explained, "My dear mother was born in Ephraim, not far from this very temple site. My father was born in Manti. Three of my four grandparents were born here in Ephraim. All eight of my great-grandparents lived in Ephraim."[43] Also present were Elders Walter F. Gonzáles, president of the Utah South Area, and Kevin R. Duncan, both General Authority Seventies. Utah governor Spencer J. Cox, a native of nearby Fairview, and Ephraim mayor John Scott attended too. Delila Olsen, a longtime resident of Ephraim, celebrated her ninety-eighth birthday and thought the prophet's coming to dedicate the site was a wonderful present. In his remarks, President Nelson recalled that shortly after the April 2021 general conference, he "received very clear instructions from the Lord that the pioneer craftsmanship of the Manti Utah Temple—set to be renovated by the Church—should be preserved and that a new temple be built in Ephraim." In his prayer dedicating the site, President Nelson petitioned that the time of construction "be a wonderful time of preparation in the lives of all who live within these precincts. May they literally become thy covenant people." As he concluded the prayer, raindrops began to fall, which some present likened to tears of gratitude and joy.[44]

Two More Temples for the Wasatch Front

Announced in 2020, these temples would continue to fill in the map of the populated Wasatch Front.

The Syracuse Utah Temple

Located west of Ogden, Syracuse and its surrounding area had grown substantially during the early twenty-first century. Despite this growth, most local Saints had no thought that there would be a temple in their community and were grateful to have the opportunity to worship in the Ogden Utah Temple, which was only about thirteen miles away. Therefore, the announcement at the end of the April 2020 general conference that the third Davis County temple would be in Syracuse came as a real surprise. Only four months later, the specific site for the temple in Syracuse was announced. It would be built on a twelve-acre site at 2500 West and 1025 South.[45]

Rendering of the Syracuse Utah Temple. Courtesy of Intellectual Reserve, Inc.

Then on February 16 the following year, the temple's design was released. It would be a comparatively large three-story building with about eighty-nine thousand square feet.[46]

Groundbreaking for the Syracuse Utah Temple was on Saturday morning, June 12, 2021. Presiding was Elder Duncan, who had grown up less than one mile from the temple site and whose great-grandfather was the first bishop of the Syracuse Ward. Mark S. and Maryanne Thayne supervised arrangements for the event.

With the easing of COVID restrictions, a group of 150 could be present. In addition to church and civic officials, selected members who were preparing to enter the

Emily Medina speaks at Syracuse Utah Temple groundbreaking ceremony. Courtesy of Intellectual Reserve, Inc.

"God wants you to have this temple. He wants you to be strengthened, to withstand the challenges of life. He wants you to have exaltation and eternal life."

temple plus others who had just recently received their temple blessings were invited. The Thaynes visited the homes of these special people in order to issue the invitations. Maryanne acknowledged that meeting children who had just been sealed to their parents, as well as couples who were about to be sealed, was a highlight for her. Youth speakers like Emily Medina were a recent addition to the programs at groundbreaking ceremonies and provide the testimony of the rising generation who serve in temples.

Also present was Elder Dean M. Davies of the Seventy, who, as a member of the Presiding Bishopric, had participated in the selection of several temple sites. He testified that "a temple represents the love of the Father and the Son, the love of living prophets and the love of members past, present, and future, all over the world."[47]

In his remarks, Elder Duncan insisted that "I love this place more than I can describe, and then to understand why we build temples and then to have one right here is indescribable." And then he emphasized, "God wants you to have this temple. He wants you to be strengthened, to withstand the challenges of life. He wants you to have exaltation and eternal life. He wants you to be saved with your family."[48]

At the time of groundbreaking, preliminary work had already begun on meeting the water needs at the site, there being a canal along part of its perimeter. Construction trailers and equipment were already present. Brent W. Roberts, managing director

Syracuse Utah Temple under construction in November 2022. Courtesy of Steve Miller.

of the Special Projects Department, indicated that about two more years would be needed to complete the temple.[49]

The Lindon Utah Temple

The scattered homes which lined the highway between neighboring settlements came to be known as "String Town." A linden tree planted by one of the original settlers became a prominent landmark and gave the community its permanent name. When it was officially incorporated in 1901, a typographical error changed the spelling to Lindon. While surrounding communities grew more rapidly, Lindon retained its more rural character. More recently, however, new neighborhoods had been created and Lindon became increasingly urban. For several years a large bishops' storehouse and cannery were in Lindon. Following the October 4, 2020, announcement that there would also be a temple there, Mayor Jeff Acerson noted with pleasure, "We're excited with what they've decided to do." He emphasized that "Lindon residents are

Rendering of Lindon Utah Temple. Courtesy of Intellectual Reserve, Inc..

The temples in neighboring Utah Valley communities are "filled to capacity once the doors open each morning—and there are always lines of youth."

all about service," so the new temple would provide another great opportunity for them.[50]

President Michael Lloyd of the Lindon Central Stake was surprised at the announcement because there were several other temples only a short drive away. Still, he noted that the temples in neighboring Utah Valley communities were "filled to capacity once the doors open each morning—and there are always lines of youth." He felt certain that "news of a future temple offers Lindon residents a sacred opportunity to better themselves and prepare to serve."[51]

On December 21, 2020, the Church announced that a three-story temple with about eighty-one thousand square feet of floor area would be located at a site near 800 East and Center Streets.[52] This was in a residential area next to a junior high school and just below the Murdock Canal. The rendering released the following June showed a temple with two spires, much like the Layton Utah Temple.[53] The heart-shaped leaf of the linden tree would be a motif throughout the structure.

Church leaders broke ground on Saturday, April 23, 2022. Elder Kevin W. Pearson, a General Authority Seventy and President of the Utah Area, addressed the group meeting in a nearby chapel: "With the dedication of the temple site, . . . may each of

Site of the future Lindon Utah Temple. Courtesy of Intellectual Reverse, Inc.

us rededicate our own lives and recommit ourselves to placing the Lord Jesus Christ and our sacred covenants at the very center of our lives." He referred to prophecies of temples covering the world and asked: "Why do we need to dot the earth with temples? The answer seems to be clear; the Lord has been hastening His work for some time now" (see Doctrine and Covenants 88:73), and he insisted that temples have "always been the greatest work on the earth." Following the gathering inside, especially invited guests walked up the hill to the site for the traditional turning of soil with gold-colored shovels. Rain had threatened, but fortunately held off. Kelly Ashburn, a high school senior invited to represent the youth, reflected that when she makes an appointment to perform temple ordinances in the Mount Timpanogos Utah Temple, she feels "as if she is making a doctor's appointment, and the Lord is the Master Physician." Eduardo Silva, an elders quorum president who grew up in Rio de Janeiro, Brazil, recalled how he and other Church members there have sacrificed to make the fourteen-hour trip to the temple in São Paulo. Both were grateful that a temple would soon be more readily accessible in Lindon.[54]

Groundbreaking for the Lindon Utah Temple. Courtesy of Intellectual Reserve, Inc.

Another Temple in Cache Valley

On Easter Sunday, April 4, 2021, in the afternoon session of general conference, President Nelson made a historic announcement—twenty new temples would be built around the world! One of these would be in Smithfield, Utah, the second-largest city in Cache Valley, just a few miles south of the Idaho border and eight miles north of Logan. Church leaders had already disclosed plans to renovate all four pioneer

Rendering of the Smithfield Utah Temple. Courtesy of Intellectual Reserve, Inc.

Lesa Stevenson, Gary E. Stevenson, Quentin L. Cook, and Mary Cook at the Smithfield Utah Temple groundbreaking. Courtesy of Intellectual Reserve, Inc.

In his prayer dedicating the site, Elder Cook prayed that the new temple might be "a beacon of light to the communities it serves."

Utah temples, although no specific date had been announced for beginning work on the Logan Temple. Still, whenever that closure came, the Saints in Cache Valley would be grateful to have a functioning temple in nearby Smithfield. Two months later, Church leaders specified that the temple would be built on a 13.3-acre site on the northeast corner of 100 North and 800 West streets in Smithfield.[55] A rendering was released in November. It would be another three-story structure with a dome-topped tower and an area of eighty-one thousand square feet.[56]

Groundbreaking was on a windy Saturday morning, June 18, 2022. Two members of the Quorum of the Twelve Apostles participated—a highly unusual circumstance. Elders Quentin L. Cook and Gary E. Stevenson were natives of Cache Valley and had graduated from nearby Utah State University. Both expressed appreciation for the beauty of Cache Valley, for the pioneers who sacrificed to lay foundations of faith in the valley, and for the strength of the present Latter-day Saints in the area. In his prayer dedicating the site, Elder Cook prayed that the new temple might be "a beacon of light to the communities it serves." Six hundred invited guests gathered at the site, while thousands of others watched by television in stake centers around the valley.[57]

Location of the Smithfield Utah Temple, which will serve patrons of the Logan Temple when that temple closes for construction. Courtesy of Intellectual Reserve, Inc.

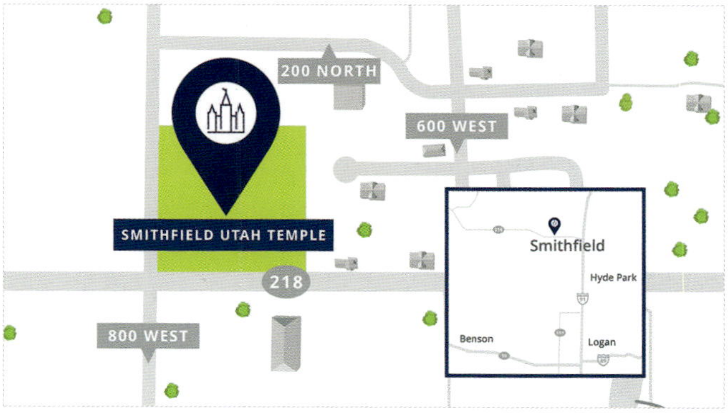

Rendering of the Heber Valley Utah Temple. Courtesy of Intellectual Reserve, Inc.

"I'm literally in tears knowing the spirit of the temple of the Lord's house will be nestled in our valley. It's like a blanket of hope and peace and love and joy."

Temples at Both Ends of Provo Canyon

In the closing moments of the October 2021 general conference, President Nelson announced plans to build thirteen new temples in locations in Asia, Africa, Latin America, and Utah. The latter would be in the Heber Valley at the upper end of Provo Canyon, and then came the surprising announcement that there would be a "reconstruction" of the Provo Utah Temple, located not far from the mouth of this same canyon.[58]

A Temple in Heber Valley

Utah's population growth was especially evident as more people established their homes along the "Wasatch Back." Many were employed locally, but a large number commuted every day through the mountains to their jobs. The Heber Valley is connected by Provo Canyon with the Utah Valley, while the Park City resort area, just a few miles to the north, is connected with the Salt Lake Valley by Interstate 80 through Parley's Canyon. The mushrooming number of Church members in Heber Valley was part of the Provo temple district, and many workers and patrons in that temple came from this area. For them the twenty-five-mile drive through Provo Canyon was often treacherous during the winter. Valley residents therefore received the news of a new temple with excitement. "My heart exploded with so much happiness," exclaimed Taunya Olsen of Heber City. "My daughter Ellie jumped off the couch saying 'No way!'—and my phone started blowing up with excitement from friends and family. I'm literally in tears knowing the spirit of the temple of the Lord's house will be nestled in our valley. It's like a blanket of hope and peace and love and joy."[59]

In September 2022 the First Presidency announced that the temple would be built on a 17.9-acre site in a residential neighborhood on Center Street about a mile east of Heber City's Main Street. The accompanying rendering was of a three-story temple with a floor area of about eighty-eight thousand square feet.[60] Like at least one other new Utah temple, it would have two baptistries. Groundbreaking was on a beautiful Saturday morning, October 8. As had been the case six weeks earlier in Ephraim, President Nelson surprised the group by presiding.[61]

Following the policy made in April 2020 to not place an angel Moroni on temples, the rendering of the new Provo Utah Temple showed that the building will return with a beautiful golden spire and without the angel.

Reconstruction of the Provo Utah Temple

President Nelson's announcement that the Provo Utah Temple would be reconstructed caught almost everyone by surprise. He indicated the change would take place "after the Orem Utah Temple is dedicated,"[62] about two years later. Ever since the similar temple in Ogden had been rebuilt during the previous decade, many people wondered if the same would be done in Provo. They now questioned the meaning of "reconstruction" and speculated about the future of the building in Utah Valley. Would the Provo Utah Temple be completely rebuilt as had been done in Ogden? Or would there only be needed upgrades to the temple's interior while the distinctive exterior was left the same? Or would the exterior be made to look more like traditional temples while leaving the efficient interior relatively untouched? Many believed that recent improvements in the temple seemed to suggest that it was here to stay.

This speculation was swirling on November 24 when the First Presidency released a rendering for the temple's new appearance, just a month and a half after President Nelson's unexpected announcement. The *Church News* referred to the rebuilding of the Ogden Utah Temple and added, "Soon, the Provo Utah Temple will go through a similar redesign and reconstruction process, resulting in a very different appearance from its present exterior."[63] There would continue to be six endowment presentation rooms, now slightly larger than those in the original temple. Like the renovated Salt Lake Temple, it reportedly would have two baptistries. Following the policy made in April 2020 to not place an angel Moroni on temples, the rendering of the new Provo Utah Temple showed that the building will return with a beautiful golden spire and without the angel.

"The Provo Temple has been a place of light and joy to so many," observed Provo's mayor Michelle Kaufusi. "The new temple will be bigger and even more beautiful. I

Rendering of the new Provo Utah Temple. Courtesy of Intellectual Reserve, Inc.

"The Provo Temple has been a place of light and joy to so many. The new temple will be bigger and even more beautiful."

have met with representatives of the Church and am eager to help them any way I can," she added. "This new temple will become one of Provo's finest gems, set against one of the most stunning backgrounds in the world, the peaks of Rock Canyon."[64]

In addition to these temples in Utah, there were plans for two others just outside of the Beehive State. The Grand Junction Colorado Temple, announced in 2021, was just over twenty-five miles from the Utah state line. The Montpelier Idaho Temple, announced in 2022, was even closer to the boundary, less than fifteen miles. Both temples would serve Latter-day Saints in Utah.

Thus, as the twenty-first century approached its first-quarter mark, Utah's map was increasingly filled in by a wave of new temples in the tops of the mountains.

Some Reflections

By the end of the nineteenth century, four temples were prominent landmarks of the Lord, all in Utah. One hundred years later at the turn of the millennium, the number of temples in the Beehive State increased to eleven. Within the next two decades that number has grown to twenty-eight and will continue forward. Many more temples will fill the communities of Utah as the work progresses and the hearts of the children continue to turn to their fathers and mothers. "With the dedication of each new temple," affirmed President Nelson, "additional godly power comes into the world to strengthen us and counteract the intensifying efforts of the adversary."[65]

As this book nears publication, the total number of temples in various phases of announcement to completion is at three hundred worldwide. As Brigham Young stepped onto the desert floor of Salt Lake Valley on July 26, 1847, he stuck his cane into the sand and announced the spot where the Salt Lake Temple would be built. Only a prophet could have foreseen what was to come in the Lord's work. President Young later shared the grander vision of temples when he stated, "To accomplish this work there will have to be not only one temple but thousands of them, and thousands and tens of thousands of men and women will go into those temples and officiate for people who have lived as far back as the Lord shall reveal."[66] Now that the Church is almost one-third of the way to a thousand temples, that milestone seems possible.

"With the dedication of each new temple, additional godly power comes into the world to strengthen us and counteract the intensifying efforts of the adversary."

But what is even more important is the impact that the covenant blessings of the gospel is making on God's children throughout the world and strengthening their relationship with Jesus Christ. For most of the first hundred years of the Restoration, Latter-day Saints who wanted the blessings of the gospel needed to do as Isaiah prophesied and go to "the top of the mountains . . . to the mountain of the Lord" in Utah. There they would receive the ordinances of exaltation (Isaiah 2:2–3). That great physical gathering of pioneers is now a chapter in western United States history.

What is just as amazing to see in the twenty-first century is the spiritual gathering in many far and near lands where temples are the crowning blessing as stakes are strengthened and can support the work of a temple. So far in the history of the Church, much work for the living and the dead has occurred in Utah, and this history has shared some of the stories of these temples. Many other books have been written about temple work among the Latter-day Saints. Theologically, the main purpose of temples continues to be for God's children to make and keep sacred covenants that will allow them to ultimately return to their heavenly parents through the merits and mercy of Christ's Atonement. This great work in temples is also fulfilling the vision of John the Revelator that the Saints will need to be "sealed in their foreheads" preparatory to the Second Coming of Jesus Christ and the inauguration of His millennial reign (Revelation 7:1–4). President Brigham Young stated,

> We are trying to save the living and the dead. The living can have their choice, the dead have not. Millions of them died without the Gospel, without the Priesthood, and without the opportunities that we enjoy. We shall go forth in the name of Israel's God and attend to the ordinances for them. And through the Millennium, the thousand years that the people will love and serve God, we will build temples and officiate therein for those who have slept for hundreds and thousands of years—those who would have received the truth if they had had the opportunity; and we will bring them up, and form the chain entire, back to Adam.[67]

Notes

1. "I Pledge My Life and . . . Full Measure of My Soul," *Church News*, June 11, 1994, 14.
2. Russell M. Nelson, "Becoming Exemplary Latter-day Saints," *Ensign*, November 2018, 114.
3. Saratoga Springs Utah Temple groundbreaking history (unpublished manuscript, 2020), 3, Church History Library.
4. Sydney Walker, "Ground Broken for the Saratoga Springs Temple," *Church News*, October 27, 2019, 24–25.
5. Valerie Johnson, "Construction to Begin on Utah Temple," *Church News*, September 15, 2019, 2; Genelle Pugmire, "What You Need to Know about the Saratoga Springs Temple," *Daily Herald* (Provo, UT), October 18, 2019, 4.
6. Saratoga Springs Utah Temple groundbreaking history, 54.
7. Walker, "Ground Broken," 24–25; Ashley Stilson, "Digging In," *Daily Herald*, October 20, 2019, 1.
8. Genelle Pugmire, "A Long-Expected Party," *Daily Herald*, November 25, 2022, 1.
9. Sarah Jane Weaver, "Layton Temple Location," *Church News*, July 21, 2019, 2.
10. Andrew Jenson, *Encyclopedic History of the Church of Jesus Christ of Latter-day Saints* (Salt Lake City: Deseret News, 1941), 419–20.
11. "Church Announces Groundbreaking for Three Temples," *Church News*, February 9, 2020, 2.
12. Scott Taylor, "A Small-Scale Groundbreaking," *Church News*, May 31, 2020, 17.
13. Danielle Christensen, "Washington County Temple Location Announced," *Church News*, November 10, 2019, 2.
14. Christensen, "Washington County Temple Location," 2.
15. Walker, "Renderings Released for Three Temples," *Church News*, April 19, 2020, 2.
16. Taylor, "Groundbreaking Makes Hollands Feel at Home," *Church News*, November 15, 2020, 4.
17. Taylor, "Groundbreaking Makes Hollands Feel at Home," 3–4.
18. John W. Van Cott, *Utah Place Names* (Salt Lake City: University of Utah Press, 1990), 372.
19. Walker, "Location Announced for Tooele Valley Temple," *Church News*, Septermber 29, 2019, 2.
20. Walker, "Renderings Released for Three Temples, *Church News*, April 19, 2020, 2; "Announcement Made Regarding 4 Temples," *Church News*, May 3, 2020, 2.
21. See the discussion at the end of chapter 6 on the history of the angel Moroni atop Latter-day Saint temples.
22. Walker, "Location Announced," 2.
23. Taylor, "New Name, Location for the Deseret Peak Utah Temple," *Church News*, January 23, 2021, 10.
24. Tad Walsh, "'This Is Where We Build the Temple': How President Nelson Selected the Deseret Peak Temple Site," Churchbeat, *Deseret News*, May 27, 2021.
25. Taylor, "New Name, Location or the Deseret Peak Utah Temple," *Church News*, January 23, 2021.
26. Taylor, "Honoring Faithful, Unified Members in Tooele Valley," *Church News*, May 22, 2021, 8–9.
27. Taylor, "How a Hasty Exit from a Temple Groundbreaking Is Emblematic of Faithful Service," *Church News*, May 22, 2021, 24.
28. Nelson, "Spiritual Treasures," *Ensign*, November 2019, 76–79.
29. Pugmire, "LDS Church Announces Site for Orem Temple," *Daily Herald*, December 12, 2019, 1.
30. Pugmire, "Orem City Council Approves Temple Zone Change," *Daily Herald*, April 16, 2020, 1.
31. Taylor, "Three Temple Sites Announced," *Church News*, December 15, 2019, 2; Pugmire, "LDS Church Announces Site," 1.
32. Pugmire, "Planning Commission Approves Change," *Daily Herald*, April 16, 2020, 1; Pugmire, "Orem City Council."

33. Pugmire, "Temple Groundbreaking Date Set," *Daily Herald*, June 25, 2020, 1; Taylor, "Renderings of Two New Temples Released," *Church News*, June 28, 2020, 2.
34. Taylor, "Temple Groundbreaking in Orem Links Past, Future," *Church News*, September 13, 2020, 6–7.
35. Taylor, "Temple Groundbreaking," 6–7.
36. Rachel Sterver and Walker, "Groundbreakings Set for Two Utah Temples," *Church News*, August 23, 2020, 6.
37. Taylor, "Three Temple Sites," 2.
38. Jason Swensen, "Taylorsville Utah Temple Already Connecting People," *Church News*, November 8, 2020, 14–15.
39. Nelson, pre-recorded announcement, May 1, 2021, copy in authors' possession.
40. Lindsey Williams, "Rejoicing 'on Both Sides of the Veil': 12 Highlights from the Ephraim Temple Announcement and Revision to Manti Renovation Plans," May 1, 2021, https://www.ldsliving.com/Rejoicing-on-both-sides-of-the-veil-12-highlights-from-the-Ephraim-temple-announcement-and-revision-to-Manti-renovation-plans/s/94261.
41. Williams, "Rejoicing."
42. "Ephraim Temple Site Announced," *Church News*, October 30, 2021, 2.
43. "President Nelson Presides at Ephraim Utah Temple Groundbreaking, Church Newsroom, August 27, 2022.
44. Weaver, "Pres. Nelson a Surprise Guest at Ephraim Groundbreaking," *Church News*, September 3, 2022, 3–4.
45. Taylor, ". . . Syracuse Utah Site Announced," *Church News*, September 6, 2020, 10.
46. "See the Just-Released Exterior Rendering of the Syracuse Utah Temple," *Church News*, February 27, 2021, 2.
47. Scott Taylor, "How Connections Became a Theme at Groundbreaking," *Church News*, June 19, 2021, 20.
48. Scott Taylor, "How Connections Became a Theme," 20.
49. Scott Taylor, "How Connections Became a Theme," 20–21.
50. Pugmire, "Mayor Has High Hopes for Temple," *Daily Herald*, October 6, 2020, 1.
51. Swensen and Taylor, "What Latter-day Saints Are Saying About New Temples," *Church News*, October 11, 2020, 14.
52. Taylor, "Site for Lindon Utah Temple Announced," *Church News*, December 27, 2020, 26.
53. "Milestones for Temples in 4 Western States," *Church News*, June 19, 2021, 22.
54. Mary Richards, "Ground Broken for Lindon Utah Temple," *Church News*, April 30, 2022, 19.
55. "Milestones for Temples," 22.
56. "Smithfield Utah Temple Exterior Rendering Released," *Church News*, November 27, 2021, 8.
57. Sarah Jane Weaver, "Two Apostles Recall Roots, Break Ground for Smithfield Temple," *Church News*, June 25, 2022, 3–4.
58. Russell M. Nelson, "Make Time for the Lord," *Liahona*, November 2021, 120–21.
59. Jason Swensen and Scott Taylor, "From Liberia to Bolivia—Reactions to 13 New Temples," *Church News*, October 9, 2021, 9.
60. "Temple Milestones in Puerto Rico, Utah, and Idaho," *Church News*, September 24, 2022, 2.
61. Jon Ryan Jensen, "President Nelson Says 'More Will Come' for Heber Valley," *Church News*, October 15, 2022, 3–4.
62. Russell M. Nelson, "Make Time for the Lord," *Liahona*, November 2021, 121.
63. Scott Taylor, "Provo Utah Temple Will Undergo Major Redesign," *Church News*, November 27, 2021, 7–8.
64. Genelle Pugmire, "New Look Incoming," *Daily Herald*, November 26, 2021, 1, 5.
65. Russell M. Nelson, "What Is True," general conference address, October 2022.
66. John A. Widtsoe, ed., *Discourses of Brigham Young* (Salt Lake City: Deseret Book, 1941), 394.
67. Widtsoe, *Discourses of Brigham Young*, 404.

Appendix:
Chronology

Provo City Center Temple, by Bruno Delfino/Unsplash.

Utah Temples Milestones

Bold = Temple dedication; *Italics = New Church President*

YEAR	EVENT
1820	Spring: The Father and the Son appear to Joseph Smith.
1823	Sept. 21: Moroni prophecies appearance of Elijah the prophet.
1830	Apr. 6: Church of Jesus Christ organized at Fayette, New York.
1836	Mar. 27: **Kirtland Temple dedicated** by Joseph Smith.
	Easter, Apr. 3: Elijah restores sealing keys.
1840	Summer: Joseph Smith teaches baptisms for the dead; performed in river at Nauvoo.
1842	May 4: Endowments given at Nauvoo in Joseph Smith's Red Brick Store.
1844	June 27: *Martyrdom of Joseph Smith.*
1846	Feb. 4: Westward exodus from Nauvoo begins.
	Apr. 30: **Nauvoo Temple dedicated** privately by Orson Hyde.
1847	July 24: Pioneers arrive in the Salt Lake Valley.
	July 26: Brigham Young sees vision and identifies site for Salt Lake Temple.
	Dec. 27: *Brigham Young sustained as President of the Church.*
1849	Fall: Addison Pratt received endowment on Ensign Peak.
1852	Endowments being given on the second floor of the Council House in Salt Lake City.
1853	Feb. 14: Site dedicated and ground broken for the Salt Lake Temple by Brigham Young.
1853	Apr. 6: Cornerstones laid for the Salt Lake Temple by Brigham Young.
1855	May 5: **Endowment House on Temple Square dedicated** by Heber C. Kimball.

1858	Spring: With approach of hostile army, temple foundations covered over.
1862	Spring: Defects discovered when temple foundations excavated, upper part replaced.
1867	Salt Lake Tabernacle entered service.
	Fall: Salt Lake Temple walls finally reach ground level.
1871	Nov. 9: Ground broken by Brigham Young for St. George Temple.
1874	Apr. 1: Commemorative box placed in St. George Temple cornerstone.
1877	Jan. 1: Baptistry and lower main assembly hall dedicated in St. George Temple.
	Jan. 11: First endowments for the dead performed in the St. George Temple.
	Mar. 1: Pattern of performing vicarious ordinances for more than relatives inaugurated.
	Apr. 6: St. George Temple dedicated by Daniel H. Wells.
	Apr. 25: Manti Temple site dedicated by Brigham Young.
	May 18: Ground broken for Logan Temple by Brigham Young.
	Aug. 21: Baptisms performed for prominent men and women at St. George.
	Aug. 29: *President Brigham Young dies.*
	Sept. 19: Cornerstones laid for Logan Temple.
1878	Oct. 16: St. George Temple's short tower destroyed by lightning.
1879	Apr. 14: Cornerstones laid for Manti Temple.
1880	Oct. 10: *John Taylor sustained as President of the Church.*
1884	May 17-19: Logan Temple dedicated by President John Taylor.
1887	July 25: *President John Taylor dies.*
1888	May 17: Manti Temple dedicated privately by President Wilford Woodruff.
	May 21-23: Manti Temple dedicated publicly by Lorenzo Snow.

1889	Apr. 7: *Wilford Woodruff sustained as President of the Church.*
1892	Apr. 6: Capstone and angel Moroni placed atop Salt Lake Temple.
1893	Apr. 5: Two-hour open house at Salt Lake Temple, first in the Church
	Apr. 6: Salt Lake Temple dedication by President Woodruff begins.
	Apr. 24: Temple dedication concludes following 31 sessions.
1898	Sept.: *Lorenzo Snow succeeds Wilford Woodruff as President of the Church.*
1901	Nov.: *Joseph F. Smith becomes President of the Church.*
1902	Larger annex built at St. George Temple.
1904	Mar. 26: Bureau of Information inside Temple Square south gate dedicated.
1916	Logan Temple thoroughly refurbished including introduction of electric lights.
1917	St. George Temple remodeled to create two additional sealing rooms.
	Dec. 4: Logan Temple fire destroys stairway and badly damages other areas.
1918	Nov.: *Heber J. Grant becomes President of the Church.*
1928	Nov. 20: St. George Temple annex completely destroyed by fire.
1939	St. George Temple reopens following yearlong construction of permanent ordinance rooms.
1945	May: *George Albert Smith becomes President of the Church.*
1951	Apr.: *David O. McKay becomes President of the Church.*
1955	Sept.: Swiss Temple first to use film in presenting endowment.
1963	May 27: Nearly completed visitors' center becomes temporary Salt Lake Temple annex.
1966	Mar. 21: New Salt Lake Temple annex enters service.
1967	Aug. 14: Plans to construct temples in Provo and Ogden announced.

Oct. 22: New Salt Lake Temple annex and North Visitors' Center dedicated by Hugh B. Brown.

1969 Sept. 8 and 15: Groundbreakings for Ogden and Provo Temples by Hugh B. Brown.

1970 Jan.: *Joseph Fielding Smith becomes President of the Church.*

Sept. 9: Ogden Temple cornerstone placed.

1971 May 21: Provo Temple cornerstone placed.

Dec. 16-30: More than 150,000 visit Ogden Temple during open house.

1972 Jan. 10-29: 246,201 visitors attend Provo Temple open house.

Jan. 18-20: Ogden Temple dedicated in six sessions by President Joseph Fielding Smith.

Feb. 9: Provo Temple dedicated in two sessions by President Smith.

July: *Harold B. Lee becomes President of the Church.*

1973 Dec.: *Spencer W. Kimball becomes President of the Church.*

1975 Oct. 13-25: 73,967 persons visit St. George Temple open house following renovation.

Nov. 11-12: St. George Temple rededicated in six sessions by President Spencer W. Kimball.

1978 June 1: South Visitors' Center on Temple Square dedicated by President Kimball.

1979 Feb. 6-Mar. 3: 213,184 visit rebuilt Logan Temple during open house.

Mar. 13-15: Logan Temple rededicated by President Kimball following renovation.

June 9: Ground broken for Jordan River Temple by President Kimball.

1981 Aug. 15: Cornerstone ceremony for Jordan River Temple.

Sept. 29-Oct. 31: 568,342 attend Jordan River Temple open house.

Nov. 16-20: Jordan River Temple dedicated in fifteen sessions by Marion G. Romney

1985	June 14-16: Manti Temple rededicated by Gordon B. Hinckley after refurbishment.
	Nov.: *Ezra Taft Benson becomes President of the Church.*
1992	May 2: Ground broken for Bountiful Temple by President Ezra Taft Benson.
1993	Oct. 9: Ground broken for Mount Timpanogos Temple by Gordon B. Hinckley.
1994	June: *Howard W. Hunter becomes President of the Church.*
	Nov. 5-Dec. 17: More than 870,000 attend Bountiful Temple open house.
1995	Jan. 8-14: Bountiful Temple dedicated in twenty-four sessions by President Howard W. Hunter.
	Mar.: *Gordon B. Hinckley becomes President of the Church.*
	May 13: Ground broken for Vernal Temple by President Hinckley.
1996	Aug. 10-Sept. 21: 679,217 participate in Mount Timpanogos Temple open house.
	Oct. 13-19: Mount Timpanogos Temple dedicated in twenty-three sessions by President Hinckley.
1997	Oct. 18-25: Approximately 118,700 visit Vernal Temple open house.
	Nov. 2-4: Vernal Temple dedicated in eleven sessions by President Hinckley.
	Nov. 17: Groundbreaking in Monticello just six weeks after announcement of temple by Ben E. Banks.
1998	July 16-18: 20,348 visit during brief Monticello Temple open house.
	July 26-27: Monticello Temple dedicated in eight sessions by President Hinckley.
2002	Nov. 2-9: Open house for newly enlarged Monticello Temple.
	Nov. 17: Monticello Temple rededicated by President Hinckley.
	Nov. 18: Angel Moroni statue placed on Ogden Temple.
2003	May 12: Angel Moroni statue placed on Provo Temple.

2006	Aug. 5: Ground broken for Draper Temple by President Hinckley
	Dec. 16: Ground broken for Oquirrh Mountain Temple by President Hinckley
2008	Jan.: *Thomas S. Monson becomes President of the Church.*
2009	Mar.: Draper Temple dedicated by President Thomas S. Monson
	Aug.: Oquirrh Mountain Temple dedicated by President Monson
2010	July 31: Ground broken for Brigham City Temple by Boyd K. Packer.
	Dec. 17: Provo Tabernacle destroyed by fire, would later become temple.
2011	Oct. 8: Ground broken for Payson Temple by Dallin H. Oaks.
2012	May 12: Ground broken for Provo City Center Temple by Jeffrey R. Holland.
	Aug. 18-Sept. 15: 404,352 persons attend Brigham City Temple open house.
	Sept. 23: Brigham City Temple dedicated in three sessions by Boyd K. Packer.
2014	Sept. 21: Rebuilt Ogden Temple dedicated by President Monson.
2015	Apr. 24-May 23: 475,542 persons visit Payson Temple open house.
	June 7: Payson Temple dedicated in three sessions by Henry B. Eyring.
	Aug. 8: Ground broken for Cedar City Temple by L. Whitney Clayton.
2016	Jan. 11-Mar. 5: Over 800,000 visit Provo City Center Temple open house.
	Mar. 20: Provo City Center Temple dedicated by Dallin H. Oaks.
2017	Apr. 2: Saratoga Springs Temple announced at general conference.
	Oct. 27-Nov. 18: 187,614 visitors attend Cedar City Temple open house.
	Dec. 10: Cedar City Temple dedicated by Henry B. Eyring.

2018	Jan.: *Russell M. Nelson becomes President of the Church.*
	Apr. 1: Layton Temple announced at general conference.
	May 20: Jordan River Temple rededicated by Henry B. Eyring.
	Oct. 7: Plans for temple in Washington County announced at general conference.
2019	Apr. 7: Plans for temple in Tooele Valley announced at general conference.
	Oct. 5: Orem and Taylorsville Temples announced at women's session of general conference.
	Oct. 19: Groundbreaking for Saratoga Springs Temple by Craig C. Christensen.
	Nov. 4: St. George Temple closes for extensive restoration.
	Dec. 29: Salt Lake Temple closes for seismic upgrade and major renovation.
2020	Mar.: COVID-19 pandemic; Church meetings and temple activity suspended.
	Mar. 18: Moroni's trumpet dislodged from Salt Lake Temple by 5.7 magnitude earthquake.
	Apr. 5: Syracuse Temple announced at general conference.
	May 23: Ground broken for Layton Temple by Craig C. Christensen.
	June: Washington County temple named Red Cliffs Temple.
	Sept. 5: Ground broken for Orem Temple by Craig C. Christensen.
	Oct. 4: Lindon Temple announced at general conference.
	Oct. 31: Ground broken for Taylorsville Temple by Gerrit W. Gong.
	Nov. 7: Groundbreaking for Red Cliffs Temple in St. George by Jeffrey R. Holland.
2021	Jan.: Tooele Valley Temple site changed and renamed Deseret Peak Temple.
	Mar. 12: Additional ordinance rooms to be built in Salt Lake Temple.

Apr. 4: Smithfield Temple in Cache Valley announced.

May 1: Manti renovation plans changed; temple announced for Ephraim.

May 15: Ground broken in Tooele for Deseret Peak Temple by Brook P. Hales.

June 12: Ground broken for Syracuse Temple by Kevin R. Duncan.

Oct. 2: Manti Temple closed for renovation.

Oct. 3: Heber Valley Temple announced; Provo Temple to be reconstructed.

2022 Apr. 23: Lindon Temple groundbreaking by Kevin W. Pearson.

June 18: Ground broken for Smithfield Temple by Quentin L. Cook.

Aug. 27: Ground broken for Ephraim Temple by President Nelson.

Oct. 8: Ground broken for Heber Valley Temple by President Nelson.

2023 Aug. 13: Saratoga Springs Temple scheduled for dedication.

Index

Ogden Sunset–from on High, by Alan Fullmer.

A

B

C

D

E

F

G

H

I

J

K

L

M

T

U

V

W

Y